Imperfect Creatures

Imperfect Creatures

VERMIN, LITERATURE, AND THE SCIENCES OF LIFE, 1600–1740

Lucinda Cole

University of Michigan Press
Ann Arbor

Published in the United States of America by the
University of Michigan Press
Printed and bound by CPI Group (UK) Ltd, Croydon, CR0 4YY

2019   2018   2017   2016   4   3   2   1

A CIP catalog record for this book is available from the British Library.

ISBN 978-0-472-07295-8 (hardcover : alk paper)
ISBN 978-0-472-05295-0 (cloth : alk. paper)
ISBN 978-0-472-12155-7 (ebook)

Acknowledgments

My grateful thanks, first, to my editor Aaron McCollough at University of Michigan Press, who perceived the academic value of this quirky project, and to Mary Hashman, Allison Peters, and others in Ann Arbor who saw it through to the end.

During the course of this research, I received help from staff at several libraries in the United States: The Newberry, University of Southern Maine, University of Illinois Urbana-Champaign, and Bowdoin College. The Kupferstichkabinett at the Staatliche Museum of Berlin provided access to the drawings of Jacques de Gheyn II, without which *Imperfect Creatures* might never have been conceived. Laura Otis, Thomas Pfau, and Heidi Hartwriter provided invaluable scholarly assistance in securing these permissions.

In the early stages of this project, Tito Chico and Cristobal Silva at *Eighteenth Century: Theory and Interpretation* gave me the opportunity to edit a special issue on animal studies. Contributors Bruce Boehrer, Erica Fudge, Laura Brown, Donna Landry, Richard Nash, Jonathan Lamb, and Cary Wolfe showed me how animal studies might be done. Rick Barney, Helene Scheck, and the readers at *Journal for Early Modern Cultural Studies*, along with participants at a 2009 Rhetorics of Plague conference, offered positive feedback and sound advice as I worked to articulate why, even prior to germ theory, vermin played crucial roles in early modern biopolitics.

Over the years, I've benefited immeasurably from the conversation, scholarship, and interdisciplinary fervor of my SLSA (Society for Literature, Science, and the Arts) family: Karen Raber (no stranger to parasites), Susan McHugh, Bruce Clarke, Nigel Rothfels, Arielle Saiber, Ann Kibbie, Christopher Morris, Spencer Schaffner, Melissa Littlefield, Carol Colatrella, Laura Otis, Stacy Alaimo, Kari Weil, and Susan Squier. The humorous, wise, and generous Richard Nash has been a pillar of support. Ron Schleifer, whose intellectual generosity is well known, gave me crucial guidance at key stages in this process. Rajani Sudan's cats run through chapter 5, and her cheerful skepticism about the anthropocene partially motivated the final pages of this book.

Colleagues at the University of Southern Maine who have supported my work in animal and ecological studies over the years include Eve Raimon, Rick Swartz, Lorrayne Carroll, Wendy Chapkis, Lauren Webster LaFrance, Kathleen Ashley, Susan Feiner, Robert Louden, and Jane Kuenz. Nancy Gish deserves special thanks for her ongoing vermin alerts and Rick Abrams for his early and invaluable comments on Shakespeare. In Piers Beirne, I found a role model and fellow traveler. Because they populated my interdisciplinary classes, USM students enabled me to write this book; from Caitlin Huber and Meaghan LaSala, I learned more than I taught. Bret Tonelli gave me courage. My friends at Bowdoin—David Collings, Terri Nickel, and Celeste Goodridge—have been good-natured, patient, and valuable listeners through the book's many stages, and endless sources of texts, food, wine, and insight.

Over the past five years, I have leaned heavily on members of my family, and this book is as much theirs as it is mine. First, my parents and my sister Melanie gave me the opportunity for concentrated work when, during my last sabbatical, they welcomed me, and the dogs, while I wrote. My mother, Jean Cole, was an unfailing source of love and inspiration. My father, Marvin Cole, passed away shortly after I completed the manuscript, and I only wish that he had seen this book in its published form. It would have made him smile. Finally, my husband Robert Markley served heroically as reality checker, mood booster, copyeditor, tea servant, and dog walker. *Imperfect Creatures* is dedicated to Bob, the most perfect of all the imperfect creatures I know.

Contents

Contents

Introduction

Reading beneath the Grain

CLOV: (*anguished, scratching himself*):
   I have a flea!
HAMM: A flea! Are there still fleas?
CLOV: On me there's one. (*Scratching.*)
   Unless it's a crab louse.
HAMM. (*Very perturbed.*)
   But humanity might start from there all over again!

—SAMUEL BECKETT, *ENDGAME*

In the last three decades, animal studies has influenced every discipline in the humanities, including literary studies, encouraging scholars to acknowledge the anthropocentrism of the stories we have been telling about ourselves and the natural world. Nuanced analyses of what Aristotle called the "more perfect creatures" have introduced new life forms into traditional literary and cultural history, so that once-overlooked references to horses, dogs, apes, bears, cats, wolves, and other beasts in early modern texts now shimmer again with complex meaning.[1] *Imperfect Creatures: Vermin, Literature, and the Sciences of Life* recovers a category of creatures—vermin—whose philosophical and literary significance in the period between 1600 and 1740 has been underestimated, if not erased. Historically, "vermin" is a slippery term because it refers neither to a particular biological classification nor to a group of genetically related animals; instead, it names a category of creatures defined according to an often unstable nexus of traits: usually small, always vile, and, in large numbers, noxious and even dangerous to agricultural and sociopolitical orders. The characteristic feature of vermin is they reproduce so rapidly and in such numbers they threaten to overwhelm their biological, environmental and—from a human perspective—sociolegal contexts.

The first full-length study of vermin in the early modern period, *Imperfect Creatures* is not a straightforward cultural history but an interdisciplinary analysis of how and why these reproducing animal populations, perceived as threats to a fragile food supply, make their way into seventeenth- and early eighteenth-century literature and philosophy. Vermin play an important role in Shakespeare's *Macbeth*; they are natural antagonists in the plague poetry of Abraham Cowley; and they enable Thomas Shadwell's satire of science, along with his critique of a parasitical social order. As the constitutionally simple beings against which the complexity of the human brain and body are defined, imperfect creatures anchor experiments in early modern neuroanatomy. And disappearing magically from Crusoe's wrecked ship, they serve as the absent center of an island economy that has grounded discussions of modern subjectivity and political economy. By bringing scholarship from agricultural history, environmental history, and medical history to bear on these and other works of literature, I argue rats, frogs, flies, and other animals located at the limits of our now-suburban zoography have shaped humanist practices, writings, and systems of thought. My historical focus is on the period 1600 to 1740, when religion, art, and science, in different ways, cast vermin as agents in studies of, and debates about, the socionatural world. Throughout this period, fleas, worms, wasps, maggots, and other swarming things carried considerable metaphysical and ethical weight, continually reshaping fundamental categories of analysis and perception.

By far, the most sustained body of scholarship on vermin during the early modern period has been written by medical and agricultural historians: the former focus on microscopy and plague treatises, and the latter focus on farming and extermination manuals. Medical historians trace a line of thought linking vermin and disease that runs through the works of Athanasius Kircher (1601–80), William Harvey (1578–1657), Robert Hooke (1605–1703), Antony van Leeuwenhoek (1632–1723), Francesco Redi (1626–97), Marcello Malpighi (1628–94), Jan Swammerdam (1637–80), and Sir William Ramsay, author of the first full-length treatise on worms in English.[2] The root of vermin is *vermis*, from the Latin word for worm, and the origin of worms was a subject of ongoing debates about the origin and nature of the universe and, in microcosm, of the human body.[3] Kircher describes the blood of those infected with plague as "so crowded with worms" that he is dumbfounded: "I have even been persuaded forthwith that man both alive and dead swarms with numberless but yet invisible little worms."[4] In his *Helminthologia* (1668), Ramsay, one of two physicians to Charles II, claims the body's "innumerable" vermin are "the most material enemy" of the physician, responsible for diseases from flux to melancholy.[5] Parasitology and medical history have generated their own subgenre of literary criticism, with critics such as Jonathan Gil Harris demonstrating how English writers imagined internal others—Jews, Catholics, and witches—as pathogens within the body politic.[6]

The work of agricultural and legal historians offers a glimpse of how humans struggled to protect an often-fragile food supply from vermin—crows, rats, locusts, and other pests. Animal trials, in particular, provide a window to assess the status of vermin as local and national threats.[7] In *The Criminal Prosecution and Capital Punishment of Animals* (1906), E.P. Evans describes attempts on the part of ecclesiastical and civil courts to punish, rehabilitate, or excommunicate insects, rooks, roosters, caterpillars, pigs, and other animals between 1266, the first recorded instance of an animal prosecution, and the eighteenth century. Nicholas Humphrey singles out a 1478 Swiss prosecution against insects called the Inger: "Thou irrational and imperfect creature[s]," the proclamation begins, are "called imperfect because there was none of thy species in Noah's ark"; they are charged with destroying or devouring "food for men and animals" and are ordered to "depart" or else present themselves for trial on the sixth day.[8] Their advocate used the usual defense that God had directed all creatures to "go forth and multiply"; the court, however, countered that because the Inger, like other insects, had not been placed on the ark but were products of spontaneous generation, they had no rights, and their defense did not hold. While animal trials were less frequent in England than on the Continent, English rats and other creatures were subject to ongoing extermination campaigns, and vermin-killing treatises described a wide range of technologies.[9] Leonard Mascall's 1590 *Book of Engines*, subtitled *Sundrie Engines and Trapps to take Polecats, Buzards, Rattes, Mice and all other Kinded of Vermin and Beasts Whatsoever* attests to the battles humans waged against creatures that threatened crops and grain supplies.[10]

By grounding my analysis in medical, agricultural, and environmental history, I explore the relationships between scientific accounts of vermin and literary and philosophical representations. Focused, as they are, on the prehistory of germ theory, medical historians often overlook the role of vermin in the everyday attempts of people in the seventeenth century to put food on their tables. Agricultural historians reverse the problem; concentrating almost exclusively on the food supply, they focus, understandably, on extermination campaigns, farming technology, and wetlands drainage, always with an eye to economic rather than epidemiological consequences. Literary critics have inherited and even reinforced this division, recognizing the importance of vermin to literature but rarely attempting to think outside of traditional disciplinary divides, seldom investigating relationships among a fragile food system, dearth, disease, and social order. Part of the problem is humanists have tended to base their analyses on culturally individuated vermin or, more precisely, on verminized individuals, such as Reynard the Fox or the other trickster figures who populate Aesop's fables. As a composite of characteristics packaged for human consumption, these speaking rats, fox, and ravens necessarily reflect to readers their own fears and desires, much as John Donne's flea becomes the emissary of the speaker's erotic ambitions or Anna Letitia Barbauld's eloquent "free born" mouse ventriloquizes Barbauld's revolutionary views. Significantly, Aesop's rat, Donne's flea, and Barbauld's mouse, unlike their real-life counterparts, travel alone. If we are to understand vermin as a category and as genuinely agential creatures in the early modern world, it is necessary to resist subjectivizing tendencies to treat dangerous and annoying animals as allegorized, isolated, domesticated, personified or even eroticized beings. In order to appreciate—indeed, even to recognize—the specific role of vermin in early modern literature, we must supplement an emphasis on individual animals or anthropomorphic representations by focusing on how writers and their readers perceived the creaturely populations who were their fellow travelers and constant, if unwanted, companions.

Imperfect Creatures, accordingly, argues what made vermin dangerous was less their breed-specific cleverness or greed than their prodigious powers of reproduction through which individual appetites took on new, collective power, especially in relation to uncertain food supplies.[11] Bitterly cold winters during the Little Ice Age brought with them not only skating parties on the Thames, the first in 1607, but widespread dearth, if not famine.[12] Temperatures in northwestern Europe dropped an average of two degrees during the period 1350–1850. During these centuries of comparatively cold winters and wet, cool summers, national policies on vermin control began to be developed; Henry VIII's 1533 policy mandating villages collect dead pests was renewed and amended under Elizabeth in 1566.[13] It required citizens to make and maintain nets and snares for trapping crows, rooks, and choughs—birds that devoured seeds before they could take root and sprout and grain before it could be harvested. Mascall estimates crows and other birds in England consumed or spoiled eight bushels of grain per parish; this amounted to 13,000 tons a year across the kingdom.[14] On the Continent, where grain prices were even higher, vermin—and especially rats and mice—began to be prosecuted vigorously during this same period. Walter Hyde's 1916 count suggests a direct correlation between climate change and the increased number of animal trials: in the fourteenth century, only twelve animals were tried; that number nearly doubled in the early days of the Little Ice Age, and then in the sixteenth and seventeenth centuries, it rose to fifty-seven and fifty-six, respectively.[15] While it is easy to dismiss the animal trials as superstitious or archaic practices supplanted by advances in philosophy and science, we should not underestimate the panic they expressed or the extent to which populations of rats, moles, rooks, choughs, and mice were perceived as eating into the health of the body politic.

To view vermin in their stark collectivity during the early modern period—as "infestations," "crowds," "hordes," and "swarms"—is to acknowledge their agency, including their role in disease. Francis Bacon observes in *Sylva Sylvarum* (1627) that during the plagues of 1624 and 1625, "many toads" with tails appeared in the ditches and "low grounds" of London, "which argueth," he writes, "a great disposition to putrefaction in the soil and the air."[16] Even in the absence of germ theory, early modern writers were attuned to the relationship between "swarms" of imperfect creatures and threats to the human body. According to Paul Reiter, Shakespeare, Defoe, Pepys, and others commented on changing weather patterns and what we now recognize as malaria, the physician Thomas Sydenham (1624–89) even noting relationships between fevers and rapidly reproducing insects. "When insects swarm extraordinarily," Sydenham writes, "and when . . . augues . . . appear early about mid-summer, then autumn proves very sickly."[17] Late seventeenth-century travel writers such as John Ovington (1653–1731) similarly remark, with horror, that "the prodigious growth of Vermin, and of venomous Creatures" during India's monsoons are seemingly both cause and effect of the "malignant Corruption of the Air," which has "direful Effects upon the *Europeans*":

> For Spiders [in India] increase their Bulk to the largeness of a Man's Thumb, and Toads are not of a much less size than a small Duck; whereby 'tis easily seen by these venomous creatures, what encouragements these infectious and pestilential Qualities meet with in this place, and

under what a contagious Influence all the Inhabitants must consequently be seated. This induc'd a Gentleman one time in the Governours and
my Company, and some other person of Note, to affirm, that he believ'd
it rain'd Frogs; because he espied upon his Hat small Frogs, about the
bigness of the end of one's Finger, when he was at a great distance from
any House or Covering, from whence they might drop.[18]

Like Sydenham and Bacon, Ovington links vermin infestations to life-
threatening effects on human health: "All Wounds and Contusions in the
Flesh," he continues, "are likewise very rarely healed here" (145). If vermin are
not quite disease vectors in such accounts, they are harbingers and agents of
malignant forces.

On transoceanic ships, the malevolent triad of illness, effluvia, and vermin was intensified. Writing from Commodore George Anson's flagship,
the *Centurion*, in the 1740s, Richard Walter describes efforts to eliminate the
"noisome stench" below decks and destroy "vermin" by cleaning, smoking the
deck, and then washing the whole ship with vinegar. Both stink and vermin
had "increased upon us to a loathsome degree," he reports, "and besides being
most intolerably offensive, they were doubtless in some sort productive of
the sickness we had labored under for considerable time."[19] Walter's phrase
"doubtless in some sort" is extraordinarily suggestive. Three quarters of Anson's crew died of scurvy and other diseases during the four years that the
Centurion spent circumnavigating the globe.[20] While the specific role of animals in shipboard illness was subject to debate, Walter joins other writers of
the period in assuming that "infection" and "infestation" are related, perhaps
different aspects of environmentally induced disease, one endoparasitic, the
other exoparasitic.

Imperfect Creatures explores the associative linkage noted by Sydenham,
Ovington, and Walter through several literary genres and across a range
of disciplines that were once folded into the broader rubrics of "natural
philosophy" or "physico-theology." In contrast to the dominant trends in
scholarship on early modern animals, represented by the groundbreaking
work of Erica Fudge, Bruce Boehrer, Karen Raber, Laurie Shannon, Donna
Landry, Richard Nash, Tobias Menely, Nathaniel Wolloch, Laura Brown,
and Jonathan Lamb, I turn away from so-called "charismatic megafauna"—
including companion species with whom humans affectively identify—in
order to analyze animals as part of dangerous or noxious collectives.[21] *Imperfect Creatures* also lies outside the tendency of animal studies to align

itself with animal welfare movements; I do not, admittedly, have an over-riding interest in the welfare of weevils. But, as Cary Wolfe argues, it is not necessary to "like" animals in order to confront speciesism or to craft a post-humanist theory of the human subject.[22] Indeed, critical animal studies, to which I am deeply committed, can only benefit by sustained critical attention to zoological outcasts, those "imperfect creatures" traditionally excluded from Noah's Ark. As the onto-historical "others" of dogs, horses, apes, and humans, vermin offer a new, post-Cartesian way to understand the material and ethical systems underwriting early modern literature: the "perfect" creatures of Renaissance humanism are, in a very real sense, dialogically dependent on "imperfect" ones. Whether depicted as frogs raining from the Indian sky, as plagues of lice swarming over bodies in Egypt, or as packs of dogs roaming the streets of London, populations of vermin move through history like locusts through a field. They contribute materially to dearth, famines, and disease—and discursively to ethical and political systems that expose or exploit human corruption, competition, violence, and vice. William Shakespeare, Abraham Cowley, George Wither, Thomas Willis, Bernard Mandeville, Thomas Shadwell, John Wilmot, Daniel Defoe, and their contemporaries write vermin into history and, in so doing, gesture toward the larger systems that define early modern culture.

ACTANT FLEAS, NESTING SYSTEMS

"Mark but this flea," writes Donne, drawing attention to a parasite that, in biting him and his lover, has "mingled" their blood.[23] In order for Donne's poem to work as a mode of playful seduction, it must figure the flea as an individuated agent, an accidental (or contingent) opportunity for the poet's sportive, metaphysical speculation. In its solitude, Donne's flea is decontextualized—not party to bodily pain, not a harbinger of a parasitical infestation that might remind us of the couple's proximity to disease and death. His flea, singled out by the speaker, allows the poem to bypass or even eclipse a larger biopolitical system in order to focus on a singularly specific and explicitly erotic situation. Metaphysical wit depends on such decontextualizing: "this flea" that joins the lovers—not "these fleas" that collectively bite and torment their hosts.

Donne's "Mark but this flea" evokes a prior tradition of already-eroticized parasites celebrated in the genre known as *La Puce*, or "Flea Searcher" paintings. In these often-puzzling and much-debated treatments of women grooming themselves, the (always invisible) flea symbolizes, for the viewer, the potential of vermin to define and cross boundaries between inside and outside, self and other, innocence and corruption.[24] Georges de la Tours' *The Flea Catcher* (1630–34), the most famous painting in this tradition, features a (possibly pregnant) young woman in a stage of partial undress, sitting before a candle in an austere room, crushing between her fingers an invisible parasite. In its apparent religiosity, de la Tours' painting often is contrasted to secular versions of the genre, such as *The Flea Hunt* (1628) by Gerrit van Honthorst, one of several flea-searcher paintings set in a richly decorated brothel, where a bare-breasted woman, usually with the help of one or more servants, investigates her naked body while two or more men look on. Within the erotic tradition, the flea serves as a point of (impossible) identification for heterosexual men, fantasizing (in the words of the seventeenth-century poet Peter Woodhouse) about being transformed into a parasite who has "free scope him selfe to sport" in the "soft bosomes" of women, even to "lower stray" at his "best pleasure."[25] For Woodhouse and the painters like van Honthorst, the flea is the inferred agent of a forbidden intimacy that, two centuries later, still finds expression in the semi-pornographic novel, *Autobiography of a Flea*.[26] The women in the flea searcher paintings and literature are always the objects of a scopophilic gaze. Having said that, the very possibility of scopophilia depends, to some extent, on the flea as an agent. Without the flea, the woman is not searching, her breasts are not uncovered, the voyeurs in the painting see only the interior of a room, and the viewer's gaze is not directed to the actions that precede the imperative, "Mark but this flea." The actions and identities of the men and women in the room are bound up in the set of relations that includes, but is not limited to, the fleas being purpled under women's fingernails.

By insisting on the agency of invisible fleas, I am invoking the post-Kantian tradition of analysis associated with, among others, the work of Michel Serres and Bruno Latour.[27] For Serres and Latour, there are no a priori distinctions between humans and nonhumans, subjects and objects, because these distinctions depend on complex relational networks of actors, forces, objects, and so on. The actor-network theory (ANT) with which their work is allied promotes a relational materiality that presupposes all entities in a system can be identified and analyzed only in relation to a larger system. Within this context, nonhumans are more than Cartesian objects or mere vehicles of our thoughts and intention; instead, they *do* things in specific sociohistorical, ecological, institutional, and psychological environments. They are, like humans, *actants* in the world. Latour coined the term *actant* to distance himself from anthropocentric accounts of intentionality; it is only through a series of networked associations that actants are provided with substance and action. Actants, he writes, "modify other actors"; they are not subjects, but "interveners."[28] In this respect, for Donne or de la Tours, fleas are actants because they compel changes in those around them: women search, men watch.

Latour's work has been useful to scholars in Animal Studies because, in the words of Erica Fudge, it allows "us a way of rethinking not only how we conceptualize the arrangements of culture and the structures of thought that organize human's perceptions of animals and themselves in the past—it might also allow us to rethink how it is that we understand the history of being human, and from that gain a better understanding of what it means to be human now."[29] In treating distinctions between agents and structures, in perceiving humans, animals, and objects as equally significant actors in dynamic and interlocking systems, historical animal studies and ANT share post-Cartesian assumptions about the socionatural world. Latour's theory of actants shifts fundamental questions from the identity of actors to their functions; the "who am I?" of western philosophy is superseded by another question: "what is my place in the system"? Moreover, the idea of system itself is destabilized: systems are not regarded as hierarchical or unidirectional arrangements of actants and forces but as what some historical ecologists call "heterarchies." Rather than emphasizing stability in ecosystems and holistic and deterministic notions of "system," many historical ecologists base their analyses on models in "which elements are unranked . . . or ranked in a variety of ways depending on conditions," or on "scalar hierarchies" in which any level of organization can affect or control temporarily others.[30] *Imperfect Creatures* offers a heterarchical reading of key texts in early modern literature in order to explore how sociohistorical, biopolitical, and ecological conditions reconfigure seventeenth-century perceptions of fleas, curs, rats, worms, and other vermin. If these are the despised and wretched creatures at the lowest rungs of the Great Chain of Being, they are also, paradoxically, crucial constituents of early modern eco-culture.

A brief look at Guiseppi Maria Crespi's flea searcher painting reveals how the concept of heterarchies can be useful as an interpretive strategy. The so-called Italian Hogarth, Crespi produced seven paintings in this genre between 1715 and 1740; most of them feature a woman delousing herself as her lapdog, a King Charles spaniel, looks on.[31] While its focus is on the woman disrobing, Crespi's painting (fig. 1) differs from works in both the earlier religious tradition, associated with de la Tours, and the overtly ribald one of the *Merry Flea Hunt*. Crespi depicts what many critics have regarded as a more realistic, ostensibly less emblematic, depiction of everyday life, possibly the first plate in a lost series about an opera singer from the lower ranks who arrives through youth, beauty, and talent to a life of luxury. Commenting on the painting's "fully detailed ambience and situation," Mira Pajes Merriman finds:

> A slightly dissolute air pervades the scene, perhaps through the suggestion made by the baby in the care of people who seem to be too old to be its parents. The ingénue—in charming disarray—takes center stage, absorbedly looking within her bodice. . . . Her profession is indicated by the announcements on the wall and primarily by the presence of the musical instrument, wholly out of place in the otherwise unrelievedly lower-class scene of hanging garlic and clay pots.[32]

This interpretation divides the painting into humans and the objects around them—garlic, pots, the spinet, papers on the wall—an "ambience" that accords with critical perceptions of seventeenth-century realism. The only action in the painting is described as a form of seeing: the woman is "looking within her bodice," oblivious to the stares of those around her. She is the only real agent in the room.

Yet from a heterarchical perspective, the painting depicts multiple actants—the young woman, the old man, the woman at the door, the baby, the dog, and the invisible flea. While all of them look at something, the organization of the painting, its kinetic energy, hinges on what we cannot see—the biting flea or louse. As in Donne's poem, then, the flea draws the viewer into a quasi-intimacy with the young woman. An irritant in a seemingly anthropocentric system, the flea provokes the action and is the source of the painting's humor. The obvious and lewd joke of most flea searcher paintings is that the female breast, which should nurse a human child, is instead the dinner table for vermin; in this painting, the flea feeds on a woman's breast, the old man feeds the child, and the dog waits to be fed. Part of a network of relations, the flea and its actions are not necessarily subordinated to an anthropocentric social order. Indeed, the more sophisticated, second order joke of Crespi's painting is all the actants are in some sense parasites, feeding off others. The baby is parasitical in an obvious sense, living on the body of the young mother. The young mother, in turn, depends on the gifts of her admirers (the spinet and the lapdog). If the old couple can be seen as the woman's parents, then they too may be living off her singing or sex work, but the lapdog may be the most overtly parasitical of the portrait's actants. Having replaced both the baby and the lover in the woman's bed, stripped of the ability to feed itself, the small dog stares at the viewers, drawing us into the system of parasitical relations.

As Latour and Serres suggest, parasitical relations need to be viewed as temporary alliances—as elements of a system that come together, disrupt previous arrangements, and then are disrupted. Nested within Crespi's painting, in this regard, is a gendered network of relations that turn on the historical association between the lower creatures and women, between vermin and female "imperfections." In Aristotelian taxonomies, modified throughout the seventeenth century, women were identified by a comparative lack of physiological development, regarded as cold and therefore imperfectly formed versions of men. As Aristotle writes in *On the Generation of Animals*:

> For females are naturally more imbecile and cold; and it is necessary to conceive the female sex as if it were a physical mutilation. Within the womb therefore the female acquires a perfect organization slowly; for the separation and distinction of the parts [by which a perfect organization is effected] is a concoction; but heat concocts, and that which is hotter is more easily concocted. Out of the womb, however, the female quickly arrives at perfection and old age. For whatever is less, more swiftly arrives at the end, as in the works of art, so likewise in the productions of nature.[33]

Morally, an "imperfect" constitution implied an "imperfect" moral nature, one lacking a masculine, guiding rationality.[34] Despite objections by Cornelius Agrippa (1486–1535) and other less orthodox thinkers, so established was this historical connection among women, insects, and constitutional inferiority that it was only in 1701 that the parasitologist Nicolas Andry de Bois-Regard congratulates his readers for having overcome the mistaken Aristotelian assumption that insects and women are intrinsically defective.[35] Writing after microscopy revealed complex nervous systems in fleas and women alike, he asserts,

That it is not at all to be wondered at, that some Philosophers have looked upon Insects as imperfect Animals, since some of them have so far been mistaken as to advance, that the Body of a Woman is an imperfect Work, a rough Draught formed contrary to the design of Nature, as if a Body perfectly proportioned, in which no irregularity can be observed, which wants no necessary part, and has none that's Superfluous [can be imperfect].[36]

Microscopy, the two-sex model, and the argument from design potentially freed women from the traditional association with imperfect creatures like flies, spiders, reptiles, and shrews.

At more or less the same time, however, women were assigned, in their roles as housewives and mothers, the function of policing the parasites in the household. "The whole Preservation of Men's Health and Strength," writes the author of a 1750 book on parasites, "chiefly resides in the Wisdom and Temperance of Women."[37] While the author of this treatise (an "Eminent Poulterer, Lately Deceased") is not the first to enjoin women to flea patrol—a famous Dutch Proverb is "Lazy mother, lousy heads"—he describes how "cleanliness," defined simultaneously as a moral and spiritual category, turns on new intimacies between women and vermin. The "greatest Slut in the World," he asserts, "does hardly smell her own House or Bed stink; For in Man is contained the true Nature and Property of all things, both of Good and Evil; therefore he is both liable, and also apt, to receive all Impressions, and to be wrought on by all things he shall either communicate with, or joyn himself to, whether it be Cleanness, or the contrary" (22). Her sense perceptions dulled by long habituation to filth, the "slut" becomes immune to the vermin around her; the good woman, in contrast, is "wrought on" by their presence and exercises "Wisdom and Temperance" in combating their filth.

In the context of this discourse of parasites and medical hygiene, some of the "realistic" elements of Crespi's painting, his highly textured "ambiance," become particularly meaningful. Herbal nosegays, including elder, fern, penny-royal, rue, mint, wormwood, and hops, were employed to ward off fleas and vermin. In the painting, herbs around the bed, intertwined garlic on the wall, the pot of water for drowning fleas, the woman's aired clothes, the open windows—all these may indicate that the poor flea-searcher (or perhaps her mother) is aware of verminous forces of corruption and is trying to combat them. Working against such efforts, however,

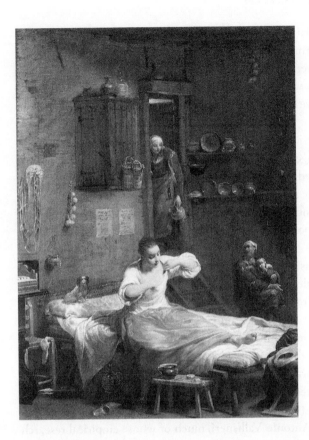

Fig. 1. Giuseppe
Maria Crespi,
Searcher for Fleas

is the presence of the dog on the bed. By the time Crespi painted, theories
of spontaneous generation used to explain the rapid proliferation of insects
had largely been replaced—thanks to Van Helmont, Harvey, Redi, and
others—by notions of biogenesis, or reproduction from eggs. Although
Robert Hooke was uncertain about the process of spontaneous generation,
later microscopy placed domestic animals unambiguously in the chain of
relations that lead to infestations:

> Fleas are produced of Eggs, which the Females stick fast by a kind of
> glutinous Moisture to the Roots of the Hairs of Cats, Dogs, and other
> Animals, and also to the Wool Blankets, Ruggs, and other such-like Fur-
> niture. Of these Eggs, a female lays ten or twelve a Day, for several Days
> successively, and they hatch in the same Order, about four or five days

after their being laid. From the Eggs come forth not perfect Fleas, but little whitish Worms or Maggots, whose Bodies have annular divisions, and are thinly covered with long Hairs. They adhere closely to the Body of the Animal, on whose Juices they feed; or they may be kept in a Box, and brought up with dead Flies, which they eat with Greediness.[38]

This popular description makes lapdogs parasitical in an originary sense; they sustain the maggots that will later metamorphose into "perfect fleas" that then begin to feed on humans. The staring dog in the young woman's bed—whatever else it says about her sexual liaisons or class relations—is already a sign of potential corruption, notice of her inadequate hygiene during a time when the policing of vermin was widely regarded as the cultural function of women.[39]

Nested within this gendered set of relations, moreover, is yet another heterarchical set of elements linking sex, species, medicine and theology. That vermin played a role in the very act of breast-feeding is always the subtext of all flea-searcher paintings. Londa Schiebinger has demonstrated the importance of work on the maternal breast to Linnaeus' (somewhat arbitrary) introduction of the term *Mammalia* to distinguish hairy animals with a four-chambered heart from others.[40] Vermin helped create the conditions for the taxonomic system she describes and to which humans are consigned. Working in the 1720s (more or less at the same time as Crespi's paintings), the Italian physician Antonio Vallisneri, much of whose empirical research was based on dissected insects, wrote a treatise on why even some newborn infants can be infected with worms. His argument is reported in the contemporary English redaction "by M. M.," *A Short Historical Account of the Several Kinds of Worms Breeding in Human Bodies*.[41] Vallisneri had argued that chyle is produced in the mother's stomach and filtered through the intestines, which "are the general Seat of *Worms*"; since milk is simply chyle "conveyed from the Bowels to the Breast," a nursing child will "receive this Verminous Progeny" should the mother (or a wet nurse) be infected (56–57). The medical issue converts into a theological one: whether these "colonies" of worms were created with humans ("originally implanted in the Body of the first Man, or Woman") or whether they emerged after the Fall as a scourge for sinful humans. Such debates similarly filter through Crespi's flea-searcher painting. Like all those in the genre, it depicts a more-than-human world in which vermin act in systems of nourishment, gender, cleanliness, the domestication of animals, and species identity. Invisible fleas disrupt interlocked systems, provoke action, forge interspecies intimacies, occasion gendered performances, and raise questions about the nature of creation, infestation, disease, and death. Vermin, in short, compel us to examine the distinctions between "inside" and "outside," self and other, nature and culture—but also "perfect" and "imperfect" creatures—that have governed centuries of liberal humanist thought.

READING BENEATH THE GRAIN

To read for vermin is not to read "against the grain," as Terry Eagleton termed his Marxian notion of critique, but "beneath the grain"—beneath the social, political, and anthropocentric modes of humanist analysis to the life-forms and energies that enable it.[42] While Eagleton focuses on the complex relations between literature and economic hierarchies of modern civilization, Michel Serres is more useful to my analysis. Serres deploys the notion of the parasite to yoke biological, information, and communication systems.[43] In French, *le parasite* (the static on a radio broadcast) signifies noise, and Serres plays on the double meaning of the term to explore irritants or interruptions within multiple systems.[44] Serres' *The Parasite*, written partly through an analysis of Aesop's fables, is notoriously difficult to adapt to familiar modes of literary criticism. On the one hand, as Latour points out, Serres is not a "critique" philosopher who "sees his task as that of establishing a distinction between beliefs on the one hand and knowledge on the other, or between ideologies and science."[45] Latour calls him "provisionally" an "anthropologist of science" who treats the sciences "as local achievements extracted from the world": "they do not replace it, and cannot be substituted for it, no more than any other metalanguage" (95). Yet because Serres refuses to follow the protocols of a single discipline, his insights have led to significant reconsiderations of the early modern period, including an important essay by Karen Raber. "There is no system without parasites," she argues, and "there is no theory of the human without them."[46] As Raber suggests, *The Parasite* opens up literary and scientific history to whole categories of creatures essential to our ecologies, creatures that have neither an obvious relation to (economic) production nor an obvious role to play in aesthetic-theological readings of the natural world. An interdisciplinary book about vermin, consequently, must be willing to be verminous—that is, to read beneath, across, and through the grain.

A broader category than parasites, although no more stable, "imperfect creatures" means different things to different early modern writers, sometimes referring ostensibly to creatures of putrefaction and, at other times, to beings regarded as anatomically or morally less complex than humans and their mammalian kin. But in the five chapters that follow, I maintain that the Aristotelian division between "perfect" and "imperfect" creatures is as historically important, in its own way, as the Cartesian distinction that has shaped our philosophical analyses of subjectivity and identity. While "imperfect creatures" are not necessarily verminous and verminous creatures not always "imperfect," the fact that these categories overlap so frequently in the early modern period is itself significant. Early modern writers, as Laurie Shannon has argued, upheld an interspecies sense of community; they "routinely understood a condition of membership and mutual participation to hold across species," rather than stressing a human-animal divide.[47] When imperfect creatures turn vermin, however, they test the limits of interspecies "cosmopolity"; a (real or imagined) ability to reproduce rapidly and in large numbers become a marker of (perceived) constitutional inferiority. What worms, rats, mice, frogs, insects, and reptiles have in common, then, and what distinguishes them from horses, elephants, domesticated canines, and even hedgehogs, is not simply a matter of intelligence or domestication, but a deeply disputed place within theological and scientific histories and their correspondent social visions.

At bottom, early modern writers had to contend with the question of how a perfect God could create imperfect creatures, those seemingly absent from the Garden of Eden. Alexander Ross's (1591–1654) exposition on Genesis puts the question this way: "Did God create in the beginning, imperfect creatures, as Bees, Waspes, and such like?"[48] To justify the ways of God to man, Ross depends on some Aristotelian casuistry: "He did not create them actually, as he did the perfect creatures, but hee created them in their causes, as hee gave that faculty to the flesh of an horse, to beget Waspes being dead" (19). In other words, although imperfect creatures were not part of the original zoography, God made it possible for them to breed through the process of putrefaction. Similarly, both John Wilkins in his *Essays Toward a Real Character and a Philosophical Language* (1668) and Athanasius Kircher in his *Arca Noe* (1675) discuss the architectures and animal populations of Noah's ark, yet neither allocates any space for caterpillars, insects, or others creatures thought to spring from dust and mud.[49] This absence symptomizes another set of theological problems: were Adam and Eve born with lice, or did those emerge after the Fall?[50] As I suggested in the previous discussion of breast-feeding women, worms and other noxious creatures cannot easily be assimilated to arguments from providential design. In fact, given their endless reproducibility and the unpredictable nature of their swarming motion, imperfect creatures may actually threaten the ideas of an orderly universe and the regeneration of Nature symbolized by Noah's Ark. When scholars ignore "imperfect creatures," they help gloss over the urgency of these seventeenth-century theological problems and downplay the ways in which so-called pests were conceived as material and ideational agents.

To be an agent, though, does not require what we now think of as ontological or taxonomic stability. Indeed, a pathologized instability is typical of most vermin and imperfect creatures. Seventeenth-century writers rarely distinguished between lice and fleas, or between rats and mice. The "ancients," writes Michael McCormick, "did not have use of the Linnaean conceptual apparatus to name and describe their animals."[51] In classical Latin, *mus*, and in Greek, *mys*, may refer to *either* a rat or a mouse; seventeenth-century writers tended to follow their predecessors in using both "rat" and "mouse" to signify common rodents. Frogs and toads, similarly, may have been distinguished in Edward Topsell's *Historie of Foure-Footed Beastes* (1607) or other texts of natural history, but poets, painters, and novelists rarely exercised such precision. This taxonomic vacillation frustrates efforts to impose a representational coherence on a particular animal in order to tell the "story" of a singular species: the ape, the horse, the rhino.[52] Vermin simply thwart such representational schema. Writing the story of the "worm," as Janelle A. Schwartz asserts, requires being attentive to representations of "everything from an earthworm to a larva to a maggot, to a flying insect, and the unknown."[53] But while vermin spoil nominalist schemes—and this is an important point—*in their categorical instability* they often constitute the temporary stability of any system in the first place. Serres claims, "We parasite each other and live amidst parasites. Which is more or less a way of saying that they constitute our environment" (10). Although it was not always apparent to early moderns who the "they" were or how "they" originated, writers from Shakespeare to Defoe similarly acknowledged the fundamental role of vermin. Reading beneath the grain allows us a more comprehensive (if shifting and squirming) appreciation of biopolitics in the period.

In the first chapter, "Rats, Witches, Miasma, and Early Modern Theories of Contagion," I confront the problem of how sixteenth- and early seventeenth-century thinkers understood the role of rats in the transmission of disease. The transmission of bubonic plague by rats was established only in 1894 when the bacteriologist Alexandre Yersin located the *Pasteurella pestis* (later, *Yersinia pestis*) bacterium in the blood of infected hosts and isolated the role of the flea as a disease vector; as the host-animal died of plague, the flea, feeding on its blood, leapt off onto another host, human or animal. Although the Chinese in the late Ming and early Qing era may have had a nascent understanding of the role of rats in the transmission of plague and although the English sometimes mentioned the role of animals as disease vectors, rats rarely make early modern lists of plague animals. Yet rats and other small animals nonetheless played an important role in linking environmental and supernatural accounts of disease. On the one hand, because they were still widely regarded as creatures of putrefaction, born of rot and corruption, rats signified, by their very presence, an unhealthy environment from which illness may emerge. On the other hand, it was widely believed that demons and witches could assume the shapes of "some small creatures" such as toads, salamanders, and rats by virtue of what is called "inspissated" air, that is, air that "partakes of some of the properties of earth."[54] Within theories of miasma, or polluted air, rodents bear an analogous (or even, for some, homologous) relationship to witches, and witches, in turn, are held responsible for physical and spiritual disease. As King James puts it in his *Daemonologie*, witches are "like the Pest."[55] I trace this constellation of witches, vermin, and "inspissated" air in contemporary treatises on witchcraft and plague in a series of engravings by the Dutch artist Jacob de Gheyn and in Shakespeare's *Macbeth*, written and performed during the London plague years of 1605–7.

In different ways, de Gheyn and Shakespeare suggest how theories of contagion developed within and were responsive to a world wracked by climatic instability and repeated local dearth, if not outright famine. Disease, plague, and famine comprise three of the four aspects of "pestilence," a term that had naturalistic and metaphysical connotations. As late as 1799, Noah Webster's *A Brief History of Epidemic and Pestilential Diseases* attempts to reconcile descriptions of plague in ancient, scriptural, and medieval sources and confronts the question of causality. Webster traces plague, famine, and war to "one common cause"—weather—or what he calls "a pestilential state of the elements, as fatal to vegetables as to animal life."[56] In a study that includes an impressive series of tables detailing the weather patterns, comet sightings, murrains, and crop failures for every recorded account of pestilence, Webster makes the case that "famine and pestilence are equally the

effects of . . . a temporary derangement of the regular operations of nature"
(86). Such "derangements" include comets, volcanoes, droughts, rains, and
overpopulated cities—any number of conditions that give rise to a corrupt
state of air. At the same time, Webster's seemingly empirical imperative is
linked to his theological effort to authenticate biblical accounts of the great
plagues of Egypt, a land whose climate, he argues, was especially conducive
to pestilence. For Webster, as for his predecessors, plague and famine appear as part of the same complex of medical, historical, environmental, and
theological discourses that are borne on the backs of frogs, flies, and the
"swarming things" of Genesis.

I bring this understanding to the next chapter, "Swarming Things:
Dearth and the Plagues of Egypt," in order to focus on seventeenth-century
adaptations of the Exodus story. At the heart of the ten plagues of Egypt
is an age-old interpretive problem: are the lice, frogs, and swarming things
to be read allegorically or literally? Is the story about political sovereignty
or natural populations? Focusing on the former, Graham Hammill has argued convincingly that plague discourse exceeds its traditional function—to
"imagine new forms of social and political control"—and instead may undermine sovereignty, narrowly conceived.[57] Like Hammill, I turn to Fou-
caultian ideas of biopower to examine plague discourse but reintroduce to
biopolitical readings the question of the animal, demonstrating how naturalistic and typological readings prove mutually constitutive. A woodcut by
Jan Sadeler (1550–1600?) depicting the plague of frogs raises critical questions about the apparent agency of vermin invading the dinner table of fashionable Egyptians. Encouraging his viewers to read history and typology as
complex overlays of natural phenomena, Sadeler underscores the interpretive problems posed by vermin: if the plagues of Egypt can be read in terms
of responses to political and moral crises—in terms, that is, of sovereign
power—they can also, like *Macbeth*, be regarded as deeply entangled in contemporary epidemiological and ecological crises, especially food shortages.
Focusing on discourses of dearth and famine in plague poems by George
Wither (1588–1667) and Abraham Cowley (1618–67), I trace their efforts to
stabilize the interpretive strategies—religious, political, and naturalistic—
that could be brought to bear on the ten plagues. Cowley's heavily footnoted
poem reflects the erudite author's knowledge of contemporary science; and
without surrendering an overarching providential narrative, Cowley brings
the biblical infestation of vermin very close to naturalistic explanation.

In the plagues of Egypt poems, where hordes of loathsome toads and armies of winged invaders darken the Egyptian skies and cover the tables of decadent slave owners, imperfect creatures constitute a kind of verminous sublime. These poems exemplify in dramatic ways the collective agency of vermin, their ability to alter domestic, national, and natural economies. At the same time that Cowley was writing, Royal Society virtuosi were pressing vermin into a different kind of service; lice, insects, frogs, and other beings were used to prove the empirical reality of what Robert Boyle called "the argument from design," the belief that providential wisdom could be read in the physiology of all God's creations. Robert Hooke's now-iconic description of the flea in *Micrographia*—a "small creature" praised for the "strength and beauty" of its limbs and parts, "adorn'd with a curiously polish'd suit of sable Armour"—brings to the fore late seventeenth-century attempts to argue that anatomical structures were, in their very complexity, evidence of providential design.[58] The next two chapters examine questions raised by the argument from design in neuroanatomy, especially in the work of the physician Thomas Willis.

Like his predecessors William Harvey and Pierre Gassendi, Thomas Willis appeals to the Book of Nature in *Cerebri Anatome* (*The Anatomy of the Brain*) (1664) and *De Anima Brutorum* (*Of the Soul of Brutes*) (1672) to provide a theological justification for comparative anatomy. Whereas Harvey had turned to "larger and more perfect animals" to demonstrate the "perfect and divine" harmonies of Nature,[59] the wisdom of the Creator, claims Willis, is manifested "even in the smallest and most despicable Animals" who share, with humans, hearts, or "so many altars and hearths to perpetuate this vital flame" of life.[60] And, like Harvey and Boyle, Willis uses resemblance to emphasize the difference between humans and animals; by "confronting these Brains," he continues, "the vast difference of the Soul of a Brute and that of a Man may . . . be shewn" (152). Yet the significance of Willis for animal studies, I argue, is not his critique of Descartes on some absolute difference between man and animal—the "more perfect" animals, Willis admits, are capable of judgment and even imagination—but his distinction between "perfect" and "imperfect" creatures. Willis reexamines this Aristotelian distinction through comparative neuroanatomy, identifying structural differences in the brains of different species by exploring the central nervous systems of oysters as well as those of humans, apes, and domesticated quadrupeds. While Willis is not the first seventeenth-century natural philosopher to distinguish between "perfect" and "imperfect" creatures, he naturalizes a theologically motivated discourse that associates instinct with a swarming, soulless form of behavior that both reason and imagination enjoin us to contain and control.

In chapter 3, "'Observe the Frog': Imperfect Creatures, Neuroanatomy, and the Problem of the Human," I suggest Willis' theologically laden anatomical writing leads to a concept of "an amphibious human," one who shares with other "perfect" creatures wit and intelligence. Comparative neuroanatomy, then, collapses the Cartesian difference between "human" and "animal"—a difference that Willis must reinstate theologically (rather than anatomically) by positing that humans alone possess an incorporeal soul, also located in the brain. A similar kind of category collapse underwrites seventeenth-century satires of Royal Society experiments on vermin. Thomas Shadwell's *The Virtuoso* mocks Sir Nicholas Gimcrack's fascination with insects, spiders, and frogs at the expense of his discovering anything useful or reinforcing the civilized virtues of wit and good nature. To read Shadwell's play within the context of Willis' experimental philosophy is to appreciate in a profound and immediate way how insects, mollusks, worms, and frogs trouble Cartesian binaries. While Shadwell's play manifests this discomfort at the level of farce, Willis' scientific work, I conclude, exhibits the two-fold process of translation/purification typical of what Latour calls the "modern constitution"; in trying to draw a line between Nature and Culture, Willis proliferates hybrid beings, notably his "Amphibious" "double-soul'd man."[61] In an important sense, "imperfect creatures" emerge, in such works, from the mud of scholastic philosophy and reappear as the introjected other of the early modern self.

In their rejection of Cartesian binaries, Willis and other comparative anatomists are important for animal studies because they promote the notion the "more perfect creatures"—always mammals—share with human beings fundamental neuroanatomical structures, including structures of feeling intrinsic to a social world. Significantly, Willis refers to the more perfect beings as "twin species" with humans, created, according to Genesis—unlike crawling things—on the fifth day. In chapter 4, "Libertine Biopolitics: Dogs, Bitches, and Parasites in Shadwell, Rochester, and Gay," I focus on the complex biological and social status of one "perfect creature": *Canis lupus familiaris*, or dogs. Donna Haraway has remarked about dogs that "the familiar is always where the uncanny lurks," and in this chapter, I explore the role of dogs in the depiction of gendered madness and disease.[62] That early modern Europeans, during times of plague, feared and executed dogs is well documented. Defoe's *Journal of the Plague Year* reports over 40,000 dogs and perhaps 200,000 cats were destroyed during the plague of 1665 (along with, I might add, a "prodigious" number of rats and mice).[63] The Restoration dog, similarly, brings together many of the thematic concerns I examine in the first three chapters: scapegoating, mimetic contagion, and the logic of expulsion; relationships among infection and infestation; and the intimate relationships among women and verminous animals. Tracing those discourses through analyses of Shadwell's *Timon of Athens* and Rochester's "A Ramble in St. James's Park," I emphasize the porous boundaries separating domesticated and verminous creatures.

"What Happened to the Rats? Hoarding, Hunger, and Storage on Crusoe's Island," circles back to rodents and explores the significant absence of rats on Robinson Crusoe's island. In marked contrast to eighteenth-century accounts of island ecologies ruined by rodent infestations, Crusoe—unlike his real-life progenitor Alexander Selkirk—suffers no depredations by rats. The economy Crusoe constructs depends, I argue, not simply on the *presence* of European corn but on the *absence* of the rats that plagued Selkirk and the millions in Europe who tried desperately to protect grain supplies from vermin. In discussing both *Robinson Crusoe* (1719) and *The Farther Adventures of Robinson Crusoe* (1719), I focus on the ways in which food accumulation and storage are essential for social virtues like compassion and benevolence, and for the reassertion of an European, civilized identity on Crusoe's island. Bees, particularly in the first half of *Farther Adventures*, help Defoe to imagine a system that might be immune to the threat posed by rats, crows, and other vermin. While Defoe joins Bernard Mandeville and others in imagining the apid colony as an alternative to constant competition for food, the hive itself, I maintain, is based on a form of organized violence, what eighteenth-century naturalists saw as the periodic "sacrifice" or expulsion of hungry drones. Generalizing from such examples, I conclude what we call "the animal" is bound not only—and maybe not even primarily—to "the human" but to fundamental questions of food and diet as well as disease.

In different ways, these chapters explore some of the implications of Serres's observation that "We have made the louse in our image; let us see ourselves in his" (7). Given the vast range of early modern texts featuring vermin, I have had to make some strategic decisions, and these chapters should be taken as necessarily exploratory rather than comprehensive. What unites them is the paradoxical logic of the parasite: vermin must be banished from biological, economic, and theological systems, and yet they remain essential to their constitution. Vermin become convenient scapegoats for those qualities that must be repressed or controlled in post-Cartesian ideals of the human, even as they return, invariably, to plague our economies and haunt our constructions of human exceptionalism. Vermin—either early modern fleas or twenty-first century "trash animals"—always plunge humans back into complex ecologies.[64] Swarming and multiplying, biting and eating, they threaten to overwhelm the orderly, theologically buttressed sociopolitical economies we tend to identify with Enlightenment and modern thought. Snarling curs, voracious rats, and omnipresent fleas mark the limits of Timon's generosity, Cowley's biblical commentary, and Defoe's colonial endeavors. Ultimately, they encourage us to rethink the constitution of "the animal" as well as the human in the ongoing development of animal studies.

CHAPTER I

Rats, Witches, Miasma, and Early Modern Theories of Contagion

Rats tenured in the academy of hunger,
Each worm an *emperor of dissolution*,
Every **beetle** a senator of the end.

—MARK DOTY AND DARREN WATERSTON, *A SWARM,*
A FLOCK, A HOST: A COMPENDIUM OF CREATURES

In sixteenth-century England, outbreaks of the plague, the persecution of women for witchcraft, and several major rat infestations occurred during an extended period of climatological instability. The Little Ice Age, between 1350 and 1850, was characterized by a general cooling, bringing about what Brian Fagan calls "a lethal mix of misfortunes": famine, serial epidemics, bread riots, and chaos. "Witchcraft accusations soared," he points out, with the greatest number of prosecutions in England and France occurring in the severe weather years of 1587 and 1588.[1] Drawing, in part, on Fagan's analysis, Emily Oster argues "in a time period when the reasons for changes in weather were largely a mystery," witches served as scapegoats for unseasonable weather that threatened harvests and outbreaks of disease; she, too, demonstrates a correspondence between the rise of the European witchcraft trials and temperature fluctuations during the Little Ice Age.[2] The environmental and epidemiological factors that contributed to witchcraft persecutions sometimes are marginalized by historians focused on sociopolitical concerns, but the roles played by climate and disease are crucial to understanding how developing theories of contagion yoked witches, rats, and plague in the early modern imagination.[3] Both witches and vermin are linked by miasmic theory to unnatural or uncanny modes of reproduction; these modes of reproduction, in turn, mimic the mysterious process of contagion, thereby reinforcing associations between rats and disease.[4] Although association does not imply causality, paying attention to how witches, rats, and plague work in concert helps us recognize the ways early modern writers and their readers understood, or misunderstood, the agency of imperfect creatures in the transmission of disease. Imperfect creatures, miasma, and witches are all parts of a generalized system of *pestilence* that generated breakdowns of the biopolitical order. What René Girard calls "the logic of expulsion" governed attitudes not only toward the infected victims of the plague but also, more generally, toward populations—human or otherwise—similarly perceived as threats to natural and cultural structures.[5]

Even in the twenty-first century, as John Kelly points out, the transmission of the plague among humans can be puzzling. Its highly mediated chain of infection can take several, not always predictable, forms. In one of the more common, a rat community's food supply is disrupted by an "ecological disaster"; the rats search for food in human settlements and, as infected rodents succumb to the plague, the parasitical flea *X. cheopis* is driven to find other hosts.[6] Once infected, humans easily spread the disease. Surrounded by death, famine, and disease, but without the benefit of germ theory, learned and popular writers alike during the sixteenth and seventeenth centuries recognized that plague was spread through contact, including contact between humans and animals, but cast about for etiological explanations.[7] George Wither claims the plague "much amazes/ The naturall man"; "he seldome findes ... The *Causes* and *Effects* agree together," and, if he does, "there is much uncertainty in either."[8] Confounded, seventeenth-century writers struggled to reconcile classical and biblical authorities and metaphysical explanations with empirical evidence and a nascent, contemporary tradition of naturalistic explanation. Anita Guerrini has argued that while physicians like Thomas Sydenham (1624–89) did not go so far as to propose "a causal explanation of the environment on disease," they did note "the concurrence of particular diseases and particular environmental circumstances."[9] Within what she calls the "pathological environment" of the early modern period, the theological notion that plague marked the corruption of a fallen, postlapsarian earth was compatible with both classical and naturalistic theories of contagion, especially that of pestilential or "bad air."

In this fluid and volatile intellectual environment, analyses of the plague frequently proceed by imagistic association. In many ways, early modern descriptions are indebted to Virgil's *Aeneid*, a text Sheila Barker argues is largely Aristotelian: for classical writers, pestilence is but "one symptom," she writes, "of nature's universal degeneration and corruption, a cycle initiated in the heavens and permeating all the lower spheres."[10] Seventeenth-century texts tend to resituate this metanarrative of "universal degeneration" within the context of Judeo-Christian theology. In his poem *Epiloimia Epe, or Anatomy of the Pestilence* (1666), William Austin draws on a compendium of etiological theories (Lucretian, Aristotelian, and Galenic) to argue that while the plague first appeared after the Flood as a sign of God's "indignation," subsequent visitations are endemic to a fallen world.[11] The earth itself is imagined as a corrupted body:

> Our *Mother Earth* some reckon such a flat,
> As *pudding* makes, and never washes *gut*:
> Eats carrion and digests not, then at last
> Belches and blows us backward with the blast.[12]

This image of a belching, farting earth (possibly recalling the London earthquakes of 1649 and 1650) drives home Austin's point that if "*Mother Earth*" can provide a "kinde embrace," she can also, and unpredictably, prove niggardly, giving food "onely fit to choke us," so that we are "starv'd at nurse."[13] In his vision of an ailing world, humans share the fate of their mother: "we must languish and be sick as ill as she."[14] Plague is the expression of a gendered earth cursed with and by human sin. Insisting that woman first "curst the earth," Austin invokes a time-worn narrative that leads from Eve, through the daughters of Gaia and Uranus, to contemporary witches, the most recent incarnations of feminized and sexualized malevolence: "Furies are females," he declares, "and who Furies made, / Gave them their whips to labor in their trade."[15] As the "*King of Mischiefs* agents," witches spread contagion:

> *Records* will tell you *Plague's* an *hellish* itch.
> That first attacks a *sorcerer* or *witch*.
> No matter in what manner they receive it,
> Whether in *pain* or *pleasure*, so they give it.[16]

If sorcerers and witches are not the only cause of plague, their sexualized alliances with the Devil make them among its first victims and the sources, directly or indirectly, of subsequent contamination.

Within the theologically charged environment of early modern Europe, the terms "plague" and "pestilence" could refer to a variety of divine scourges:

disease, famine, bad air, crop failures, murrains, or infestations of animals, ranging from rats, to lice, to locusts. Because "pestilence" includes crop failure brought about by infestations, vermin serve as a kind of missing link or excluded middle in seventeenth-century theories of contagion. In his influential treatise, *On the Demon-Mania of Witches* (1580), Jean Bodin discusses the case of four would-be witches in Constance accused of stirring up a storm that, in his words, "ruined the fruit for four leagues around."[17] In Bodin's providentialist view, Satan often tries to take credit for natural disasters, sometimes convincing his witches that "they bring, or drive away the plague and tempest and famine" when, instead, Satan simply has forecast a divinely sent storm.[18] Nonetheless, moral corruption, "blasphemies," and "atheism," claims Bodin, breed "evil spirits," "plagues," "wars," and "famine" (145). This list of dire natural, metaphysical, and sociopolitical phenomena, suggests that, in plague discourse, categories are never really distinct. Then it is hardly surprising that, in a revealing simile, Bodin conflates witches with "vermin":

> Not that it is impossible to drive witches away completely without there always being some, who are just like toads and grass-snakes on the ground, spiders in houses, caterpillars, and flies in the air, who are engendered by corruption and who attract the poison from the earth, and the infection from the air. But well cultivated land, purified air, and cleared trees are not so subject to this infection. And if one lets the vermin multiply, it engenders corruption and infects everything. (145–46)

"Engendered by corruption," witches, like toads, caterpillars, and flies, invite or impel plague-like conditions: they "attract the poison of the earth, and the infection from the air." By superimposing the discourses of moral corruption on those of natural infestation, Bodin makes the referents of his phrase, "the vermin," difficult to disentangle. Witches, toads, flies, spiders, and so on are all catalysts for ecological and epidemiological corruption. While verminous conditions can be rectified, to some extent, by "purifying" the air through cultivation and reclaiming wastelands for productive uses, Bodin's language of infection thwarts attempts to distinguish between vermin infestations and witches' curses.

In conflating witches, plague, and vermin, Bodin blurs the lines between miasmic pollution (infection) and verminous corruption (infestation): "If one lets the vermin multiply," he insists, "it engenders corruption and in-

fects everything." His fusion of infection and infestation may strike us, looking back from the perspective of germ theory, as typical of a prescientific
worldview, but this linkage reflects the fundamental precepts of miasmatic
theory, which held that "contagion could not adequately explain widespread
epidemics; rather, a tainting of the atmosphere as a whole was responsible."[19]
Understood as a compound of tiny particles, air was imagined as carrying
mysterious motes that infected bodies, which then could infect the bodies
of others. Drawing on contemporary humoral theory, the physician Thomas
Lodge explains infection in such terms in his treatise on the plague, published in 1603. "Contagion," writes Lodge, "is an evil qualitie in a bodie, communicated unto an other by touch, engendring one and the same disposition
in him to whom it communicated."[20] Plague, he continues, "proceedeth from
the venomous corruption of the humors and spirits of the body, infected
by the attraction of corrupted aire, or infection of evil vapours, which have
the property to alter mans bodies, and poysons his spirits after a straunge
and dangerous qualitie" (B2v). For Lodge, ecological disruption ("corrupted
aire") is internalized as communicable disease, "the venemous corruption"
that infects and disseminates its deleterious effects. Like Bodin's "infection
from the air," Lodge's "infection of evil vapours" links disease to atmospheric
disturbances. "Pestilent sicknesses," Lodge claims, are heralded by regions
"troubled with thicke, cloudy, moyst, and ill smelling vapors," with the wind
coming from the south.

Theories of putrefaction are apparent in Bodin's warnings about "poison
from the earth" and Lodge's concern with warm and "ill smelling vapors" and
played a crucial role in early modern biotheological discourses. They also ensured that imperfect creatures, the animals most closely associated with rot,
became further enfolded in the contagious cluster of witches, plague, and bad
air. Still widespread in the sixteenth and early seventeenth centuries was the
ancient assumption that rats, mice, toads, and other denizens of the witches'
kitchens were generated spontaneously from putrefaction. This belief, found
in Ovid's *Metamorphoses* and many other classical texts, was reinforced in
one of Europe's most important sixteenth-century works of natural philosophy, Giambattista Della Porta's neo-Pythagorean *Natural Magick* (1584).
Della Porta, citing Pliny, among others, claims "Mice are generated of Putrefaction"; after the flooding of the Nile, mice emerge with "their fore-parts
living and their hinder parts being nothing but earth."[21] The early sixteenth-
century philosopher and alchemist Henry Cornelius Agrippa (whose work
was translated into English in the seventeenth century) described all ani-

mals generated without "Manifest seed" as "Monstrous," and claimed mice "sometimes are generated by Coition, and sometimes of the putrefaction of the Earth."[22] Unwilling to reject classical authorities outright, many other sixteenth and seventeenth-century natural philosophers equivocated, creating in their accounts of imperfect creatures a tension between sexual reproduction and spontaneous generation. Acknowledging there is "some dispute" among his sources, a somewhat skeptical Edward Topsell nevertheless cites Pliny and other ancient writers in his *Historie of Foure-Footed Beastes* (1607): "the generation or procreation of Myce, is not onely by copulation, but also nature worketh wonderfully in engendering them by earth and small showers."[23] Rats, in Topsell's view, "belongeth also to the rank of mice" and are similarly creatures of putrefaction; their long and "venomous" tail "seems to partake with the nature of Serpents" (519). Topsell's strained morphological analogy between rats' tails and poisonous snakes exemplifies the ways in which the category of "vermin"—useless or "Monstrous" animals—could expand (or contract) to accommodate any species linked metaphorically to disease, witches, slime, or even "small showers." Rats and mice, then, shared with other imperfect creatures—frogs, toads, worms, and scorpions among them—a suspicious origin in putrefying matter and ambiguous modes of reproduction.

Early modern questions about the reproductive agency of rodents complicated their role in sixteenth- and early seventeenth-century theories of contagion. Instead of looking for evidence that rats were (or were not) perceived as disease vectors in a twentieth- or twenty-first century sense of the term—as hosts for the plague, bacillus—we should think of them as actants, as mediating agents within interanimating cycles of bad weather, environmental stress, corrupted air, moral degeneration, and communicable disease. What Edward Green argues about African theories of disease also might be applied to early modern understandings of contagion: "indigenous contagion beliefs express essentially the same process of infection as modern germ theory attempts to, but in an idiom to which we are unaccustomed."[24] The writings of fifteenth-, sixteenth-, and seventeenth-century physicians and theologians are full of uncanny moments in which the etiology of disease is described in a rhetoric that seems familiar in its depiction of complex networks of relations and causation, but links (for us) what appear to be unlikely and even implausible elements. In his *Discours des Sorciers* (1610), Henri Boguet begins with a complaint that witches, with Satan's help, "cause cankerworms, rats, and other vermin to waste the fruit, even as they de-

plete the fertilization in the soil." Rather than seeing these creatures as naturalistic instruments of evil, he quickly conflates rats and witches: there is
hardly a country, he asserts, "not infested with this miserable and damnable
vermin."[25] This verbal slippage between destructive animals and metaphysical agents allows the rubric "damnable vermin" to suggest that both rodent
infestations and witches' satanic designs blight harvests.[26] In such texts, rats
and mice scurry through early modern theories of contagion by virtue of an
ontological instability that makes them amenable, if not foundational, to
both naturalistic and theocentric theories of disease.

It would be convenient to argue that some writers, under the empirical imperatives of seventeenth-century natural philosophy, grew skeptical of
witchcraft and began to recognize a direct, causal relationship between rats
and disease. Perhaps a few did. In her article on plague and Continental art,
Baker suggests, as early as the fourteenth century, travelers in Europe had
observed an association between shipboard rats and the spread of plague,
a point she uses to examine rat infestations in paintings by Raphael and
Poussin. Another work, Vincenzo Cartari's 1556 *Le imagini de I dei de gli
antichi*, she claims, offers what appears to be a "scientific explanation," linking
dead rats to pestilence.[27] Yet proximity does not imply causation. In his report on rodents in Spain, for example, Topsell links rats and plague without
recognizing a modern understanding of zoonotic disease: "There are such a
number of these mice in Spaine," he writes, "that many times their destruction caused pestilent diseases, and this thing hapned amongst the Romaines
when they were in Cantabria, for they were constrained to hier [sic] men
by stipends to kill the mice, and those which did kill them, scarse escaped
with life."[28] What Topsell probably means by his statement, "their destruction caused pestilent diseases," is the sheer number of rodent corpses created
a noxious breeding ground for all sorts of diseases. His account, in this manner, links mice and disease through theories of bad air.

Even though early modern writers operated without the explanatory
power of germ theory, they often suggested that rats and mice played a
quasi-pathological role in the spread of the plague. Writers on witchcraft,
in particular, often reinforced a complex chain of associations that linked
rodents to miasma, miasma to witches, and witches to famine and disease.
Their ontological instability allows rodents, like witches, to embody mysterious forms of contagion mimicked by their unnatural modes of generation.
Ironically, in other words, it is *by virtue* of their slippery natures that rats
can appear in early modern accounts of pestilence as something *resembling* a

disease vector. In their relationship to moisture and "bad air," rodents herald disease; as instruments of God's wrath, they are heaven's gluttonous emissaries. They move easily between the medical and religious imaginaries, yoking what, for us, appear to be very different worlds.

METAMORPHIC RATS AND FROGS:
THE DRAWINGS OF JACQUES DE GHEYN II

The intricate and mysterious associations among vermin, witches, and disease were a popular subject in the visual culture of the early modern period, particularly in the dramatic series of etchings by the Dutch artist Jacques de Gheyn II (c.1565–1629). In traditional visual depictions of witchcraft from Breughel to de Gheyn, rodents are rendered alongside salamanders, serpents, scorpions, and other imperfect creatures in genre paintings of "the witches' Sabbath" or the "witches' kitchen" in which several (usually old) women mix potions and raise storms while their animal consorts look on.[29] Verminous familiars in de Gheyn's early seventeenth-century drawing *Witches' Kitchen* link his work to Breugel's *St. James and the Magician Hermogenes* in which demonic beings are raised from a miasmic cauldron. Its dank subterranean setting, as Claudia Swan notes, is "the diametric opposition of the polished Dutch domestic interior." In this work, witches cajole, rather than combat, traditional household enemies, such as toads and rats, in ways that suggest de Gheyn's understanding of the popular view that the "devil vexes and confounds by purposeful inversion; the force of evil is compelled to invert."[30] Such typical examples of demonic "inversion" may make his depiction of witchcraft seem "largely conventional,"[31] but several of de Gheyn's other sketches or drawings jarringly juxtapose portrayals of witches with naturalistic images of imperfect creatures.

Take, for example, his *Study of Hermit Crab and Witchcraft* (fig. 2). Swan argues convincingly that the crab and the scenes of witchcraft are linked by the former's emblematic nature as a figure (like the moon and woman) of inconstancy and mutability.[32] The crab's association with witches is reinforced by its backward and sideways movement: "Witches," writes Nicholas Remy in the *Daemonolatreiae libri tres* (1595) "love to do everything in a ridiculous and unseemly manner. For they turn their backs toward the Demons when they go to worship them, and approach them sideways like a crab."[33] At the same time, crabs, like rats, were often regarded in the popular imagination

as creatures of putrefaction. In describing "monstrous generations" not produced "according to the Laws of Nature," Agrippa includes in this category
the usual suspects (gnats generated from worms, wasps from a horse, bees
from an ox), and "a Crab" whose "legs being taken of[f], and . . . buried in
the ground" will later (presumably) emerge as "a Scorpion."[34] De Gheyn's
creatures in this sketch, similarly, are both "zoomorphic" and markedly
arthropod-like. Arthropods include *crustaceans* (such as shrimp, lobster, and
crabs) and *chelicerata* (such as spiders and scorpions, along with insects).
These animals have in common an exoskeleton, jointed appendages, and a
segmented body. Behind and to the right of the accurately rendered hermit
crab, a group of creatures troubles species identities. One clearly sports an
exoskeleton, a kind of shell, on which, strangely, a naked human form clings
like a barnacle. The short, broad cockroach-like being in the middle of the
demonic group exhibits qualities of humans and arthropods, as do the two
beings with long, segmented proboscis. In another version of hybridity, the
segmented bodies of arthropods are mimicked in the humanoid form of the
skeletal man on the right of the drawing.

Fig. 2, Jacques de Gheyn II, *Study of Hermit Crab and Witchcraft*

If de Gheyn's *Study of Hermit Crab and Witchcraft* links witchcraft and crabs through an emblematic tradition, its metamorphic associations among witches, insects, and crabs stage the complexities and ambiguities of seventeenth-century theories about generation, putrefaction, and the role of imperfect creatures. In visually undoing traditional boundaries between the natural and the monstrous, the stable and the metamorphic, and the "real" and nightmarish renderings of hybridity, de Gheyn's sketch deals not in questions of belief but in images of what Karen Barad calls entanglement—the irrevocable materiality and contingency of representation/reality.[35]

In a related sketch, *Witches and Frogs* (fig. 3), de Gheyn interrogates the problem of generation. Three amphibious chimera—frogs endowed with marked secondary sexual characteristics—surround a book of spells. In this instance, creatures that ambiguously might reproduce "outside" the laws of Nature through spontaneous generation have anthropomorphized female breasts and oversized male genitalia, as though they were reproducing monstrously through sexual intercourse.

Fig. 3. Jacques de Gheyn II, *Witches and Frogs*

An obvious interpretation of these figures would see the frogs (and the rats discussed in fig. 4 below) as witches in the process of transformation, their amphibious bodies beginning to assume the postures and disposition of humans. This reading is in keeping, again, with theories of bad air. Kramer and Sprenger argue demons and witches can assume a bodily form only with the aid of "inspissated" air. Devils and disembodied spirits," they contend, "can effect this condensation by means of gross vapours raised from the earth, and by collecting them together into shapes in which they abide, not as defilers of them, but only as their motive power which gives to that body the formal appearance of life."[36] Even under such circumstances, however, witches cannot assume "natural" shapes "except in the case of some small creatures" such as toads, salamanders, and rats.[37] De Gheyn's strange depiction of demonic transformation similarly endows imperfect creatures with a kind of "motive power," a "formal appearance of life." Yet what make his amphibians seem especially "monstrous" are their breasts and genitalia, the secondary sexual characteristics tagging them as desiring creatures; if these metamorphic frogs are capable of human sexual desires, the drawing suggests, they are also capable of other kinds of agency. De Gheyn's imperfect creatures, in other words, are not, like those in the "witches' kitchen," silent witnesses to human manipulations of the natural world, but active agents of desire and disorder.

This sense of ambiguous agency marks de Gheyn's *Study of Two Rats and Three Frogs* (1609) as well (fig. 4). The strangely humanoid flayed rats and three frogs grasp sticks in ways that simultaneously suggest *both* aspiring ro-

Fig. 4. Jacques de Gheyn II, *Study of Two Rats and Three Frogs*

dents, trying to walk, *and* disabled humans, struggling to avoid falling down. Given their extended bellies, the rats seem both pregnant and starved.

The frog to the right of the rats lounges languidly atop what appears to be a pile of coins. Most striking about this image is that de Gheyn's naturalistic technique—specifically, the fine and accurate articulation of muscles in rest and motion—is entangled with cultural representations of seemingly bestial or immoral aspiration and acquisitiveness. The effect, to say the least, is discomfiting. While Swan admits "it is difficult to reconcile the epistemological underpinnings of de Gheyn's naturalistic works with the tone, subject matter, and effect of his demonological pictures," she tries to split the difference by arguing that de Gheyn, skeptical of witchcraft, portrays what he regards as effects of a diseased imagination.[38] Following this assumption, one might regard the transformation of the animals in *Study of Two Rats and Three Frogs* as an example of a belief in demonological transformation from which the artist distances himself.

But questions about whether de Gheyn actually "believed" in witches do not, and should not, obscure the naturalistic theories of transformation, putrefaction, and inspissation on which he draws. His uncannily anthropomorphic vermin exist in a world, both historical and imaginative, alive with trans-species relationships. In de Gheyn's "imperfect creatures" struggling to assume human postures, we find iconic images of a socionatural world that has not yet been neatly divided, as ours has, into the "social" and the "real," or into distinct realms of religion and science.[39] The humanoid musculature of the rats and frogs implies the human and the verminous are always emergent qualities, transformative rather than static. In this sense, de Gheyn's creatures are not the beings with which we are familiar. Pre-Cartesian, animated by forces that humans share, their appetites, secondary sexual characteristics, and even their tails are entangled in the epistemological and ontological questions of what it means to be "human." On the one hand, the rats' serpentine appendages serve a tropological function in their phallic suggestiveness. Topsell writes that rats, "when they are in copulations, ... embrace with their tailes, filling one another without al delay."[40] On the other hand, however, Topsell's description is not "merely" symbolic: the tail of the rat is actually part of a complex vascular system used for cooling and heating that operates much like a penis, swelling and shrinking in accordance with the function it performs.[41] De Gheyn's rats inhabit both of these realms, the tropology of folk belief and the science of empirical observation. They entangle, in Barad's sense, humans, witches, and vermin in recursive hybridities.

VERMIN IN *MACBETH*

In ways that play on the themes of de Gheyn's drawings, Shakespeare's *Macbeth* exploits the associations between natural and spiritual contagion, drawing on seventeenth-century demonology and miasma theory to stage imagistically the relationship among vermin, plague, and witches. Shakespeare's tragedy was written and first performed sometime between 1605 and 1607 during the height of one of London's plague seasons.[42] As F. P. Wilson notes, the language Ross uses to describe Macbeth's Scotland very well could have been used to characterize plague-ridden London.[43] Under Macbeth's rule, "sighs and groans and shrieks that rend the air / Are made, not marked" and

> . . . violent sorrow seems
> A modern ecstasy. The dead mans knell
> Is there scarce asked for who, and good men's lives
> Expire before the flower's in their caps,
> Dying or ere they sicken.
>
> (4.3.169–74)[44]

References to pestilence and the human devastation of a plague-ridden city or kingdom abound throughout the play. Storms, murrains, and crop failures are the calling cards of the three witches in act 1. A "feverous" earth and crop failures are alluded to in the second act and again in act 4. Indeed, Macbeth's rise to power and subsequent rule are cast as a kind of epidemiological horror, the contagion in the body politic mirroring that of the natural world.

One of the most insistent patterns of imagery in Shakespeare's tragedy links the moral and political state of Scotland to atmospheric disturbances and miasma. The play begins with the three witches crying, "Fair is foul and foul is fair, / Hover through the fog and filthy air" (1.11.11–12). Subsequent invocations of "filthy air" similarly confuse or conflate the two realms. In the first act, Banquo describes the witches emerging from the kind of miasma associated with disease, bad air, and moral corruption: the "earth hath bubbles, as the water has / And these are of them" (1.3.79–80). Later, in Shakespeare's staging of a masque-like witches' Sabbath, Hecate announces she will "raise . . . artificial sprites" out of a moondrop "distilled by magic slights" (3.5. 23, 26). Hecate's "little spirit," her imp, "sits in a foggy cloud" (3.5.34–35). In its uneasy ambiguity, this language describes the "inversions" and equivocations typical in early modern demonology ("Fair is foul and foul is fair"), and, at the same time, gestures toward the climatic instability of weather patterns during the Little Ice Age, when persistent storms off the North Sea battered the Scottish Lowlands and England.[45] The cold, foggy, and rainy climate of Macbeth's Scotland foreshadows and evokes miasmic associations that make atmospheric, moral, and political corruption seem mutually constitutive. "Infected be the air" the witches "ride" on, curses Macbeth, and "damned all those that trust them" (4.11.115).

In *Macbeth*'s generally theocentric view of multiplying "evil," swarming vermin play analogous roles in the spiritual, agricultural, and ecological economies. The traitor Macdonwald, for instance, is described as a kind of breeding ground for the carriers of pestilence, the flies and vermin that carry moral corruption as well as disease: "Worthy to be a rebel, for to that / The multiplying villainies of nature / Do swarm upon him" (1.2.10–12). This imagery recalls not only Bodin's creatures of putrefaction, but also the language of James I's *Daemonologie* (1597). In a dialogue between Epistemon and Philomathes, James, like many of his predecessors, describes witches as a kind of spiritual pestilence.[46] Witches, Epistemon says, are especially harmful to those who are "of infirme and weake faith," to which Philomathes responds, "Then they are like the Pest, which smites these sickarest [sic], that flies it farthest and apprehends deepliest the perrell thereof."[47] Philomathes invokes the idea that the very fear of contagion makes one vulnerable to it; and Macbeth, who allows his "vaulting ambition" to get the better of his loyalty, seems to invite the witches' spiritual pestilence to corrupt his soul. After he murders Duncan, Macbeth becomes linked metaphorically to witches, vermin, and other creatures of putrefaction: "O, full of scorpions is my mind, dear wife!" (3.2.59). If scorpions breed spontaneously from putrefaction, Macbeth is now the origin and incubator of his own putrefying sin. Although, for Malcolm, Macbeth's corruption assumes satanic proportions— "Not in the legions / Of horrid hell can come a devil more damned / In evils to top Macbeth" (4.3.57–59)—Shakespeare keeps alive the notion that moral corruption and infection are mutually constitutive: the hero's mind, like his wife's, is "infected" by things "unnatural" (5.1.61–63). As the Doctor says of Lady Macbeth, "Unnatural deeds / Do breed unnatural troubles; infected minds / To their deaf pillows will discharge their secrets" (5.1.61–63). The language of infection, then, is of a piece with the filthy air, scorpions, and swarming evils that plague the kingdom.

To acknowledge vermin—spiders, frogs, rats, and other creatures pre-

sumably born of rot and companionate with witches—as signs and symptoms of both spiritual and physical contagion in early modern literature does
not mean that one can definitively answer questions (long central to scholars
of early modern witchcraft and to some critics of *Macbeth*) about whether
Shakespeare and his audience actually "believed" in witches and their demonic familiars.[48] Indeed, these presumed creatures of putrefaction may
complicate our views about which animals can serve as familiars, and why.
Diane Purkiss reads familiars as "collaborative construction[s]"—that is, as
compromise formations between elite and popular versions of witchcraft—
that render the "witch a perverse kind of mother."[49] The filial relationship
she describes perhaps explains the witch's relationship with Graymalkin in
Macbeth, but rats and other less perfect creatures bring with them discursive
assumptions that undermine, rather than reinforce, filial—indeed, intersubjective and affective—relations. Composites of ideological and natural materials, affiliated with disease, and characterized by their ability to refuse a
stable shape at all, verminous familiars pose, rather than answer, questions
of knowledge and belief. In *Macbeth*, Shakespeare exploits the epistemological as well as ontological instability of rats and other imperfect creatures to
explore the complex relationships among vermin, disease, and witchcraft.
Refusing to provide answers, the play stages the many ways its audiences
might imagine the relationship between spiritual corruption and pestilence.
    Rodents are used to evoke the general context of pestilence very early in
Macbeth. One of the witches, describing her revenge on a woman who had
refused to share some food, envisions herself tracking the woman's husband
across the seas:

> Her husband's to Aleppo gone, master o'th' Tiger.
> But in a sieve I'll thither sail,
> And like a rat without a tail,
> I'll do, I'll do, and I'll do.

(1.3.7–10)

At least since the eighteenth century, this odd image has been treated as a
curious example of Elizabethan folklore. Glossing this stanza in his 1773 edition of Shakespeare, George Steevens writes, "it was imagined" that "though
a witch could assume the form of any animal she pleased," she could not alter
her sex: "the tail would still be wanting."[50] Yet given the emphasis on pestilence elsewhere in the play, Shakespeare's rat is a telling choice. What makes

the rat—rather than, say, a toad—an especially powerful vehicle for *Macbeth*'s witch is its suggestion not only of famine and "filthy" air but also of a toxic sexuality. In addition to proliferating through putrefaction, rats were figured, when full grown, as among the most lustful of creatures. Topsell refers to the white mouse as a long-standing image of lust, but "all mice," he asserts, are "most desirous of copulation."[51] Rats, in his mind, are even more sexually dangerous than mice, capable of going into something resembling elephant musth, excreting a toxic fluid: "For if the urine do fall upon the bare place of a man, it maketh the flesh rot unto the bones."[52] The bodily fluids of rats eat away at human flesh, and the danger posed by their "urine" is itself a refracted image of pestilential decay.

For Shakespeare's audience, however, the greatest danger posed by rats' "copulation" is their prodigious power of reproduction. Because they are able to reproduce quickly and in mind-boggling numbers, rats are a constant threat to human food supplies, a danger magnified during periods of bad weather and bad harvests. Topsell claims mice conceive every fourteen or sixteen days, exceeding "all other beasts" in the "number they bring forth"; a contemporary scholar estimates two black rats and their progeny, breeding continually for three years, can produce 329,000,000 offspring.[53] During a period in history when the cost of grain increased roughly in an inverse ratio to income, the productive capacity of rats and mice posed significant threats to life and livelihood: "the lower the income available to a household, the greater was the dependence on grain,"[54] and, therefore, the greater the danger posed by rodent infestations.

Europeans of all social classes were familiar with stories about famines caused by rats and mice, notably the biblical account of the plagues in Egypt, but contemporary narratives were common as well, especially stories of rats on board ships. Garcilaso de la Vega, to take one prominent example, tells his readers about the "great Destructions and even Plagues" that struck Peru in the sixteenth century, "caused by the incredible multitudes of Rats and Mice" that stowed away on Spanish ships. "Swarming all over the Land," these voracious rodents ate seeds and killed fruit trees, nearly forcing the colonists to "abandon their Dwellings," had not "God in mercy caused that Plague to cease on a sudden" when it was at its extremity.[55] In a similar vein, Samuel Clarke's account of the first English Bermuda plantation describes a "great Plague" visited on the English by "reason of a few Rats." Having infested a meal ship, they "multiplied so exceedingly" on the island that despite efforts to eradicate them using cats, dogs, ratsbane, and traps, and then even setting the woods on fire, the rats took over the island. By eating "all up," they precipitated a devastating disease. Clarke ends his narrative with a strangely hybrid explanation—part theological, part empirical; eventually, supplies from England and "some rest and ease" helped the disease to abate and "suddenly it pleased God (by what means was not known)" to "take [the rats] away."[56]

Read within the context of, and against, such narratives, Shakespeare's image of the would-be-demon rat simultaneously evokes and displaces a theocentric discourse of the plague, food shortages and infectious disease. As Deborah Willis argues, Shakespeare invokes or stages scenes of feeding or deprivations of food throughout *Macbeth*, even as "the witches' motives and the extent of their powers remain maddeningly opaque."[57] This ambiguity may be explained, in part, by recognizing within plague discourse, witches functioned as both carriers and symptoms of a mysterious and destructive mode of contact. They are, as Philomathes says in James I's *Daemonologie*, "like the Pest," and contagion, as we have seen in Austin's *Anatomy of the Pestilence*, was baffling enough to elicit a variety of explanations, with most commentators agreeing its origins taxed the capacity of human understanding. In their mysterious origins and connection to pestilence, witches share the opacity of vermin. The latter, at least, could be recuperated into a theological discourse as providential scourges of humankind's sins. In his *Curiosities: or, The Cabinet of Nature* (1637), a popular commonplace book, Robert Basset poses the question of why "unnecessary frogs and Mice doe breed ... of their owne accord, seeing other animals for Mans use breed not, but by propagation?" The answer, he asserts, lies in the power of God. Because plagues of mice are connected to other seemingly random natural disasters, such as floods and droughts, he reasons rodents must be instruments of divine power. "Even as the High Procurator of the great World, provides store of all manner of Viands for his little world (Man)," humankind remains prone to sin:

So also [God] chastiseth this neglecting Man, when he subtracts and withdrawes from him the fruits of water, earth, Ayre, and beasts for mans owne faults: Wherefore sometimes waters either abound by inundations, sometimes by Drought are extenuated, and scarce; sometimes the Ayre by contagion infects, sometimes fire rageth so, that from whence these breed, it can no more be certainly arrived, than whence the swarmes of these Animals. And the innumberable diseases of man do also breed.[58]

In Basset's theocentric view, the "innumerable diseases of man" are analogous to these "swarmes" of mice, inexplicable and dangerous, but permitted by God as scourges to humankind.

As Shakespeare's witch suggests, the battle for human souls is waged in often explicitly sexual terms. Very early in learned witchcraft literature, such as in Heinrich Kramer and James Sprenger's *Malleus Maleficarum* (1486), witches are represented as "enemies of the human race" not only because they "change the perceptions and befoul the emotions of man" (mental or psychological contagion) and "bring diseases" (epidemiological contagion) but because, among their "thousand ways of doing harm," they have power over human sexual function and appetite.[59] Not surprisingly, sexualized rodents are part of the witches' arsenal for tempting and bedeviling humankind. William Drage's 1665 treatise *Daimonomageia* includes cases of witches sending their "Imps, or young Spirits, into . . . the form of Mice, sometimes of Flies," who then bewitch cattle and men and blast "Plants and Fruits of the Earth."[60] John Barrow recounts the story of his son's possession by demons who appear in the form of rats and tempt him with "Pasties" or sweet food. "Then they would demand his Soul," writes Barrow, "bidding him give it to the Devil, but he refused to condescend to them."[61] Underscoring the characteristic conflation of metaphysics and materiality in witchcraft literature, Barrow's demon-rats cast their temptation in a diabolical image of food consumption: the demon-rats use a sweet to appeal to the young man's appetite rather than an adult sexual desire. In this manner, they link forbidden desire, damnation, and the specter of demonic possession in the entwined terms of eating and sexuality.

For Shakespeare's witch to imagine herself in the form of the rat, then, is in keeping with a long-established relationship among contagion, consumption, and sexuality—specifically, with unnatural modes of reproduction—evident in her threat to "drain" the sailor "dry as hay" (1.3.18). Since demons were thought to materialize from inspissated air, without a natural bodily form, they were often imagined as collecting semen from humans—ideally, according to Kramer and Sprenger, to have

semen removed by a witch during the "carnal act." Carnally gathering semen is better than semen produced through "nocturnal pollutions" since
the latter, they write, "arises only from the superfluity of the humours."[62]
In imagining herself draining the sailor "dry as hay," Shakespeare's witch
may therefore be announcing (albeit in a near-comic revenge fantasy) a
sexual encounter that gives her the opportunity to collect his semen, if
not his soul: "I'll do, I'll do, and I'll do." The copulating and childless
other of the childless Lady Macbeth, the witch is poised, like both Macbeth and his wife, for a yet-to-be-named mode of evil. Her unnatural act
of copulation must be cast in the form of a familiar, the rat whose form,
thanks to the inspissated air, she is presumed (in popular imagination)
to be able to assume. Rats, sexuality, and "filthy Aire" remain embedded
in the mutually reinforcing languages of vermin infestations, plague, ecological stress, and moral blight that characterize Scotland under Macbeth's unquiet rule.

SCAPEGOATS AND MOUSETRAPS

While Shakespeare's randy witch only fantasizes about turning rodent,
the persistent association between witches and rats provoked one late
seventeenth-century physician, writing sixty years after *Macbeth*, to mount a
defense not only of the humans accused of witchcraft but of their pet vermin
as well. Referring to a 1645 case in which a woman was executed for keeping
a frog in a box, Thomas Ady argues, "Oathes that have been usually taken
against many person in that kinde, are not to be regarded":

> [If] such a one hath been seen to have a Rat or Mouse creep upon her, or
> under her Coats, or was heard talking to her Imps, these are not mate-
> rial testimonies, but are foolish and senseless arguments, not grounded
> in the Word of God . . . For it is as lawful to keep a Rat or Mouse, or
> Dormouse, or any Creature tame, as to keep a tame Rabbit, or Bird; and
> one may be an Imp as well as another.[63]

In deliberately blurring distinctions between "vermin" and domesticated
creatures, Ady argues forcefully that keeping mice or rats does not prove
"that the Devil is in it." He warns judges and jurymen against reasoning from

the appearance of the usual cast of familiars—"Mice, Dormice, Grasshoppers, Caterpillars, Snakes"—to the assumption that these creatures are evidence of demonic forces at work. Ady even claims he knew a "Gentleman" who, "to please his Phantasie in trying conclusions, did once keep in a Box a Maggot that came out of a Nut, till it grew to an incredible bigness."[64] The quasi-scientific interest in "trying conclusions," he argues, trumps allegations and superstition.

Ady's "defense" of imperfect creatures as pets raises, from a different perspective, the crucial question of the extent to which early modern writers and readers could disentangle the empirical, theological, and folk attributes of vermin. In her foundational article on vermin in the early modern period, Mary Fissell demonstrates how fabular and popular depictions of vermin reflect contemporary social problems. Early modern vermin, she argues, shared three characteristics: "they ate human food; they were cunning; and they understood symbols." As a combination of "projections, fantasies, identifications" and real flesh and blood animals, vermin "threatened the always tenuous balance between ease and hardship, satiety and starvation, enough and not-enough."[65] Twenty-five Norwegian or grey rats, according to one historian, "eat as much as one human being does, and they foul much more food than they eat."[66] Rats and other swarming creatures posed fundamental challenges because, in significant numbers, they assumed a collective identity and agency. This collective agency, in turn, paradoxically endowed vermin with legal and spiritual status. All across Europe in the fifteenth and sixteenth centuries, they were hauled into court—at least symbolically—and prosecuted.

Recorded early modern prosecutions against rats and mice include trials in Berne (1451); rats and moles at Nimes (1479); rats at Autumn (1500–30); vermin at Lausanne (1509); rats at Langres (1512–13); field mice at Glurns (1519); rats at Lausanne (1522); and rats in Spain (throughout the sixteenth century).[67] As late as 1651, the Catholic Church in Germany was publishing exorcisms, like the following:

> I exorcise you, you pestiferous worms, mice, birds, or locusts and other animals through God the omnipotent Father and through Jesus Christ His Son and the Holy Spirit who proceeds from both, so that you depart without delay from these fields, or vineyards, or waters and no longer live in it but move to those places where you are unable to harm

anyone, and for the sake of the almighty God, and heavenly hosts, and God's Holy Church you will be cursed wherever you go. You are accursed and made to decrease from day to day, and diminish until nothing of you shall be found in any place unless it be necessary for the wealth and use of mankind.[68]

This exorcism, with its blanket condemnation of worms, mice, birds, and locusts, seeks to turn the logic of scapegoating or expulsion from a single sacrificial animal to entire populations of vermin. The unintentionally comic quality of this curse to "diminish" the offending vermin highlights the helplessness of early modern communities confronted by infestations. The recourse to exorcism reasserts the status of vermin as part of a divine creation precisely so they can be threatened with a kind of bestial excommunication. Unlike the sacrificial goats of the Old Testament, rodents (like all "imperfect creatures") are difficult to expel precisely because they shape the very agricultural ecologies—"fields," "vineyards," and "waters"—that define the early modern world.

The logic of expulsion intended to protect the foodstores "necessary for the wealth and use of mankind" also took more material forms. During the early modern period, a number of widely distributed technologies—including traps, poisons, professional exterminators, and specially-designed barrier devices—constituted the arsenal directed against vermin. Mice and rats affected households of every rank, often in numbers referred to as "prodigious" and in swarms described as "armies." Consequently, almost every castle and community employed not only a priest but a ratcatcher, some of whom became legendary in song and literature. Like the rats he hunted, the ratcatcher occupied a kind of double role: as both an abject, semimystical figure, a kind of "vermin-whisperer" capable, like the Pied Piper, of moving large populations through mysterious means, and a scientific husbandry professional, part chemist, part engineer. During the sixteenth century, ratcatchers developed an impressive number of methods for exterminating or otherwise controlling rodents and other pests. Leonard Mascall's 1590 *Booke of Engines* (a compilation from previous sources) provides recipes for dozens of poisons and thirty-four different traps, many of which make their way into the art and literature of the period. The most well-known of these "mousetraps" is on the right panel of the Merode Altar; one appears in the "mousetrap scene" in *Hamlet*, and another at the end of Christopher Marlowe's *The Jew of Malta*.[69]

The Jew of Malta appeared shortly after Mascall's *Booke of Engines* and is full of rodent-like poisonings, including those of Abigail and the nuns. After a career of murders and gloating about his prowess as a killer, Barabas finally dies when he falls into the trap he set for the Turks—a pot of boiling water. As it is depicted onstage, Barabas has created a "mill trap" (also called a "fell-trap" or "pitfall-trap"), which, as David Drummond points out, is "apparently the earliest known example of an ever-set, multi-catch mouse-trap."[70] This contraption is designed to control rodent infestations because it does not have to be reset after every kill. The author of *The Compleat French and English Vermin Killer*, commenting on this trap one hundred years after Mascall, claims it can promote the demise of "40, 50, nay 100" rats "in one Night."[71] His version (Figure 5), involves putting oatmeal and butter on one end of a plate suspended from two sticks and positioned over water; when the rat ventures out on the platform for the food, its own weight depresses the baited side of the platform and dumps it into water, which is sometimes laced with arsenic, and sometimes, as in the *Jew of Malta*, placed over fire.

The fact that the contemporaries of Marlowe, Shakespeare, and de Gheyn felt the need for a trap that kills in double and triple digits reinforces the magnitude of the problems faced by English farmers and citizens. Yet Marlowe's use of a fell-trap to finish off his Machiavellian hero suggests the extent to which the problem of vermin control could be refigured as a way to deal with threats posed, for instance, by Turks and Jews, to a body politic defined by the ostensible logic of Christian communion. Rats, worms, and other "pestiferous" creatures can (in theory) be exorcised, but conflating the racial or religious "other" with vermin produces a chilling rationale for containment or extermination that, as I argue in chapter 5, comes into play on Crusoe's island.

Unlike the cats massacred during the French Revolution, rats cannot easily function as scapegoats for socioeconomic and political problems, in part because the threat they pose to food supplies and their possible role as disease carriers leave them outside a normative socioagricultural order.[72] Yet as *Macbeth* and *The Jew of Malta* suggest, vermin mark the absent center of the ritual expulsions that define Europe's relationships with its own "alien" populations. In the modern world, René Girard argues, the simple act of scapegoating—choosing an animal to sacrifice for a community's sins—is replaced by "a spectacle of secret substitutions" in which one victim is substituted for another. Such scapegoating substitutions usually go unnoticed, he claims, remaining "only as a trace," but occasionally, as in the destruction

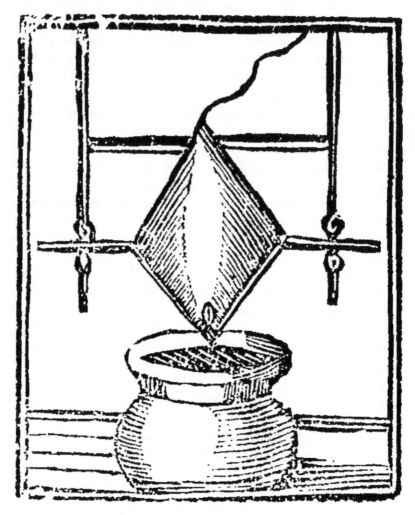

Rats and *Mice* to kill.

Fig. 5. The Fell Trap

of European Jews by the Nazis, "they can reappear in forms more virulent than ever and on an enormous scale."[73] While the subject of genocide, then and now, lies beyond the scope of this book, the logic of what Girard calls "mimetic contagion" can displace a community's sins onto another ethnic or national group. Vermin define both the subject and processes of mimetic contagion, and, as we have seen in this chapter, Turks, Jews, devils, witches, and rats exist along a chain of substitutions that operates by this logic of always-imperfect expulsion. What has made modern forms of genocide thinkable, in an important sense, are the very technologies developed to address rampant food insecurity: the threats posed by the vermin that populate plague discourse and biopolitics during the early modern era.[74] Girard notes plague "is never present alone" but is part of a "thematic cluster" that links venom, poison, moral corruption, dearth, and putrefaction in mutually reinforcing discourses.[75]

In the seventeenth century, George Wither's *Britain's Rembrancer* drops the rats from its account of the plague, but retains the witch, reimagined as a feminized basilisk, who turns "her poison" on individuals. Characterizing the plague as a kind of airborne "venom," a "*Maladie*" that manifests a "spreading Nature," Wither imagines a feminized figure of Pestilence, armed with a "venom'd speare, which, where it toucheth, fills/ The veines with poison, and distracts, and kills." The sorceress Pestilence is a master of poisons—"of the pois'ning Art [she] hath found the height"—because her acts are highly mediated: "she knows how to poison by conceit" (43). Poisoning "by conceit" suggests both a kind of agency and an unsettling obscurity about the connections among the disease, its sources, and its victims. Much like most of the so-called "imperfect creatures," the plague "neither certaine forme, not habit wears." Contagion defies epidemiology: "*Pestilence*," Wither writes, "doth show her selfe inclin'd / So variously she cannot be defin'd" (116). This inability to locate a single cause for evil and infection characterizes the "thematic clusters" that make vermin a critical component of the threats that troubled early modern society

In the next chapter, I revisit the relationship among imperfect creatures, epidemiological crisis, and ecological uncertainty in examining what is perhaps the most verminous narrative in the Western world: the Genesis account of the ten plagues of Egypt. In seventeenth-century redactions of the biblical narrative by Wither and Abraham Cowley—two of the most popular writers of the period—famine, disease, and pestilence take the form of rapidly reproducing frogs, locusts, lice, and other mysterious swarming creatures. Empirical and theological accounts of pestilence remain mutually constitutive, and Cowley's efforts, in particular, to untangle the two open up a series of questions about the "rise" of seventeenth-century "science." As I argue in chapters 2 and 3, vermin populate the discourses of natural philosophy as surely as they do early modern legal, literary, and demonological texts.

CHAPTER 2

Swarming Things
Dearth and the Plagues of Egypt in Wither and Cowley

Eate as it becommeth a man those things which
are set before thee; and devoure not, lest thou be hated.

—KING JAMES BIBLE 1611, ECCLESIASTICUS 31:16

In his 1616 treatise, *The Fall of Man, or the Corruption of Nature*, Godfrey
Goodman exhorts his readers, "let not the plagues of Aegypt seem so incredible," when, within living memory (1580), swarming mice infested Essex
and made it "almost [un]inhabitable."[1] The corruption of nature, he asserts,
has spread throughout the animal world: even domesticated creatures "who
were made onely for mans vse and seruice" have "cast off their yoake, and are
now become dangerous and obnoxious to man" (219). Goodman's characterization of a deeply corrupted nature in the early seventeenth century turns
on an extended analogy between the Egypt of Exodus and the England
of James I: both are plagued (at least in Goodman's imagination) by large
beasts of prey and by vermin. "Wee stand not onely in feare of fierce Lions,
cruell Tigers, rauening Wolues, deuouring Beares," writes Goodman, "but
Gats, Flies, and the least wormes doe serue to molest vs" (219). As his title
suggests, the fall of man is bound inextricably to the corruption of a natural
world, figured not only by traditional images of wild beasts (all but extinct
in seventeenth-century Britain) but by small, noxious creatures, ubiquitous
and familiar vermin.

During the sixteenth, seventeenth, and eighteenth centuries, biblical accounts of infestation by lice, flies, locusts, frogs, and other unidenti-
fied swarming things were deeply embedded in scientific and political, as
well as religious, culture. For religious writers, Europe was subject to real

plagues, pestilence, and famine that reinforced the experiential authenticity of Exodus and evoked, conceptually and typologically, the corresponding idea that England was being punished for its collective sins. Indeed, several seventeenth-century writers on the plagues of Egypt were thrown into jail, accused of comparing England's leaders to the wicked Pharaoh.[2] Invocations of and allusions to the Old Testament plague narrative always involved the danger of topical interpretations of Exodus as political allegory, even as writers registered contemporary concerns about the environment and natural world. Given their hermeneutic multiplicity, plagues of Egypt narratives, as Goodman's text suggests, offered tempting opportunities to explore biopolitics throughout the seventeenth century. Focusing primarily on plague poems by George Wither (1588–1667) and Abraham Cowley (1618–67), this chapter traces conflicted and complex attitudes about the relationships among environmental, political, and religious narratives as they are figured through the swarms of verminous things.[3] Republicans and royalists alike draw on typological uses of the plagues of Egypt narratives to reinforce, or subvert, different visions of God, King, and Nature.

Vermin—and especially plagues of vermin—were popular subjects for theological writers, like Goodman, partly because they functioned as markers for what now we would call anxieties about environmental degradation. During the Little Ice Age, populations of hungry animals or insects often meant the difference for individuals, families, villages, and cities between sufficiency and hardship, even between life and death. Cold temperatures, rainfall shortages, and easterly winds brought with them crop shortages, reflected in higher grain prices.[4] Increases in grain prices created food insecurities and nutritional deficiencies that, in turn, made already vulnerable populations more susceptible to disease.[5] In 1533, Parliament passed an act requiring citizens to make and maintain nets and snares for trapping crows, rooks, and choughs, birds that fed on seeds before they could sprout and take root. In 1566, under Elizabeth, the earlier act was "revived," but this time it was expanded to include a larger range of vermin, including foxes, weasels, otters, rats, mice, and moles.[6] When James ascended to the English throne in 1603, he drew up an elaborate plan (and corresponding taxation) for improving agricultural conditions in England, in part by controlling vermin This draining of the fens did not actually occur on a large scale until Charles I, and then drainage and enclosure may have worsened, rather than improved, the vermin problem. Michael McCormick argues land clearing and grain production increased food sources for rats, even as it deprived some of their predators—primarily owls, foxes, and weasels—of their natural habitats.[7] Paradoxically, then, the clearing of wetlands may have contributed later in the century, particularly in 1665–66, to the increase of vermin and the ferocity of plague.

On the Continent, where grain prices were even higher, vermin—especially rats and mice—were prosecuted for their depredations. While pigs, dogs, and other mammals were, into the eighteenth century, sometimes charged and tried in ecclesiastical courts, vermin constituted a much bigger problem, evident by a greater number of prosecutions. Livestock and most stray mammals could be seized by humans and penned or chained, but "continuing infestations of insects and other vermin," writes Dannenfeldt, seemed to require metaphysical aid, what C.P. Evans calls "sacerdotal conjuring and cursing."[8] Unlike *Thierstraten*, the category of capital punishments brought against pigs, cows, and other domestic animals for homicide, *Thierprocesse* were proceedings brought against rats, mice, locusts, weevils and other vermin "in order to prevent them from devouring the crops, and to expel them from orchards, vineyards, and cultivated fields by means of exorcism and excommunication."[9] Once the insects and vermin were warned against the destruction of crops, they were sometimes subjected to the "*anathema maranatha*" or cursed in the name of the Lord.[10] This seemingly bizarre reaction to vermin infestations on the part of ecclesiastical authorities stemmed from uncertainties about the ultimate source of insects or rats, sent either by God or by Satan as a punishment for, or as a mark of, sin. Evans notes:

> If the insects were instruments of the devil, they might be driven into the sea or banished to some arid region, where they would all miserably perish; if, on the other hand, they were recognized as the ministers of God, divinely delegated to scourge mankind for the promotion of piety, it would be suitable, after they had fulfilled their mission, to cause them to withdraw from the cultivated fields and to assign them such a spot, where they might live in comfort without injury to the inhabitants. The records contain instances of both kinds of treatment.[11]

Such proceedings testify to conceptual struggles to incorporate vermin into theological and political systems so their power could be contained or destroyed. In this sense, "sacerdotal conjuring and cursing" join nets, traps, engines, and other devices as strategies to shore up humankind's dominant

Ranarum, Ciniphum, Mufcarum funditur agmen.   Et terra natis corporibufque nocent.   Exod. 8.

Fig. 6. Jan Sadeler, *The Plague of Frogs* (1585)

place in an already corrupted natural world. Biblical vermin provided writers and their readers ample precedent for interpreting "the corruption of nature" in simultaneously theological and material terms.

BIOPOLITICS AND THE PLAGUES OF EGYPT

The plagues of Egypt were a typological touchstone for depictions of a fallen world and a warning to the corrupt times. Intrinsically political, the Exodus story became a popular subject during the politically and ecologically troubled sixteenth and seventeenth centuries, as writers and artists tried to warn frightened audiences about punishments that they, unlike their pagan predecessors, might still be able to avoid. In retrospect, early modern accounts of the plague can be read through the context of what Foucault calls "bio-power," one of the mechanisms through which "modern Western societies took on board the fundamental biological fact that humans are a species."[12] The plagues of Egypt, individually and collectively, bring with them disruptions to the social order, biopolitical disruptions often figured, both in art and literature, in terms of vermin and the threats they pose to food supplies. One of the more interpretively rich representations is Jan Sadeler's 1585 version of the plague of frogs, partly because it brings into clear relief the zoopolitics of Egypt's degradation. Here imperfect creatures invade and overrun a sociopolitical body arranged for humans and normally populated by them and their domestic animals. Sadeler renders the frogs naturalistically, with attention to their anatomy and genuinely omnivorous diets. A dozen or so hungry amphibians assail an Egyptian dinner table laden with plates of fish. Although we tend to think of frogs as living on insects, they also readily consume small fish and sometimes even other frogs; because the Egyptians share with supposedly loathsome creatures similar appetites they are dragged down to the level of voracious, invading vermin. At the bottom right of the plate, one of the frogs seems to be staring down a dog for table scraps, a staged competition that suggests a larger economy of consumption and scarcity. Such trans-species encounters raise the question of fundamental Aristotelian categories: who or what can be considered vermin? The frogs? The dog? The Egyptians? Distinctions among ostensibly distinct orders of being threaten to collapse. In the lower left corner, also at ground level, are an African, a monkey, and a frog engaged in what appears to be another scene of consumption. The monkey eats a piece of fruit with his left hand and reaches out to a frog with his right; compositionally and strategically, the monkey, the frogs, and dog—at a level below the African boy, who, in turn, is below the aristocratic Egyptians—are identified as competitors for food resources and perhaps as vermin, too. While this remarkable print doubtless stages familiar sociopolitical hierarchies, it also suggests that vermin are not particular animals, or a static category of creatures, but are determined by their position in shifting set of agricultural, theological, and political relations.

Sadeler also manages to incorporate the historical and narrative dimensions of the Exodus story. Whereas most other artists render the ten plagues sequentially—one plague per plate—Sadeler depicts the second, frogs, in the foreground, while in the background, lice (the third plague) and flies (the fourth) attack horses beyond the gates of the city. Superimposing the diachronic on the synchronic, he encourages us to read typology and history simultaneously; by virtue of their progression in a series, Sadeler's creatures appear as part of a *telos*, as punishments at the hands of an angry God, who replaces excess with scarcity. The biopolitics of this woodcut, then, are bound to food shortages, or what Foucault calls "misfortune in its pure state." As Foucault argues in *Security, Territory, and Population*, political thought traditionally has addressed scarcity in one of two ways. First, it can be seen as "cosmological-political": "bad weather, drought, ice, excessive humidity, or anything that is outside one's control" leads to scarcity, one of the "fundamental forms of bad fortune for a people and for a sovereign."[13] Second, scarcity may appear as "juridical-moral," as punishment for man's sins: either God uses "nature" to punish humankind—scarcity itself is seen as a form of punishment—or

> ... man's evil nature [influences] scarcity by figuring as one of its sources, in as much as men's greed—their need to earn, their desire to earn even more, their egoism—causes the phenomena of hoarding, monopolization, and withholding merchandize, which intensify the phenomena of scarcity.[14]

If writing about the plagues of Egypt, from either perspective, is necessarily a political act in the seventeenth century, it is one capable of being interpreted in myriad ways. Interpretations of the ten plagues—"cosmological-political" and "juridical-moral"—were deeply entangled with contemporary epidemiological, political, and ecological crises. To read such crises from a narrow political perspective is to foreclose the semiotic possibilities provoked by Sadeler's vermin, to sacrifice his disturbing vision of the place of the human polis within a less-than-predictable bioworld.

It is within this broader understanding of biopolitics that early modern commentaries on the plagues of Egypt can be read. In a very real sense, seventeenth-century English men and women were faced with the Egyptian Pharaoh's dilemma: how to interpret and respond to unpredictable infestations of vermin, dearth, and disease, a crawling and destructive creaturely landscape. James I, Charles I, Charles II—and Cromwell, the Lord Protector—could be perceived as standing in for the stony-hearted Pharaoh, bringing increasing destruction on a land and its people. Early modern writers were well aware that seventeenth-century England witnessed four distinct and major outbreaks of plague—1603, 1625, 1636, and 1665—three of which coincided with significant political events: the death of Elizabeth, the death of James and coronation of Charles I, and the declaration of war on the Dutch.[15] As the sinful sovereigns of a corrupt nation, monarchs could be accused of having caused scarcity by provoking God's wrath. Even if plague and dearth were regarded as "cosmological-political," a matter of misfortune, queens and kings could be held responsible for their failure (again like the Pharaoh) to respond to conditions of dearth and disease appropriately—to develop, for example, anti-hoarding policies during periods of grain shortage. By treating the plagues of Egypt as a theological text, poets like George Wither, writing in periods of civic unrest, could maintain the fiction that exegesis transcends sectarianism and politics. In so doing, they could evade the legal consequences of being seen as critical of the political order.

So commonly did people read plague narratives as veiled commentary on the fate of sovereigns that Wither, who dedicated his *Britain's Remembrancer* to Charles I, admits some readers may see his lines as dishonoring the monarch: "*My Lines are loyall,*" he insists, "*though they bold appeare.*"[16] Insisting Charles has not been on the throne long enough to judge his rule as either "good or ill" (17), Wither offers his poem as a holy tribute and acknowledgement of monarchical power: "O! let my *Poeme* be / A sanctified *Sacrifice* to thee" (32). At the same time, distinguishing between the piety of the monarchs and the corruption of their subjects, Wither represents himself as a prophet who holds up "*a Glasse*" by which the king may "*Behold (without the hazard of infection) / The horrid* Pestilence *in her true form, / Which in your Kingdome did so lately storme*" (19). This image of the poem as a "glasse" for a diseased kingdom captures Wither's two-fold ambition to reflect the reality of plague and dearth in England, even as he frames and shapes those realities in ways meant to explore fundamental questions about the relationships among politics, religion, and the environment.

In Michael Drayton's *Moses, His Birth and Miracles* (1604), written after the plague of 1603, food scarcity and theories of contagion come together in a poetical and deeply topical description of the ten plagues.[17] Personifying Egypt as a menstruating female, Drayton describes how God turned the "Christalline" river Nile into a "black lake or setled marish (*sic*)"; fish and serpents die, other animals fly from the "contagious stinke," and the clean cisterns and reservoirs of Egypt become "poys'ned" (146). After this God-inflicted menstrum, a second plague of frogs is born out of manure. The "soyle, that late the owner did enrich/ Him his faire Heards and goodly flocks to feed" now becomes a "common ditch" where "in their Todder loathly Paddocks breed" (147). Agricultural and domestic spaces metamorphose into breeding grounds for vermin. The land subsequently becomes alive with the bodies of amphibians "as though in labour with this filthy frie/ Stirring with paine in the parturious throwes."

People from windowes looking to the ground,
At this stupendous spectacle amazed,
See but their sorrow every where abound,
That most abhorring whereon most they gazed.
Their Troughes and Ovens Toadstooles now become,
That Huswifes wont so carefully to keepe,
These loathsome creatures taking up the roome,
A croking, there continually do creepe.

(147)

In Drayton's poem, as in Sadeler's print, frogs corrupt food systems and thereby disrupt domestic and political order. Manuring and related practices of good husbandry produce a living mass of creeping things rather than sustenance for people and flocks. Similarly, the implements and efforts of housewives—their tables and ovens—become filled with croaking frogs and toads rather than bread and meat. Drayton envisions the second plague as a kind of agricultural inversion, the spaces of food production and consumption usurped by creatures unnatural to cultivation.

His dense descriptions draw on a variety of myths, beliefs, and observations about the generation of frogs. "Loathly Paddocks" breed in their own "Todder," an archaic word form that refers to the "spawn of a frog or toad," a "slimy gelatinous matter" (OED). Drayton's is the only example of this word offered in the OED, but it seems to refer to the egg sacs of frogs which, when laid on land rather than water, were often kept moist through a combination of saliva and urine. Since frogs, moreover, are not all sexually dimorphic, and—even if they are—are notoriously difficult to sex, Drayton plays on the widespread belief that frogs were the product of spontaneous generation. This belief, which can be traced back to Pliny, had not been dispelled completely even as late as 1646, when Thomas Browne refers to the common garden or grass frog—"Temporariae"—as being born without the act of copulation.[18] The discourse about frogs, moreover, is always marked by associations with the Whore of Babylon, who spewed an unholy mass of amphibious creatures from her mouth. Topsell writes about a woman giving birth to frogs, and Alexander Ross, a seventeenth-century natural philosopher, claims to have seen a person whose swollen belly was "full of small toads, frogs, evets, and such vermin usually bred in putrified water," simply by having drunk from a puddle.[19] But what makes Drayton's frogs "loathsome" is that, in a fallen world, they not only compete for food but threaten to "tak[e] up the roome" of copulation, gestation, and the feeding practices crucial to domestic and social order. The plague of frogs—an image invoked by writers of different political affiliations and theological beliefs—acts as a kind of ideological substrate: frogs function as both the material causes of ruined harvests and subsequent dearth and as evidence of a providential punishment for humankind's sins. If Graham Hammill is right in his argument that Drayton, instead of "retreating from politics into nature forces a damaged vision of nature into the sphere of politics," vermin function as the greatest evidence that sovereign power can enact violence in the name of "life."[20]

DEARTH, PESTS, AND *BRITAIN'S REMEMBRANCER* (1628)

In his list of "pure misfortunes" that plague sovereigns and peoples, Foucault lists a series of weather events and "anything that is outside one's control," but he does not mention small, hungry animals that compete with humans for food. Within the Christian tradition, however, the Four Horsemen of the Apocalypse—War, Famine, Disease, and Death—were more often than not accompanied by vermin, "given power," according to Revelations 6:7–8, to "kill with sword, and with hunger, and with death, and with the beasts of the earth." George Wither's *Britain's Remembrancer* begins with a description of how Famine follows the devastation of crops by vermin. Wither acknowledges the roles of bad weather and poor farming but devotes most of his energy to personifying Famine as a general commanding a host of "Troups" that include caterpillars, locusts, birds, and worms:

> The crawling *Caterpillars*, wastfull *Flyes*,
> The skipping *Locust* (that in winter dies)
> *Floods, Frosts, & Mildewes, Blastings, Windes, & Stormes,*
> *Drough, rav'nous Fowles, & Vermine, Weedes, & Wormes:*
> *Sloth, Evill husbandry,* and such as those,
> Which make a scarcenesse where most plenty grows.
>
> (41)

Aided by "Sloth" and "Evill husbandry," Famine destroys the "plenty" that was universally taken as a sign of God's favor. In Deuteronomy 9:8, God reminds the Jews coming out of the wilderness of all that should make them grateful: in the promised land, "thou shalt eat bread without scarceness, thou shalt not lack any thing in it; a land whose stones are iron, and out of whose hills thou mayest dig brass." Abundance is both the cause and effect of virtue, scarcity a sign of sins that pervade the socionatural world. Wither's poem admonishes the evil behaviors that bring vermin down on the land as a token of God's displeasure.

Wither was in London during the plague of 1625 and later sided with Parliament during the Civil War. A republican poet who admired Edmund Spenser, Wither took seriously his prophetic role. David Norbrook regards him as the "most ideological" of the Spenserian poets, a group that included Fulke Greville, Samuel Daniel, Drayton, Phineas and Giles Fletcher, and Wither's lifelong friend, William Browne.[21] By 1628, Wither had twice been thrown in prison (once around 1614, again in 1621) for presumably libelous, allegedly anti-royalist rhetoric. Norbrook also cautions us, however, against reading his poetry too narrowly as a straightforward articulation of republican ideals because Wither's politics are often ambiguous and because the "motivating force behind [his] political ideas" was not a particular form of government but "a strong belief in an impending apocalyptic transformation."[22] In this respect, the *Remembrancer* looks forward to a conversion heralded by verminous harbingers. As a generic hybrid, *Britain's Remembrancer* walks a fine line between moral exhortation and targeted satire. Claiming in a dedication to Charles that he was "*call'd . . . to make this Declaration*," Wither compares his muse to a falconer who would "*spring / Those fowles that have been flowne at yet by none / Ev'n those, whom our best* Hawks *turne taile upon*" (6–7). His hunting metaphor—note the pun on "fowles"—characterizes his work as too threatening for other "Hawks," and invites, without overdetermining, allegorical interpretations of his targets. If his raptor muse proves insufficient, Wither claims,

> I can unkennell such an eager packe
> Of deep-mouth'd Hounds, that they afraid shall make
> Our sternest Beasts of prey, and cunning'st Vermine,
> Ev'n from the Fox-fur, to the spotted Ermine.

(7)

Poet turned hunter, he will deploy his hounds against those who threaten humans ("Beasts of prey") and those who compete for food supplies ("Vermine"). This animal imagery folds easily into the political, juridical-moral rhetoric of scarcity identified by Foucault. Clergymen and peers, who wear fox and ermine, are the targets of Wither's hunt, the "sternest" and "cunning'st" beasts, whose greed and sin threaten society.

Britain's Remembrancer was written shortly after one of the century's worse food crises—England's bad harvest year of 1622–23—followed by a severe outbreak of the plague in 1625. Wither remained in London throughout this period. The subtitle of his poem declares unambiguously its occasion and purpose: "Containing A Narration of the PLAGUE lately past A Declaration of the MISCHIEFS present And a Prediction of JUDGMENTS to come If Repentance prevent not." The title page announces a "Premonition" of a "dismall Cloud exceeding black" extending over the sinful island of England with "thicke foggie Vapours" that threaten to "darken MERCIES beames" (title page). Drawing on the imagery of climatic crisis, inspissated air, and disease that Shakespeare had used in *Macbeth*, Wither imagines sin and social corruption in quasi-biblical forms. Within the "dismall Cloud," the speaker "did behold All Plagues and Punishments" (title page). Then, "with a trembling heart," he sees rays of mercy piercing the cloud, making their way through those "Exhalations" and revealing the following inscription:

> BRITAINES REMEMBRANCER. . . . These words me thought The Storme is, yet, delaid, And if ye doe not penitence defer, This CLOVD is only, a REMEMBRANCER. But, if ye still affect impiety, Expect, ere long, what this may signifie.

Crucial to Wither's apocalyptic imagination—his rhetoric of fear and divine retribution—is a comparison of England's present condition of scarcity and disease to the depths of pestilential catastrophe to which it could descend. The aptly-named "Remembrancer" functions prophetically. It reminds the English they face future torments unless they amend their behavior, a warning that is conveyed by harrowing descriptions of the nation's recent past.

Despite—or in conjunction with—its apocalyptic rhetoric, Wither's poem offers relatively sophisticated and nuanced accounts of both scarcity and disease as they were understood in the seventeenth century. Significantly, Wither demonstrates a sensitivity to the local nature of food shortages and, therefore, to the differences between "dearth" and "famine." As John Walters, among others, has argued, in contrast to Scotland, Ireland, and most of its "Continental neighbors," England "had slipped the shadow of famine at an early date" and certainly during Wither's lifetime.[23] England's

dearth was local, never as widespread as on the Continent, in part because
by the early sixteenth century towns in England, including London, had
erected storage granaries that helped them weather difficult harvest years
and combat vermin infestations. England also developed anti-hoarding policies and a national market in wheat through which local shortages could
be mitigated.[24] Walter estimates that improved agricultural methods may
have "doubled gross yields between the early sixteenth and mid-seventeenth
centuries" and that, by the late seventeenth century, England, in fact, had
become an exporter of grain.[25] Contemporary diaries and literary accounts,
including Wither's poem, nevertheless reveal a people alarmed about uncertain weather, bearing witness "to the shock of harvest failure on a society for
which bread was still literally the staff of life." [26] And even with improved
technology, some years—the 1590s, 1622–23, the 1640s—brought with them
severe harvest failures in a significant portion of England.

Wither's understanding of the English situation is reflected in his description of dearth as at once ecological and theological. One of God's
"Hoast of Plagues" is "Dearth," who is commended by "Justice" and "Mercy" to
visit England, so as "to make us feare"

A *Scarceness*: she should scatter here, and there,
A *Floud*, or *Tempest*; and at sometime bring
A *droughty Summer*, or a *frosty Spring*,
Or *Meldewes*, to remember us, from whom
The blessings of a plenteous yeare doe come.

(79)

"Scarceness" is regional, associated with storms that God has "scatter[ed]
here, and there" or precipitated by intermittent—"sometimes"—cold, wet
summers or "frosty" springs, the unstable seasonal effects characteristic of
the Little Ice Age. Such weather brings "Meldewes," a phenomenon not yet
recognized as fungal, but which was widely known to be associated with
moisture that produced a destructive white coating on plants. In *King Lear*,
a facetious Edgar ascribes such destruction to "the foul Flibbertigibbet" who
"makes the hare-lip; mildews the white wheat, and hurts poor creature of
earth" (III.iv.113–17); Hamlet, in a more naturalistic image, complains that
Gertrude's new husband "is like a mildwe'd ear / Blasting his wholesome
brother" (III.iv.64–65).[27] Wither's similar characterization of mildew as
weather-related reflects a widespread understanding that precipitation can

devastate harvests. Like droughts and unseasonal frosts, mildewed crops ground an injunction to his readers to embrace virtuous behavior. "Mildewes" serve as a stark warning that conditions may worsen, reminding an ungrateful people about the source and significance of God's bounty. Indeed, later in the poem, meditating on God's mercy to England, where, their "Granards filled," the English "feast" while others "fast" (247), Wither reminds his readers that they, too, had experienced dearth before the coming of the plague.

> The Winter last before the Pest began,
> Throughout some Northern Shires a Famine ranne,
> That starved some; and others were faine,
> Their hungry appetites to entertaine
> With swine and sheep, and horses, which have dy'd
> By chance.
>
> (247)

Plenty can quickly turn into dearth, and dearth into famine, during which Londoners could find themselves, like the hungry northerners, turning carrion-eaters and feeding on fallen livestock. By emphasizing this harbinger of disaster, Wither treats real food scarcity in Foucault's juridical sense as a sign of a "loving ... *Father's* rod" (248), as a merciful, motivating warning that, if heeded, would have spared England the plague that followed.

In contrast to conditions in England, widespread starvation on the Continent is a sign, for Wither, of God's judgment against Catholics, whose dietary practices feature slimy, verminous creatures. Wither's descriptions of European famine foods—foods of last resort during times of agricultural failure—are among the most harrowing and fascinating of the poem. Famine, he insists, taught Spaniards how to "dresse / Their Frogs," Germans how to "make a dinner or a supper on a Snake," Italians how to feed on the slimy snail, and Irishmen "to live upon a weed / That growes in Marshes" (41). (This weed may be Irish moss, a form of kelp.) Foods we now often regard as staples of particular national diets become the unclean objects of consumption. This pestilential diet marks the lives of sinful populations at the mercy of extreme weather conditions, poor farming practices, and providential punishment. "Those dainty pallats which could relish nought/ But what was set farre off, and dearly bought," writes Wither, have been so starved, or "dieted," by Famine, "that they could feed / On moldy scraps; and beg them too for need" (42). Foreign luxury has given way to verminous feeding practices. Wither then personifies "Famine" as an evil mother who, rather than supplying her family with healthy meals, forces them to consume dried animal skins and rodents: "The broiling of old shooes, was her device / And so was eating Carrion, Rats, and Mice" (42). Sin leads to scarcity, scarcity to desperation, and desperation to the collapse among categories—vermin, leatherwork, food. Indeed, "Famine" encourages cannibalism: "This Hag, hath Townes and Cities famished / With humane flesh, the hungry men hath fed" (42). Cannibalism is the ultimate act of degradation and depraved minds, and this feminized evil the logical end of humankind's sin.

Famine, then, compels humans to sink radically below their privileged species position and behave like mosquitoes, worms, and other "imperfect creatures" who "feed on mouldy scraps," "suck their horses blood," and "feed on Pigeons dung" (42). In effect, Famine inverts the presumably natural food chain, in which humans kill, dismember, cook, and consume selected animals, usually medium-size mammals or birds. Graphic descriptions of filial cannibalism instead connect humans to some insects, spiders, rats, and other animals that were thought to kill and eat their own young. Wither describes how mothers in Famine's dark and horrible household, mothers who would normally suckle their young, use them to sustain their own life. Famine

> ... is that unequall'd cruell-one,
> Who urg'd a *Mother*, once, to kill her *Sonne*,
> And make unnaturally that cursed wombe
> Which gave him being, to be made his tombe.

> (42)

The child returns in pieces to the mother's belly, first as food and then as excrement. Wither had precedent for baby-eating mothers in the Bible: Deuteronomy 28:56–57, and 2 Kings 6:28–29. Josephus provides an extended account of a Jewish woman consuming her child during the siege of Jerusalem, and versions of this tale circulated in the seventeenth century.[28] Shakespeare draws on the image in *Titus Andronicus*; Tamora unwittingly eats her own children, baked into a pie.[29] Wither's version, however, is not the stuff of revenge tragedy but a marker of ecospiritual apocalypse, a collapse of a gendered social, ecological, political, and natural order.

This apocalypse, the end point of Wither's prophetic nightmare, is fully imagined in Canto Eight. Despite all the warnings to the English, God eventually visits plague on humans, animals, and the lower ecosystem, "on each person, place, and ev'ry thing": the "pleasant soyle, wherein such plenty growes, / And where both milke and honey overflowes" are made "barren" (513). The land is stripped of wheat, grass, and corn, and the fields and lakes made empty; God drives away "pleasant Fowles" and "all those Fish that play / Within [England's] waters" (513). The result of sin is a fallen world unfit for humans:

> The very Climate, and thy temp'rate ayre,
> Shall lose their wholsomnesses, for thy offenses;
> And breed hot *Fevers, Murraines, Pestilences,*
> And all diseases. . . .
>
> (255)

In a poetic rendering of Goodman's vision of the "corruption of Nature," Wither describes common spaces—towns, cities, churches—given over to vermin and wild beasts: "the places where much people meetings had / Shall vermine holes, and dens for beasts be made" (514–15).

This ecological collapse ushers in the reign of vermin. As their punishment for idleness and luxury, diseased women will wear "deformity" rather than jewels "about their faces," and God, unleashing a horde of pricking insects, will

> Scourge thee with *Scorpions, Serpents, Cockatrices,*
> And other such; whose tailes with stings are armed,
> That neither can be plucked forth, nor charmed.
>
> (151)

In keeping with the juridico-political discourse of scarcity, such verminous and pestilential conditions are both causes and effects of spiritual corruption. People, Wither warns, will eat without being "suffiz'd" and, suffering more than "scarcity of bread" and "temp'rall food," will be deprived of the "meat / Whereof the faithful soul desire to eate" (515). To avoid this hell-on-earth, they must immediately turn to Christ—to a Christ, we are reminded, who in John 6:35 occupies the place of food: "I am the bread of life. Whoever comes to me will never be hungry, and whoever comes to me will never be thirsty."

The eight cantos of rhymed couplets that constitute *Britain's Remembrancer* consistently blur differences among religious, medical, and ecological devastation. If the poem breaks down barriers between genres, as Norbrook maintains, that is in part because Wither seeks to create a collective or working memory, yoking as many discourses as possible.[30] From this perspective, religious, medical, and agricultural histories (along with specific farming and medical practices) provide a common frame of reference for a dark, even apocalyptic vision. The performative nature of Wither's task is aptly reflected in his title—"Remembrancer"—which turns the poet into a vehicle for, or a recorder of, a social and moral activity that helps constitute a community of readers who abjure the sins he describes. Weaving together narratives and folk memories of starving peoples, mothers eating babies, and present hardships, *Britain's Remembrancer* reinforces a providential explanation of Britain's hardship and points towards a redemptive future. Wither relocates the plagues of Egypt—or at least *some* of the plagues of Egypt—to seventeenth-century Europe, thereby evoking and naturalizing the power of God as dramatized in the biblical narrative.

In comparing his contemporary, disease-ridden England to the Pharaoh's Egypt, Wither walks a fine line between naturalized explanations and typological readings. He warns that, should England "remain impenitent,"

> those plagues will all
> Descend on thee, which did on *Egypt* fall
> *Blood, Frog,* and *Lice,* great swarms of uncouth *Flies,*
> Th'infectious *Murraine,* whereof Cattle Dyes;
> *Boiles, Scab[ies],* and *Blaine;* fierce *Hail, & Thunderstorm;*
> The *Locust,* and all fruit devouring *Wormes.*

(517)

Although Wither's long poem depends on naturalistic interpretations to enforce his descriptions of famine, dearth, and scarcity, his treatment of the Exodus story in Canto Eight incorporates an emphatic allegorical dimension. Vermin proliferate. "All those *Plagues* shall fall on thee," he continues, "According as the *Letter* doth imply, / Or, as in *mystick* sense they signifie" (517). Using noxious animals to represent human failings is a familiar rhetorical strategy in early modern literature. Both Jacobean tragedy and natural philosophy employ beasts and bugs to signify the traits of humans who fall into violence, greed, gluttony, and dishonesty. Wither uses this tactic in describing the "curse of *ravenous beasts*" that will fall on the "wicked kingdome": "No Tygers Lyons, Wolves, or Beares" will ravage "thee," he explains, somewhat laboriously, but men and women will be assaulted by "beastly minded men" who are "farre/ More cruel than those bloody spoilers" (516). In warning his readers about the plagues that will be visited on England, Wither is hardly subtle about the allegorical interpretations he wants them to draw. "*Lyons*" are "*Tyrants*," he clarifies; "*Tigers*" are "men of no compassion"; "Theeves" and "outlaws vile" are "*Beares*" and "*Wolves*." Beasts of the more perfect variety are linked to particular moral weaknesses, to humans who fall into bestial sins. In contrast, however, imperfect creatures are linked to a collective national and even ethnic failure. "Most loathsome *Frogs*," he claims, bred in "unwholesome fens, and ditches," should be read as a "race impure, / Of base condition, and of birth obscure" (517). Like the frogs of Exodus, they will spread over wholesome fields and "make unwholesome (by their sluttishnesse) / Thy kneading troughs, thy ovens, and that meat / Whereof thy people, and thy Princes eat" (517). But these amphibians figure more than a threat to food supplies. As part of Wither's typology, they explicitly link vermin to "a nasty *Generation*," "Unworthy either of the reputation / Or name of men" (517). Imperfect creatures offer Wither opportunities to characterize the nature of good and bad government in class-based and ethnic terms.

Allegory, in other words, shades into a kind of sociopolitical literalness: moral corruption ("sluttishnesse") disrupts the agricultural economy of the kingdom, and the low-born "brood," evil upstarts (like Shakespeare's Bushy, Bagot, and Green in *Richard II*) rise to "sing" in the King's chambers, "spewing evil in bragging, reviling, ribaldries, and slanders" (517). This "nasty *Generation*" of counselors easily metamorphoses into the third plague: "as Lice" they "shall feed / Ev'n on the body whence they did proceed; / Till poverty, and sloven'ly, and sloth" have consumed them (518). On the one hand, the comparison of government officials to frogs and lice invokes a tradition of stage characters who embody similarly verminous qualities, like the "parasite" Bosola in Webster's *The Duchess of Malfi*. When Ferdinand recruits Bosola as his "politic dormouse" and gives him the prestigious (and ironic) position of Master of the Horse, Bosola asks: "What's my place? / The provisorship o' the horse? Say then my corruption/ Grew out of horse dung" (I.i.273–74).[31] In this image, the double-dealing and self-loathing parasite identifies himself with leeches, lice, and other vermin ostensibly engendered by mud or slime, thereby transforming himself into a soulless thing born of putrefaction. On the other hand, however, given Wither's emphasis on the "nasty *Generation*" of evil counselors in Stuart England, Egypt's verminous plagues lend themselves to particularistic readings. As God's punishment of a stonehearted leader and a luxuriant people, they signal not a millenarian end to history itself but to a particular regime.

As Graham Hammill has argued in the cases of Thomas Dekker and Michael Drayton, plague poems are always ways of reading the sovereign body.[32] Wither's *Remembrancer* is—despite his lengthy pleas to the contrary—no exception. Without the providentialist structure of Exodus— the punishment of Pharaoh for enslaving the Israelites—the plagues become merely a sequence of horrors. The difference between invoking the millenarian end of time, signaled by the Four Horsemen of the Apocalypse, and the plagues of Egypt with their swarming creatures, then, is this: the Exodus tale places the poet-prophet and his readers in the symbolic position of wandering forty years in the wilderness, beset by dissension, greed, sin, and heresy. The reward of reading the politics of Exodus "correctly" in its "mystick sense" is, however, not a transcendence of sin through repentance but an endorsement of Wither's critique of corruption, his allegorizing of verminous behavior. The end of Wither's providential politics is a return to politics, to the kinds of extermination campaigns promoted by ratcatchers and described in Mascall's *Booke of Engines*.

COWLEY, FROGS, AND THE HAND OF GOD

In his groundbreaking account of agriculture in early modern England, *God Speed the Plough*, Andrew McRae argues that population explosion, from around 2,000,000 in 1500 to approximately 5,000,000 in 1660, was the "most important social development of the period," leading to soaring prices and schemes to promote increased agricultural production, including national projects for draining the wetlands.[33] *God Speed the Plough* ends with a brief discussion of Abraham Cowley, whose work, maintains McRae, "helped to define the revised ethics and aesthetics of rural property."[34] In contrast to Wither's tendency to allegorize natural phenomena, Cowley seeks to bridge the gap between the theological and metaphysical. Even in his *Davideis*, written as a youth at Cambridge, Cowley attached to the religious poem notes demonstrating his acquaintance with natural philosophy: the origin of winds and comets, accounts of thunder, and theories of gravity are joined to his description of hell.[35] Later, he proposed an agricultural college, inspired by Virgil's Georgics, and outlined in his *Essays* an ethos of improvement that influenced eighteenth-century agricultural practices. Cowley was admitted to Cambridge in 1664 for the M.D.[36] A founding member of the Royal Society, he brings his lifelong fascination with medicine and natural philosophy to bear on his reading of the plagues of Egypt. Acknowledging forthrightly the epistemological problems of interpreting the Bible, his poem, *The Plagues of Egypt*, includes copious notes almost three times the length of his pindaric.[37] In this metacommentary, Cowley attempts to control a cacophony of exegetical debates about the extent of God's power, natural laws, and relationships between humans and other animals. In the poem and its appended metacritical commentary, we see how animals—and especially vermin—once again provoke competing theological and epistemological interpretations.

On the whole, Cowley's notes attempt to make recent studies in natural philosophy consistent with the Hebraic and classical accounts of natural disaster, thereby synthesizing ancient and modern learning. One of the most troublesome questions raised by Exodus for natural philosophers was about the status of the serpents that the Pharaoh's magicians conjure up in response to the snake produced by Aaron's rod. Cowley summarizes in his notes the four dominant interpretations of this episode and his arguments against them: the Egyptian serpents are mere illusions (Josephus); the Magicians, through the Devil, did in fact create true serpents; they were true serpents but the products of spontaneous generation, rather than the Devil (Thomas Aquinas); and the Devil performed a sleight-of-hand by removing the rods and replacing them with serpents (248–49). Cowley supports the last view, arguing it "Agrees better with the Swiftness of the Action" (249). His poem resolves the interpretive problem by turning the Egyptian priests into mere jugglers or magicians. When the magicians mutter "secret Sounds," their "servile Gods" or "evil spirits . . . snatch the *Rods* away / And *Serpents* in their place the airy *Juglars* lay" (236). In addressing the status of the serpents, Cowley walks a fine line between naturalistic and religious interpretation, acknowledging the power of occult forces to switch out the rods and serpents without people noticing but insisting on this power as kind of theatrical effect. Thus, he points out in a previous note that various translators have rendered the magicians as "Venefici," "Poisoners," "Wisemen," "Inchanters," "Astrologers," "Philosophers," and "Witches" (248). Cowley's preferred term is "Sorcerers," and his account of the serpents emphasizes the creative power of God over an anthropomorphized and material Nature. The "Hebrew-

Serpent" flew on the Egyptians ones, breaking their backs, devouring them almost at once: "So much was over-power'd / By *God's* miraculous *Creation* / His *Servant Nature's* slightly-wrought and feeble *Generation*" (237). In effect, the serpents are divided into two species—the agents of God's miraculous power and the vermin that are physiologically inferior, "slightly-wrought" and "feeble" (237). As he writes in a later note, "I cannot believe that *God* and the *Magicians* had the same *Agents*" (257). The instability of the category of vermin forces readers to confront profound epistemological uncertainties; vermin raise questions about origins and power that can be resolved only by recourse to theological or extra-natural explanations.

Cowley's strategy, though, is to use disagreements between theological explanations as the basis for offering more naturalistic accounts. In his poetic rendering of the plague of frogs, after the Nile has turned to blood,

> The *River* yet gave one *Instruction* more,
> And from the rotting Fish and unconcoted Gore,
> Which was but *Water* just before,
> A loathsome *Host* was quickly made,
> That scal'd the Banks, and with loud Noise did all the *Country* invade.
>
> (237)

The traditional theological question that troubled commentators was whether or not the frogs were newly created by God or, in keeping with ancient theories of spontaneous generation, created by natural means. Cowley shifts the focus of argument from the question of the frogs' origin to the ways God can alter, at will, the natural behaviors of entire animal populations. Drawing an analogy between the tainted Nile and the natural properties of blood "which when it corrupts *Boils* and burns as it were in the veins," Cowley asserts it is "no wonder" that water "corrupted in this manner . . . produc'd a great Number of *Frogs*" (250). If the river changed temperature, it could, like corrupted blood, give rise to living things. The real "Wonder," he continues, is "that the Number was so infinite, in that it was so suddenly produc'd upon the Action of *Aaron*, and that contrary to their Nature, [the frogs] came to molest the *Egyptians* in their very Houses" (251–52). Cowley's frogs are not in themselves vile—a "race impure," as Wither asserts—but a problem precisely because they *deviate* from their natural character. Cowley's frogs "mount up higher/ Where never *Sun-born Frog* durst to aspire," placing their "slimy Members" in silken beds in a "*Luxury* unknown before to all the *Watry Race*" (238). Although produced "naturally" within seventeenth-century understandings of spontaneous generation, frogs become providential agents sent to punish the Egyptians.

In its treatment of frogs as a "race impure, / Of base condition, and of birth obscure," *Britain's Remembrancer* alludes to the still-active notion that amphibians are sexually indeterminate and derive from putrefaction. Many years later, Alexander Pope exploits this association in his *Epistle to Dr. Arbuthnot* in the figure of the sexually ambiguous Bufo, that "Amphibious Thing!" who flatters and lies his way into dinners and courts.[38] Cowley, in contrast, generally rejects allegorical, satirical, or particularist interpretations, preferring instead to synthesize classical and biblical accounts of the plague of frogs through natural philosophy. Even as he follows Wither and other religious writers in maintaining that Exodus is the prime example of the divine violence exacted against an unregenerate people, Cowley emphasizes the frequent character of such events and their historical (if not entirely material) nature. Citing "profane Histories," he writes in his notes:

> *Athenaeus* in his eighth Book, Chapt. 2. reports that in *Paenoa* and *Dardanium* (now call'd *Bulgary*) there rained down so many *Frogs* from Heaven (that is, perhaps, they were suddenly produc'd after great Showers) that they fill'd all the Publick Ways, and even private Houses, that their Domesticall Furniture was cover'd with them, that they found them in the very Pots where they boil'd their Meat; and that what with the Trouble of the *Living* and the Smell of the *Dead ones*, they were forc'd at last to forsake their Country. And *Pliny* reports in his eighth Book, Chap. 29. That a whole *City* in *Gallia* hath been driven away by *Frogs*, and another in *Africk* by *Locusts*, and many Examples of this kind might be collected. (251)

Cowley explicitly characterizes such periodic explosions of animal populations as "Judgment[s]" exacted against nations, as punishments that ought to "be attributed to the same Hand of God, though the *Rod was Invisible*" (251). From his perspective, then, profane histories can reinforce the authenticity of the biblical narrative. As significantly, they make the "Hand of God" part of a universal, rather than exclusively, Christian history. This history is the responsibility of natural philosophers, as well as theologians, to elucidate.

Cowley's Christian rationalism is evident in his determination to distance himself from suspect theories of spontaneous generation, as in the third plague, the plague of biting insects. The biblical noun *kinnim* refers to an insect that has been variously interpreted as lice, gnats, mosquitoes (common around Egypt), and sand fleas. Cowley writes in his note, "What kind of *Creature* this was, no Man can tell certainly" (251). Ultimately, however, he agrees with his contemporaries Benedictus Pererius and Levi Rivet that the biblical *kinnim* was probably "some new kind of Creature, called Analogically by an old known Name" and emphasizes, as he does in discussing the first plague, a distinction between "magick" and God's creative force: "the *Magicians* could not counterfeit this *Miracle*, as it was easy for them to do those of the *Serpents*, the *Blood*, and the *Frogs*, which were things to be had every where" (252). Instead, the "swarming things" defy the "*Sorcerers mimick Power*" and testify to the power of God in punishing the Egyptians:

> They stroke the *Earth* a *fertile* blow
> And all the *Dust* did straight to stir begin;
> One would have thought some sudden *Wind* had been
> But, Lo, 'twas nimble *Life* was got within!
> And all the little *Springs* did move,
> And every *Dust* an arm'd *Vermine* prove,
> Of an unknown and new-created Kind,
> Such the *Magick-Gods* could neither *make* nor *find*.
>
> (238)

This stanza reinforces the voluntaristic power of the Judeo-Christian God over the natural world in generating "an unknown and new-created Kind."[39] In such passages, Cowley demonstrates how old theories of spontaneous generation can be given theological explanations, even while leaving the accounts of Pliny, Africk, and other ancients more or less intact. Rather than allegorizing the vermin, assigning them a "mystick sense," Cowley reanimates and naturalizes them, casting them as the "little Springs" of God's voluntaristic power.

While Cowley's *Plagues of Egypt* has sometimes been read as political allegory, it is difficult to reconcile allegorical readings with the poet's copious notes. In many cases, the notes approach the length of mini-essays and attest not only to Cowley's vast knowledge of biblical commentary on Exodus but to his naturalist's interest in plant and animal populations.[40] His accounts of plagues four (flies), five (pestilence), and eight (locusts), in particular, reflect his preoccupation with agricultural reform. The domestic animals struck down by pestilence are drawn with the sensitivity usually reserved for executed human martyrs: the "labouring Ox drops down before the *Plow*"; chickens, "the Crowned *Victims*," are "to the *Altar* lead," where they "Sink, and prevent the *lifted Blow*" of beheading (239). These "useful" animals are innocent of humankind's sin, and Cowley conveys their almost anthropomorphized suffering in a series of poignant images. The starving sheep that "refuse to feed"

> bleat their innocent Souls out into Air;
> The faithful *Dogs* lye gasping by them there;
> The astonish'd *Shepherd* weeps, and breaks his tuneful *Reed*.
>
> (240)

Pestilence breaks down the agricultural system by striking down perfect creatures and thereby disrupts complex interdependencies and affective relationships among domestic animals, shepherds, companion species like dogs, and the larger, imagined ecosystem of ancient Egypt.

In his description of the eighth plague, Cowley anthropomorphizes the locusts in a very different manner. The "Infant Corn" is blasted by a "scorching Wind" of "greedy *Locusts*":

> ... where-e'er
> With founding Wings they flew,
> Left all the earth depopulate and bare,
> As if *Winter* itself had march'd by there.
> Whate're the *Sun* and *Nile*
> Gave with large Bounty to the thankful soil,
> The wretched *Pilagers* bore away,
> And the whole *Summer* was their prey.
>
> (241)

His notes on this passage make no particular theological argument but enumerate historical accounts of locusts that document the size of their swarms, the havoc they wreak on crops, and, most significantly, the seeming coordination of their attacks: "Wonderful are the Things which Authors report of these kinds of Armies of *Locusts*, and of the Order and Regularity of their Marches" (255). Cowley recounts how, in 852, locusts, "in manner of a formed Army," descended on Germany, their "Captains" marching ahead to choose the "most opportune Places for their *Camp*" (255). Eventually, the locusts were "driven by a violent wind into the *Belgick Ocean*" and drowned; their bodies, however, covering an area some twenty miles wide, washed back on shore, causing "a great Pestilence in the Country" (255). This account demonstrates the power of God to punish sinners and characterizes God's power as a principle of order and regularity; the locusts become a military wing of divine punishment. In this context, Cowley quotes St. Hier: "When the Armies of Locusts came lately into these Parts, and filled all the Air, they flew in so great Order, that Slates in a Pavement cannot be laid more regularly, neither did they ever stir one inch out of their Ranks and Files" (255). While the image of the locusts as scourges of an angry God comes as no surprise in the writings of a Christian theologian, Cowley finally turns to Pliny and quotes, without commenting on, the ancient naturalist's description of locusts that "*pass in Troops over great Seas, enduring Hunger for many days in the search of foreign Food*" (255). Their numbers are so great, according to Pliny, that they sometimes "*overcast the Sun, whilst People stand gazing with Terrour, lest they should fall upon their Lands*" (255). Locusts, then, appear in Cowley as *both* a specific instrument of God's punishment of the Egyptians *and* a threat to all agriculturalists—a threat that pervades ancient and modern history. By interweaving classical, medieval, and biblical accounts, Cowley effectively yokes biblical and natural history in a manner consistent with the Royal Society's defense of what Robert Boyle and others called physico-theology.

Implicit in these notes on the plague of locusts—and in Cowley's interpretation of Exodus as a whole—is a new attitude toward vermin. On the one hand, far from being the devil's misshapen emissaries, as they are for de Gheyn, locusts and other imperfect creatures are agents of God's power. Indeed, they constitute a kind of verminous sublime, a spectacle of natural forces marshaled to punish sinful communities by devastating crops and disrupting animal-human economies that depend on annual yields of grain. On the other hand, vermin incite humans to employ their God-given reason in finding ways to strike back against invasions and infestations. Thus, Cowley's note on locusts ends with another quotation from Pliny pitched in a decidedly practical, rather than Miltonic, vein: "*In the Country of Cyrene there is a Law to make War against them thrice a Year, first by breaking their Eggs, then by killing the young ones, and lastly, the old ones, &c.*" (255). Citing this ancient attempt to eradicate locust populations, Cowley implicitly moves beyond a purely theological interpretation of the plague of locusts and toward a practical solution for working farmers—a specific historical instance of the kind of rational response to vermin infestations that he champions in "Of Agriculture." Cowley's verminous sublime, coupled with a dose of useful knowledge, edge the demonic forces associated with vermin in *Macbeth* offstage, or at least to the wings.

Admittedly, despite the lengthy engagement with natural philosophy in *The Plagues of Egypt*, Cowley is not completely above using vermin as allegorical machinery in the service of a larger political agenda, most notably in *A Vision, Concerning His Late Pretended Highnesse, Cromwell, the Wicked*, published in 1661. Given the poem's extended conceit linking vermin, Cromwellians, and war, it is easy to see how Cowley can be described as a "pew-ranting Anglican."[41] Cowley compares the "Tyrant" Cromwell both to a "mischievous Serpent" and to the rod that scourges the land: "A Tyrant is a Rod and Serpent too," he writes, "And brings worse *Plagues* than Egypt knew" (591). Cowley compares the plagues of lice, flies, and locusts to invasive bands of religious dissenters:

> What croaking Sects and Vermine has it sent
> The restlesse Nation to torment?
> What greedy Troups, what armed power
> Of Flies and Locusts to devour
> The Land which every where they fill?
> Nor fly they, Lord, away; no, they devour it still.
>
> (592)

Even in this allegorical rendering, however, politics and natural philosophy reinforce one another. What makes the image effective is more than an allusion to the Old Testament; it is a concrete knowledge of how similarly armies of men and armies of locusts behave. This analogy registers Cowley's and his readers' sensitivity to the fragile relations among "Flies and Locusts," consumption, national politics, and food systems. "Croaking sects" situates this mid-seventeenth-century version of biopolitics in the context of royalist nightmares of "greedy Troups." To "devour," a word Cowley repeats several times, is to "swallow" greedily, voraciously, recklessly—to eat, in other words, like a wild, predatory animal rather than a supposedly civilized human. "Eate as it becommeth a man," we are told in the original King James version of Ecclesiasticus, ". . . and devoure not, lest thou be hated." In the poet's dark satiric vision, the Civil War made prey of human beings, the verminous armies of the Parliamentarians—rather than the singular tyranny of Macbeth—stripping people of land, life, and sustenance.

VERMIN, REFORM, AND THE BALANCE OF NATURE

In works both before and after the Interregnum, Cowley answers prophets of doom, like Godfrey Goodman, by denying that humans sink naturally under the weight of a universal principle of decay. Goodman distinguishes between creatures created by God and the ephemeral offspring of a corrupted nature: if nature were "sound and entire," he reasons, she would have given vermin "a more noble birth, and a longer continuance of life; but being defectiue, and not able to produce couragious Lions, braue Vnico[rn]es, fierce Tigers, stout Elephants, shee makes it her taske and imployment to be the mother, and mid-wife of wormes, of gnats, and of butterflies, wherein she seemes most to abound, and to bring forth a very plentifull brood."[42] If Goodman's imperfect creatures call into question the nature of life and emphasize the sinfulness of humanity, most of Cowley's vermin reinforce his view that "The world's a scene of changes, and to be Constant, in Nature, were Inconstancy."[43] Mutability functions as evidence of God's power and providence in the world; this dynamic universe and unified vision of physical reality similarly underwrites the argument from design popularized in the 1660s.

Even worms, therefore, must have their place in Cowley's natural order. His iconic essay "Of Agriculture" makes apparent his understanding of "corruption" as a physical process in which vermin play important roles. A sardonic, if biologically accurate, depiction of parasites occurs in his poeticized herbal, *Plantarum Libri Sex* (*Six Books of Plants*), in which a personified wormwood (*Artemisia absinthium*) praises its own medicinal efficacy. In having the bitter-tasting wormwood celebrate its victories over Death, Cowley veers into a sardonic digression, into the discourse of the parasite:

> (Voracious Worm! Thou wilt most certainly
> Heirs of our bodies be whene'er we die;
> Defer a while the meal which, in the grave,
> Of human viands thou ere long must have.)
> Those vermine infants' bowels make their food,
> And love to suck their fill of tender blood:

They cannot stay till Death serves up their feast,
But greedily snatch up the meat undress'd.
Why should I speak of fleas? Such foes I hate,
So basely born, ev'n to enumerate;
Such dust-born, skipping points of life, I say,
Whose only virtue is to run away.[44]

Born with infants (or passed though the mother's milk), worms live in and on "infants' bowels" and will be the "heirs" of the body at death. The birthright of parasites is set against the origin of "basely born . . . fleas" who, moreover, do not present wormwood—toasting its own healing prowess—with the kind of challenge that it ostensibly seeks. To the extent that Goodman imagines an ongoing corruption in nature, Cowley offers a naturalist's antidote to specific instances of "corruption" (Artemisia indeed has antibacterial properties) and parodies the hierarchy of humankind, perfect, and imperfect creatures on which Goodman relies.

Plantarum Libri Sex is typical of Cowley's later writing, which often presents the relationship between humans and animals as a darkly comic series of nested connections, too complicated to be collapsed into hierarchical or metaphysical schemes. Cowley is the author, after all, who complains in "Of Agriculture" that while "metaphysic"—which "may be anything or no"—is considered part of the arts and sciences, plant and animal husbandry are not. His championing of an agricultural, rather than metaphysical, order is historically significant; "Of Agriculture" was incorporated in the nineteenth century into the mission statement of land-grant colleges and universities across the United States. Yet his conception of order itself, as the personified wormwood testifies, is shot through with the ironies and complexities of a divine and mysterious creation.

Even in his theological writings, Cowley's treatment of the human-animal relationship is described in the inversions and indirections characteristic of a dynamic natural order. In his Pindaric based on Isaiah 34, written before *The Plagues of Egypt*, Cowley describes impending devastation: rivers and lakes overflow with human blood; rotting corpses, infecting the air, beget plagues and "putrid Venoms;" and streets are overtaken by serpents, wolves, ravens, and owls (225). Terrified by vermin, humankind becomes subjected to animals. Cowley's note explains this inversion: "Though *Beasts* were first *created* in time, yet because *Man* was first and chiefly designed, and they only in order to him, the Right of *Primogeniture* belongs to him, and therefore all Beasts at first obeyed and feared him" (229). Yet "Man," ostensibly "*Gods and Angels Kin*," has abdicated his dominion, or has effectively relinquished his moral claims to "the Right of *Primogeniture*." Correspondingly, Cowley's Pindaric offers a strong (mis)reading of Isaiah 34:5 in that men, rather than animals, are figured as sacrificial offerings. The original King James version reads: "For the sword of God is filled with blood, it is made fat with fatness, and with the blood of lambs, and goats, with the fat of the kidneys of Rams." Cowley, invoking the horrors of the Civil War, describes the ritual slaughter to which sinfulness has led:

> *God* does a solemn *Sacrifice* prepare;
> But not of Oxen, nor of Rams,
> Not of Kids, nor of their Dams,
> Not of Heifers, nor of Lambs.
> The *Altar* all the *Land*, and all *Men* in't the *Victims* are.
>
> (224)

Cowley's contemporaries typically interpreted this biblical verse allegorically—lambs mean the "common people"; goats signify political leaders; rams represent magistrates. In his notes, Cowley takes issue with this interpretation, which he regards as overly ingenious: "these two . . . interpretations of *Goats* and *Rams*, seem very slight and forced; the Meaning is, that all sorts of men shall be sacrificed to God's Justice, as lambs, goats, and rams were wont to be" (228). While admitting the "Text seems . . . quite contrary" to his view, Cowley nevertheless insists on the necessity of the interchangeability of men and beasts: "the Names of *Beasts* in that Place must necessarily be understood, as put for *Men*; all sorts of Men" (228). His emphasis on the generic collectivity—"all sorts of Men"—as sacrificial offerings robs them of their agency: rather than sacrificing *to* God to forgive their sins, they are sacrificed *by* God because of their sins.

Cowley's somewhat torturous misreading, it seems, articulates a model of collective identity that includes animals, and especially domestic creatures.[45] Throughout Cowley's work, domestic animals are portrayed in a manner that, a century later, could be termed sentimental. As in his poetic treatment of faithful dogs and innocent sheep dying for humankind's sins in *The Plagues of Egypt*, Cowley's "translation" of Isaiah similarly emphasizes the innocence of perfect creatures:

Since wicked *Mens* more guilty Blood to spare,
The *Beasts* so long have sacrificed been,
Since Men their *Birth-right* forfeit still by Sin,
'Tis fit at last *Beasts* their *Revenge* should have,
And *sacrificed* Men their better *Brethren* save.

(224)

Anticipating that many of his readers will take issue with his assertions that beasts are the "better Brethren" of "Men," an explicit inversion of God's having granted Adam dominion over beasts, Cowley addresses the problem in his notes. "We should not be angry or ashamed," he writes, "to have [Beasts] called our *Brethren*, for they are literally so, having the same *Creator* or *Father*" (229). Indeed, Cowley expands this kinship to include vermin. Quoting Job 17:14, he asserts that "the Scripture gives us a much worse Kindred: *"I have said to Corruption, thou art my Father; and to the Worm, thou art my Mother and my Sister"* (229). Although in this reference to Job Cowley may appear to align himself with Goodman, Wither, and others for whom the verminous nature of man is a foundational principle of Christian theology, his allusion seems a bit tongue in cheek. He deploys ironically humans' kinship to vermin so that vermin can function, as they do in his agricultural essay, as an incitement to moral reform.

In *The Plagues of Egypt*, "reform" seems to imply accepting God's ability to perform divine violence, but increasingly in Cowley's work, it comes to be associated with a kind of self-fashioning through retirement from the city, the proper use of medicine, and the stewardship of the land. By virtue of his interest in natural philosophy, Cowley rewrites the plagues of Egypt and the prophecies of Isaiah, making vermin signs not of an originary corruption, but of intensifications of natural, even, commonplace phenomena. Vermin infestations speak to a neglect of the land. As such, they are subject to naturalistic as well as spiritual corrections, primarily through techniques of good husbandry. As he writes in "Of Agriculture," agriculture can and will exist without philosophy and the other arts, but "no one other" can exist "without this": agriculture "is like Speech, without which the Society of Men cannot be preserv'd" (653). Recognizing the role of vermin in nature, Cowley mounts a powerful ideology of improvement, agricultural as well as spiritual. In contrast to Macbeth's Scotland, Cowley's England can be redeemed by shared knowledges and technologies instead of through another ostensibly restorative regicide.

John Ray's *Wisdom of God Manifested in the Works of Creation* completes the rehabilitation of vermin foreshadowed in Cowley's works. With William Derham, the naturalist and divine, Ray articulates what he regards as the "use value" of "*Animalcula*" discovered under the microscope, arguing that in their aquatic versions they "serve for Food to some others of the small Insects of the waters."[46] He extends the same line of argument to "noxious Insects." In response to why so many are "produced," he claims, first, that what might appear noxious "to us, are salutary to other Creatures." Poultry feed on spiders and peacocks prey on serpents, both demonstrating that while a sting or bite may be poisonous, that effect is neutralized when the creature is taken "entire into the Stomach."[47] Second, Ray points out that even venomous creatures "afford us noble Medicines" and rarely use their sting unless "assaulted or provoked."[48] "Lastly," he continues, God sometimes uses such creatures "as Scourges, to chastize or punish wicked Persons or Nations, as he did *Herod* and the *Egyptians*":

> No Creature so mean and contemptible, but God can, when he pleases, produce such Armies of them as no humane Force is able to conquer or destroy, but they shall of a sudden consume and devour up all the Fruits of the Earth, and whatever might serve for the Sustenance of Man, as Locusts have often been observed to do.[49]

Those who use the existence of noxious creatures to argue against the wisdom of God, he concludes, might equally argue against the "Prudence and Policy" of any state that keeps forces for its own protection. Such forces share with populations of insects rudeness and insolence but are "necessary, either to suppress Rebellions, or punish Rebels and other disorderly and vicious Persons, and keep the World in quiet."[50]

Ray's *apologia* for swarming things emphasizes their use value in terms that recall the medical and moral qualities outlined, earlier in the seventeenth century, in Thomas Moffet's foundational *Insectorum Theatrum*. Ray justifies his comments on vermin by involving the principles of a "balance of nature," an argument that, as Frank Egerton demonstrates, had its roots in Herodotus, Plato, and Cicero.[51] The idea of a balance of nature turns on the following assumptions: populations of species remain essentially stable; when "eruptions" occur, the balance in the long run will be restored; and all species have a specified place in the structure of nature. Predatory species have low reproductive rates, and the species on which they prey have much higher ones.[52] Synthesized in the seventeenth century, these ancient balance-of-nature arguments, filtered through the imperatives of Protestant theology, helped formed the roots of modern ecological thinking.[53]

What ideas of the balance of nature did not bring with them, however, was a wholesale rebranding of swarming things as genuinely viable food sources for Europeans, despite some persuasive arguments about the nutritional value of locusts and other creatures. Reporting in 1697 on swarms of locusts that had recently devastated Ireland and promising to avoid "bare Hearsays," the naturalist and physician Thomas Molyneux describes how the locusts consumed so many trees and hedges that summer looked like "the depth of winter."[54] Swarms then spread into houses "where," he writes, they "would often drop on the Meat as it was dressing in the Kitchen," and fall from the ceilings "into the Dishes as they stood on the Table" (744). A second generation of locusts, still in the maggot stage, crept underground, devouring the roots of corn and grass, thereby ruining "both the support of Man and Beast" (744). But in a move worthy of Defoe's Crusoe, Molyneux's tale avoids environmental disaster by taking a providentialist turn. The "rage" of this plague was checked by both by fortunate winds and the foresight of a God who allowed the locusts to serve as a substitute food source for starving animals (745). Swine and poultry, Molyneux reports, began to watch for the locusts to fall from trees:

> And when they came to the Ground eat them up in abundance, being much pleased with the Food, and thriving well upon the Diet. Nay, I have been assured that the poorer sort of the *Native Irish* (the Country then labouring under a Scarcity of Provision), had a way of dressing them, and lived upon them as Food; nor is it strange that what fattened our domestick Poultry and Hogs, should afford agreeable and sufficient Nourishment for the Relief of Man. (746)

Molyneux's description of the locust infestation demonstrates a nascent (if theologically structured) understanding of how humans and the "more perfect" creatures not only share basic food sources and appetites, but how they can survive in a shared agricultural and ecological system under threat.

In his letter, Molyneux imagines a holistic ecology based on the recycling of locusts into a providential agro-economy. This agro-economy is remarkable in its inclusion of the imperfect creatures that had been banished from the Garden of Eden, booted from Noah's Ark, and converted to a benign, buzzing landscape in seventeenth-century georgic. What enables his strange utopia are two rhetorical moves: first, Molyneux demonstrates the double-sided nature of plagues—as scourges, as in Sadeler, but also, following Cowley, as incitements to practical salvation. Second, he shows how locusts, usually regarded as an "unclean" food, may be reinterpreted through Mosaic law into a viable part of a providentially sanctioned food system. "Forseeing the great Dearth and Scarcity that these Vermin might one Day bring upon his People," writes Molyneux, Moses "gives them a sort of Hint what they should do" when the locusts and beetles have destroyed provisions (753). Rather "than starve," Moses tells them, "they might eat, and live upon, the filthy Destroyers themselves, and yet be Clean" (753). While most Western scholars are unlikely to find in Molyneux's remarkable description of beetle nutrition an example to imitate, it does raise questions not only about the role of imperfect creatures in Judeo-Christian dietary practices, but also about their continuing constitutive functions in our systems of thought.[55] I explore the latter problem in the next chapter by focusing on the scientific perceptions of imperfect creatures, particularly in the works of the comparative anatomist, Thomas Willis. If Cowley begins poetically to reassess the role of vermin in a traditional balance of nature, Willis, working in a different part of natural philosophy, challenges the fundamental, Aristotelian precepts of a more-than-human world divided into perfect and imperfect beings.

CHAPTER 3

"Observe the Frog"
Imperfect Creatures, Neuroanatomy, and the Problem of the Human

Beasts are either perfect or imperfect.
—THOMAS BROWN, *NATURE'S CABINET UNLOCK'D* (1657)

Thomas Shadwell's 1676 comedy *The Virtuoso*, a pointed and very popular satire of the Royal Society, lambasts Sir Nicholas Gimcrack, a would-be experimentalist who embodies the follies of pursuing impractical knowledge rather than managing his family and finances. His rebellious nieces, Clarinda and Miranda, describe Sir Nicholas to their suitors, Bruce and Longvil, as "A sot that has spent two thousand pounds in microscopes to find out the nature of eels in vinegar, mites in cheese, and the blue of plums," and who "has studied these twenty years to find out several sorts of spiders, and never cares for understanding mankind."[1] The seeming triviality of Sir Nicholas's pursuits is celebrated enthusiastically by his parasitical friend, Sir Formal Trifle:

> [N]o man upon the face of the earth is so well seen in the nature of ants, flies, humble-bees, earwigs, millipedes, hog's lice, maggots, mites in a cheese, tadpoles, worms, newts, spiders, and all the noble products of the sun by equivocal generation. (III.ii.1–5)

Throughout the play, Sir Formal's rhetoric, as Andrew Black has suggested, is essential to making Sir Nicholas's seemingly useless knowledge significant—or significant sounding.[2] Responding to Sir Formal's compliment, Sir Nicholas eagerly adds: "Indeed, I ha' found more curious phenomena in these minute animals than in those of vaster magnitude" (III. iii.6–7). Yet, even given Shadwell's satiric intentions, the Virtuoso is self-aware enough to insert himself into some illustrious company, going back to Sir Francis Bacon. Writing in 1627, Bacon emphasized the ability of what were still called "insecta," or creatures born of putrefaction, to serve as exemplars of the wonders of the Book of Nature: "the Nature of Things," he writes in *Sylva Sylvarum* "is commonly better perceiued, in Small, than in Great, and in unperfect, than in perfect, and in Parts, than in whole: So the Nature of Vivification is best enquired in Creatures bred of Putrefaction."[3] Long before professional exterminators penned works like John Southall's *A Treatise of Buggs* (1730), vermin were enlisted to advance inquiries into the very nature of life.[4]

Throughout the seventeenth century, creatures ostensibly born from mud or dung—including flies, gnats, frogs, earthworms, eels, and snakes—had served as experimental subjects for Ulessa Aldrovandi, Thomas Moffet, Francesco Redi, Antony van Leeuwenhoek, Martin Lister, Robert Hooke, Jan Swammerdan, and Marcello Malpighi, among others; all of these natural philosophers sought to dispel theories of spontaneous generation. With the invention of the microscope, Bacon's "unperfect" beings ("the noble products" of Sir Formal's "equivocal generation") took on new significance because, as Hooke argued in *Micrographia*, fleas, mites, gnats, and other "little objects" can, by virtue of the microscope, "be compare'd to greater and more beautiful Works of Nature," like a "Horse, and Elephant or a Lyon."[5] Although the microscope became a key technology in bringing vermin into the order of a providentially designed world, as Tita Chico argues, it also posed some difficult theatrical problems for Shadwell; audiences can no more can see through the lens of a microscope than they can spot the lunar creatures that Baliardo claims to have spied through his telescope in Aphra Behn's farce, *The Emperor of the Moon* (1688).[6] Sir Formal's rhetoric is one of Shadwell's strategies for trying to make vermin visible, as well as risible.

But it is not the only one. *The Virtuoso*'s funniest and best-known scene demonstrates a kind of verminous experiment different from those Hooke or Bacon had in mind. Gimcrack's swimming lesson depends on Shadwell's satiric parody of the Royal Society's close observation of imperfect creatures and on what Chico identifies as the shared illusional space of the theater and the laboratory.[7] As Gimcrack's young (and unfaithful) wife takes Bruce and Longvil to see the Virtuoso in action, she explains: "He has a frog in a bowl of water tied with a packthread by the loins; which packthread Sir Nicholas holds in his teeth, lying upon his belly on a table; and as the frog strikes, he strikes; and his swimming master stands by to tell him when he does well or ill" (II.i .295–99). The libertine heroes come upon the harnessed Sir Nicholas being egged on by Sir Formal, as the Swimming Master delivers a blow-by-blow commentary of the action: "Ah! well struck, Sir Nicholas. That was admirable; that was as well swum as any man in England can. Observe the frog. Draw up your arms a little nearer, and then thrust 'em out strongly. Gather up your legs a little more. So. Very well. Incomparable" (II.Ii.6–10). The satire in this scene cuts in two ways. In one respect, Shadwell takes aim at the overblown rhetoric and seemingly impenetrable jargon that critics of the Royal Society invariably mocked. "So it is wonderful," Sir Nicholas says to Sir Formal, "to observe the agility of this pretty animal which, notwith-standing I impede its motion by the detention of this filium or thread within my teeth which makes a ligature about its loins, and though by many sudden stops I cause the animal sometimes to sink or immerge, yet with indefati-gable activity it rises and keeps almost its whole body upon the superficies or surface of this humid element" (II.ii.15–23). Gimcrack's language under-mines the Royal Society's ostensible goal of clear and concise prose—the ideal, as Thomas Sprat put it, "to return back to the primitive purity and shortness [of language], when men deliver'd so many *things* almost in an equal number of *words*."[8] In another respect, the Swimming Master's in-junction to "observe the frog" demonstrates how close the Baconian injunc-tion to study "the Nature of Things . . . in unperfect" creatures comes to self-parody—verbally, theatrically, and conceptually. The actor playing Sir Nicholas has to mimic the motions of the frog because members of the au-dience, even in the comparatively close quarters of the Restoration theater, could not *see* a frog onstage. The animal has to be conjured into imaginative existence; much like the unseen fleas in Crespi's paintings, imperfect crea-tures can be made visible only (or primarily) in the actions, descriptions, and metaphors of the humans who share their environment. While perfect crea-tures (such as Launce's dog Crab in Shakespeare's *Two Gentlemen of Verona*) frequently upstage actors, this is one case in which an imperfect creature, with Sir Nicholas serving as his surrogate, steals the scene. The Swimming Master's injunction to "Observe the frog" suggests the power of unseen ver-min to provoke and organize human activity, including an understanding of the natural world. The frog (presumably without being onstage) becomes the absent, normative center—a creature doing what comes naturally—of a satiric world given to presumption, imitation, and self-parodic folly.[9]

The comic nature of the swimming lesson should not distract us from acknowledging its experimental structure. Gimcrack's experiment plays with similarities and dissimilarities between the amphibian and human body; the intellectual efforts of the virtuoso become tethered, both literally and figuratively, by a thread to the musculature of a frog. The scene is funny because it forcibly yokes two presumably unlike things—the experimental subject and object, the human and the frog—thereby collapsing differences between the high-minded scientists and the struggling member of a lower species; it is analytically important, however, because it reminds us that animals, both more and less "perfect," were foundational to experimental science and efforts to reimagine the "human" in ways compatible with changing views of the natural world.

This posthumanist insight has driven work in early modern animal studies. Unlike many contemporary philosophers who found in Descartes a fundamental frame for understanding the posthumanist project, historicist scholars have uniformly cautioned against treating the Cartesian "beast-machine" as the dominant cultural metaphor, especially in early modern English literature.[10] As Erica Fudge argues, many "modern critics read the Cartesian human back onto pre-Cartesian writings, even while those critics are assessing the workings of Aristotelian psychology. In so doing, they implicitly and anachronistically assert that the Cartesian human is the only model of the human available."[11] Fudge, Bruce Boehrer, Karen Raber, Richard Nash, Laura Brown, Laurie Shannon, and Jonathan Lamb, among others, have rehistoricized this discourse of the human in the seventeenth and eighteenth centuries, demonstrating, in different ways, the often peripheral role of Descartes in English scientific and literary texts. What Shannon calls "Descartes's indelible formula" of the human-animal divide is often projected, ahistorically, back on to early modern texts.[12]

Shadwell's Virtuoso, like Jonson's Volpone before it, rejects Cartesian distinctions, creating a satirical space for more nuanced, less theologically univocal perceptions of human-animal connections.[13] More precisely, it draws on an additive model of the soul inherited from Aristotle and reworked through the various branches of natural philosophy. The Virtuoso opens with Bruce and Longvil satirically comparing the "race of gentlemen" in Restoration London to ill-bred horses (I.i.21–24), and then to vegetables ("untimely fruit") rotting on the vine: "These are sure the only animals that live without thinking," complains Bruce about men of the town: "A sensitive plant has more imagination than most of 'em" (I.i.60–63). While it may appear that these opening salvos collapse a normative difference between the "human" and the "animal" conceived as a binary, the presence of vegetables indicates that Bruce draws on an additive or tripartite model of the soul, in which souls can be vegetative (nutritive, or what is termed "vital"), animal (sensitive or corporeal), and rational (intellectual or noncorporeal). The tripartite model of ensoulment destabilizes any opposition between the "human" and the "animal," or, to put it another way, forces those terms into a chain of zoopolitical differences.[14] Indeed, concepts of the "sensitive soul" or the "soul of brutes," defined as "an heap of animal spirits everywhere diffused thorow the Brain and Nervous Stock," seems ready-made for a lusty satire on human pretensions.[15] The play's witty heroines, Miranda and Clarinda, describe Sir Samuel Hearty, a would-be wit, as "a well-educated spaniel" (I.iii.28–29), and Snarl, a hypocritical declaimer against vice, as both a "mad dog" in need of worming (I.ii.38–39) and as a "stingless drone" (I.ii.135). For his part, Snarl repeatedly labels Miranda and Clarinda "paltry, lazy cockatrices," that is, cockroaches (I.ii.81–82). Later, in Act 2, this promiscuous universe of animal spirits is materialized in Gimcrack's claims to have transfused the blood of a sheep into a madman, an account that makes a mockery of what Boyle defended as the "usefulness" of laboratory science.[16] Gimcrack's "patient" goes from "being maniacal or raging mad" to "wholly ovine or sheepish," with "wool growing on him in great quantities," and a "sheep's tail" growing "from his anus or fundament" (II.ii.190–95). Humans, dogs, sheep, cockroaches, frogs, horses, and spiders seem to exist as part of the same order of life and with the same basic nervous system; Gimcrack's experiments, as John Shanahan aptly puts it, make "basic ontology problematic."[17]

Seventeenth-century neuroanatomy similarly thwarts any simple and stable human-animal difference. A decade before *The Virtuoso* was performed, the English physician and comparative anatomist Thomas Willis published *Cerebri Anatome* (1664), a groundbreaking study in work on the brain, followed by the Latin edition of *De Anima Brutorum* (1672), or *Of the Souls of Brutes* (trans. 1683). In these texts, Willis describes neurological structures in oysters, worms, and other creatures in order, he says, to show the "vast difference" between the souls of these creatures and those of humans (*AB* 44).[18] With contemporary interest in neuroanatomy, cognitive science, and MRIs, Willis's often-neglected works are again being read and his influence reassessed.[19] Willis's lectures on anatomy were transcribed by Boyle and Locke, and he was widely regarded as being "tutor" to the latter.[20] Shadwell may or may not have known any of the Oxford physician's works.[21] Both, however, were the heirs of Aristotle's *De Anima* and its driving assumptions that humans shared with other animals a "corporeal" or "sensitive" soul, responsible for autonomic functions as well as memory, imagination, and certain forms of intellection. In the seventeenth century, Pierre Gassendi (following Aristotle) claimed that because animals show evidence of memory and other functions, they must have souls. Willis attributes these characteristics to a "corporeal" or "brute" soul shot through with "animal spirits," which, in turn, were connected to the brain; his work "transformed the traditional three-part soul . . . into the corpuscular philosophy of the nervous system."[22] His 1683 treatise *Of the Soul of Brutes* offered empirical evidence for a sensitive soul "Common to Brute Animals with Man" (*AB* 1), even as it sought to establish a rational or incorporeal soul that, located in the brain, ostensibly controlled the corporeal one. Taking issue with both Lucretius and Descartes and focusing on comparative anatomies of creatures from oysters, to chimps, to humans, Willis examined the brains of the "more perfect Brutes" and the nervous systems of "unperfect" ones. What emerged from his investigations are not absolute differences between humans and animals but a spectrum of physiological distinctions and similarities.

Rather than add Willis's experiments to the list of *The Virtuoso's* sources, I want to read Shadwell's comedy and Willis's neuroanatomy contrapuntally in order to emphasize the ways in which late seventeenth-century satirists and natural philosophers challenged the Cartesian assumption that the souls of men and the souls of animals were distinct.[23] Together, Willis's scientific analyses and Shadwell's trenchant satire on scientific texts and practices reveal the extent to which our own habits of analysis are shaped by often unacknowledged Cartesian values and assumptions, if by "Cartesian" one means a strict metaphysical dualism naturalized by formalist interpretive procedures. A default Cartesianism imposed on British seventeenth-century natural philosophy results in missed opportunities, occlusions, and elisions; we tend to overlook the experiments that structure, categorize, and carve up biological systems.[24] By examining the ways in which Willis and Shadwell treat the continuum of human-animal relations, we can, however, regain some sense of how Bacon's "unperfect creatures" helped to shape understandings of human physiology and the human soul.

"TWIN SPECIES"

Natural philosophers, from Bacon on, argued that the lower creatures shared a complex sensory system with humans. Bacon claims in *Sylva Syl-*

varum that the *"Insecta* have *Voluntary Motion,* and therefore *Imagination,"* a belief he supports by the evidence of ants going "forwards to their Hills" and bees who "admirably know the way, from a Flowry Heath, two or three Miles off, to their Hives" (177). While he is willing to admit that gnats and flies have a more "mutable" imagination than bees and ants, he insists most of the "insecta," just like dogs, apes, and humans, have more than one "sense of Feeling" located in the head (177). Reasoning from the example of bees, he argues "if they goe forthright to a Place, they must needs have Sight: Besides, they delight more in one *Flower,* or *Herbe,* than in another, and therefore have *Taste:* And *Bees* are called with *Sounde* upon *Brasse,* and therefore they have *Hearing;* Which shewith likewise that though their *Spirit* be diffused, yet there is a *Seat* of their *Senses* in their *Head*" (177). By "*spirit*" Bacon means the animals spirits that, as George Rousseau argues, were in the forefront "of all theories explaining life" between 1400 and 1800.[25] The head, or "*Seat* of the *Senses,*" housed or served as a kind of switchyard for the animal spirits. The central clearinghouse for these sensations constituted the corporeal or sensitive soul.

In the seventeenth century, after William Harvey's work on circulation, these unseen "vital spirits" began to be conceived as part of a network conjoined by blood; the brain, according to Zimmer, "worked like a bellows, pulsating and driving the spirits in to the nerves."[26] Neuroanatomists sought to identify what was described variously in the seventeenth century as a fluid, an ether, or a fire "which mediates between mind and body in the eternal search for consciousness, emotion, and memory." [27] The cornerstone of this tradition was Willis's 1664 *Cerebri Anatome,* the first text, according to Rousseau, to argue unequivocally that the "seat of the soul is strictly limited to the brain."[28] *Cerebri Anatome* went through four editions within a year; over the next century, these ballooned into twenty-three editions.[29] The project of *Cerebri Anatome* is in keeping with Willis's theological imperative: to locate in the animal body proof of divine workmanship. Unlike Descartes, Willis promotes a method to establish an empirical (rather than philosophical) basis for the relationship between neuroanatomical form and behavioral function.

In his first chapter, Willis defends his comparative method, claiming not only that "humane Heads" are less readily available for dissection than those of other creatures and the "immense bulk" of the human head can itself be a "hindrance" to anatomical investigation, but, significantly, that quadrupeds can stand in for humans, given marked similarities between their brains (*CA*

6). Based on this "compared Anatomy" between "Beasts" and men, he declares his method is able to reveal "the impressions, influences, and secret ways of working with the sensitive soul" (CA 6). Summarizing the differences readers should expect to encounter between "perfect" and "imperfect" creatures and explaining the organization of his treatise, Willis writes:

> Concerning the Heads of living Creatures . . . it was observed . . . that there was a notable Analogy between man and four-footed Beasts, also between Birds and Fishes; For when the first Inhabitants of the new-made World were produced, as one day brought forth Fowls and Fishes at once, another in like manner Man and four-footed Beasts; so there is in either twin species a like form of the Brain; but between the Child of the former, and this of the following day, there is found a great difference as to those parts. For as much therefore as Men and four-footed Beasts have got more perfect Brains, and more alike among themselves, we have Ordered our Observations from their Inspection; Then afterwards we shall deliver the Anatomy of the Brain in Fowls and Fishes. (CA 6)

The organization of *Cerebri Anatome*, then, mirrors a theological order, in which creatures of the waters and sky were created on the fifth day, and man and other beasts on the sixth. (Genesis 1:20–31) (That God created "creeping things"—themselves regarded as "imperfect" on day six as well does not seem to trouble Willis's scheme.) In this theocentric view, humans and quadrupeds are "twin species" in the same way birds and fish are; their analogous brains both reflect and reaffirm their origins and place in the divinely created order of nature. Although this "twinning" of humans and higher creatures creates practical opportunities for the comparative anatomist in articulating the windings of the sensitive soul, it also poses a theological danger because these similarities cannot override the physiological differences that underwrite human exceptionalism.

Willis argues that similarities, and therefore differences, are located, in part, in the cerebral cortex or the surface of the brain, which distills and distributes the animal spirits. Produced by arterial blood, the animal spirits are conveyed to the grey cortex, "and then carried through white matter, the brain stem, and through the nerves into the rest of the body: muscles, organs, and fibrous membranes."[30] Higher cognitive faculties require "free and changeable" pathways for the circulation of the animal spirits (CA 60). Therefore, the texture of the cortex—even more than brain size—seems to be responsible, in Willis's mind, for the uneven distribution of memory, imagination, and intellection across species. The cortices of humans and the more perfect animals are characterized by variegation—"uneven and broken, with turnings, and windings and rollings about, almost like those of the Intestines" (CA 59)—but the brains of "lesser four-footed beasts" and "Fowls and Fishes" are "plain and even" (CA 59). In human brains, the pathways are

> far more and greater . . . than in any other living Creature, to wit, for the various and manifold actings of the superior faculties . . . Those Gyrations or turnings about in four-footed beasts are fewer, and in some, as in a Cat, they are found to be in a certain figure and order: wherefore this Brute thinks on, or remembers, scarce anything but what the instincts and needs of Nature suggest (CA 59–60).

In this neuroanatomical drama of difference, four-footed beasts share with humans a birthday and a brain that distinguishes both species from fish and fowl, but their status as "twin species" is qualified by the comparatively less complex brain texture of quadrupeds. Willis's method enables finer distinctions than gross neuroanatomy, and many of these reinforce culturally specific stereotypes and biases. His description of the cat's regular arrangement of neural tissues, for example, offers an anatomical corollary for "typical" feline behavior, which was thought to be driven less by memory or learning than by predatory and instinctive actions.[31] To have a species' cerebral "Gyrations" appear in "a certain figure and order" is to characterize its ability to learn in a qualitatively and quantitatively different manner from humans. A more regular "order" of brain tissue limits the cat to "comprehend or learn by imitation fewer things, and those almost only of one kind" (CA 60). For Willis, neuroanatomy is destiny.

These structural correlations between form and function also obtain in other parts of the brain. Willis is "especially intrigued," according to Hans Isler, by the quadrigeminates, including the pons and the medulla, that "convey the natural impulses from the cerebellum to the cerebrum where they cause moods that result in more or less purposeful movements."[32] Domesticated farm animals—Willis mentions sheep, cattle, goats, and swine—seem to have small pons and large quadrigeminates.[33] In his mind, this neuroanatomical arrangement signifies the predominance of instinct and a paucity of emotional capability; but in animals with strong emotions, those species in which intelligence dominates instinct, this "relation," as Isler notes, "is reversed."[34] Formulating a law of comparative anatomy, Willis claims the preceding correlation "holds good in most Animals which I have yet happened to dissect," including a monkey. The largest pons, logically enough, are to be found in humans, whose greater passions require more complex housing and transportation arrangements. Man "is wont to be suddenly and vehemently disturbed," he writes, "therefore the Promptuary or Store-house is required to be more large, in which a greater plenty of Spirits may be kept, to be bestowed on such inordinations of the Affections" (CA 100). Yet Willis implicitly rejects a Cartesian division between humans and those animals that seem closely related in terms of brain structure. As in the human brain, the neuroanatomy of three "more perfect" creatures reflects some fundamental similarities to humans in their behavior: "Next to a man," Willis notes, "this part [the pons] is greatest in a Dog, Cat, and Fox" (CA 100), and the underdeveloped quadrigeminates in these animals indicate their *inability* to rely exclusively on instincts: "in a Man, a Dog, Fox, and the like, who are more apt to learn and acquire habits, these Prominences are very small; and these Animals being newly born, are furnished with only a rude and imperfect sense; besides, they are found wholly unapt to seek out their food" (CA 101). As his use of the phrase "wholly unapt" suggests, these creatures need a form of animal socialization, a model to imitate, in order to learn how to hunt.

As this account implies, Willis opposes "instinct" to "wit," a faculty intimately related to passion, which, in turn, is intrinsic to the sensitive soul. "They in whom the Affections are wont to predominate," Willis writes, "and who are furnished with a certain wit, (as besides Man, are Dogs, Foxes, and some other hotter Animals) are less powerful in Instinct" (CA 101). The brains of dogs and foxes (the cat, once mentioned, drops out of the chain of equivalences) show physiological evidence of their intellectual and behavioral similarities to humans. The sensitive or corporeal soul, therefore, provides a neuroanatomical basis for a kind of "twinning" apparent between humans and perfect creatures that resonates throughout Restoration literature—particularly in satires that call into question humans' pretense to have mastered the sensitive soul and its corporeal appetites. Although Willis was not focused on apes, an uncommon experimental subject in the 1660s, his work influenced Edward Tyson's *Anatomy of a Pygmy* (1698), another scientific treatise that destabilized, intentionally or not, Cartesian assumptions about humans and animals. In his 1695 letter to John Dennis on comedy, the playwright William Congreve concedes he is disturbed by "seeing things, that force me to entertain low thoughts of my Nature," and then admits he "could never look long upon a Monkey, without very Mortifying Reflections; tho [he] never heard any thing to the Contrary, why that Creature is not Originally of a Distinct *Species.*"[35] Congreve's "mortifying Reflections" stem from his and his culture's nagging fear that the physiological similarities between humans and the "more perfect" creatures may undermine the philosophical and religious principles that grant what he calls our "God-like *Species*" dominion over the rest of creation. His triple negations ("never heard . . . to the contrary . . . not Originally") signify a marked anxiety about maintaining humankind's privileged position in creation. Willis and other advocates of the tripartite or additive model of the soul contribute to such anxiety because their ambiguous chains of species distinctions do not readily conform to Christian notions of absolute spiritual difference. As the Earl of Rochester's famous portrait reminds us, monkeys, too, can be poets.[36]

Congreve's uneasiness with the human resemblance to monkeys, in turn, leads back to the question of how to differentiate human wit from animal intelligence. In this regard, Willis's neuroanatomy resonates with his contemporaries' efforts to define exactly what "wit" is and how it divides the "true" wits of Restoration London from pretenders to wit. In a passage in *The Virtuoso* that mimics hundreds of others in late seventeenth-century comedy, Miranda disparages Sir Samuel Hearty's pretensions to being a wit by turning him into a satiric hybrid. Although Sir Samuel *"takes himself to be a wit,"* his wit, she claims, is imitative and dog-like: he has "as many tricks as a well-educated spaniel" and "some tricks of a man, too" (I.ii.27–33). That he nevertheless can "pass muster among the young gay fellows of this town, and [can] sing all the new tunes and songs in the playhouses" suggests that differences between true and false wit are not invariably apparent; so there is no confusion about his status the audience has to be told he is spaniel-like (I.ii.27–33). Indeed, this comparison of Sir Samuel's wit to a spaniel's both confuses and clarifies his intellectual stature. John Dryden, in a well-known passage, constructs his definition of wit by analogizing it to a "nimble spaniel" who "beats over and ranges through the field of memory, till it springs on the quarry it hunted after; or, without metaphor," he continues, "which searches all over the memory for the species or ideas of those things which it designs to represent."[37] Despite Dryden's effort to dispense with figurative language, the "faculty of imagination," even "without metaphor," is constituted spatially ("searches over") and therefore does not really dismiss the spaniel simile as much as anthropomorphize it. Like Willis's attribution of "a certain wit" to dogs and foxes, Dryden's metaphoric spaniel and Shadwell's Sir Hearty co-implicate human intellect and the sensitive soul in culturally resonant ways.

It is worth pointing out, however, that even so-called vermin could be pressed into the service of framing human wit. In an extended image, William Davenant into "The Author's Preface" to his heroic poem, *Gondibert*, describes wit as "the laborious, and the lucky resultances of thought, . . . a Web consisting of the subtilest threads."[38] "Like that of the Spider," Davenant continues, it "is considerately woven out of ourselves; for a Spider may be said to consider, not only respecting his solemnesse and tacite posture (like a grave scout in ambush for his Enemey) but because all things are done either from consideration or chance; and the works of chance are accomplishments of an instant, having commonly a dissimilitude; but hers are the works of time, and have their contextures alike."[39] Davenant's considering spider becomes, at least metaphorically, a creator contemplating strategies and technologies realized in material ways. In anthropomorphizing the spider, Davenant uses a language of "time" and "contextures" to evoke a kind of motivated intelligence that conforms more closely to Bacon's idea of insect imagination than it does to Dryden's example of wit, his spatial metaphor of a spaniel ranging over the fields. If Davenant is right that wit is the consequence of both "laborious" design and "lucky" circumstance, and if such design is best realized by the spider, Davenant effectively extends to the mind Bacon's observation that principles of physiology are "commonly better perceiued, in Small, than in Great, and in unperfect, than in perfect" creatures. Paradoxically, human exceptionalism rests on similes that liken humankind to the very beings from which "man" is trying to distinguish "himself."

For his part, Abraham Cowley in his much-anthologized "Ode of Wit," elevates this tendency to describe human wit through animal behavior to the status of a biblical exemplum:

In a true Piece of *Wit* all things must be,
    Yet all things there *agree*.
As in the *Ark*, join'd without force or strife,
All *Creatures* dwelt; all *Creatures* that had *Life*.

                                               (4)

Although, as I argued in the previous chapter, Cowley tried to bring a seventeenth-century naturalistic perspective to his verses on the plagues of

Egypt, he resorts to the archetypal Ark to analogize wit as characterized by a capaciousness and unity, "without force or strife."[40] Yet as his curious half line "all *Creatures* that had *Life*" seems to imply, vermin generated by putrefaction may be excluded from this image, just as, presumably, inelegant or inappropriate things must be banished from "a true Piece of *Wit*." Yet wit remains a kind of human-animal hybrid; Cowley's insistent negative catalogue of what wit is *not*—homonyms, puns, bombast, or "some odd *Similitude*" (4) ultimately calls attention, in its own way, to the differential economy of wit and satire. This differential economy turns on animals. To be a seventeenth-century wit like Davenant, Dryden, and Cowley—indeed, like Bruce and Longvil—is to master constitutive metaphors of animal behavior and deploy them to other humans. In *The Virtuoso*, a play that satirically suggests Sir Nicholas can claim no right of precedence over a frog, images of vermin ground this chain of similarities and differences.

PATHOLOGY, POSTHUMANISM AND PURIFICATION

As Willis's *De Anima Brutorum* suggests, the problems of characterizing "a certain wit" in animals are entangled with those of human and animal ensoulment. Once British natural philosophers rejected the Cartesian beast-machine metaphor (implicitly or explicitly), the empirical difficulty of identifying what elevates human intelligence above that of the perfect creatures becomes crucial to the emergence of a range of biological and medical sciences. In *We Have Never Been Modern*, Latour argues seventeenth-century natural philosophers did not inherit a world divided neatly into persons, who had souls, and things, which did not. While "modernity," he argues, usually is defined by the advent of humanism, this construction itself is a product of what he calls "the modern constitution" because "the human" remains asymmetrical, essential to "the simultaneous birth of non-humanity—things, objects, or beasts."[41] The hallmark of modernity is the will to purify, to establish a clear Nature-Culture divide that allows "modern" culture to distinguish itself from its own past, from nonmodern peoples and from a world of de-animated things, including animals. Purification, therefore, involves the political, scientific, and conceptual practices of proliferating distinctions and taxonomies: "Century after century," writes Latour, "colonial empire after colonial empire, the poor premodern collectives were accused of making a horrible mismash of things and humans, objects and signs, while their accusers finally separated them totally."[42] Modern science, as it is traditionally depicted, is given the task of sorting out, identifying, classifying, and regularizing the "horrible mishmash" that pervades the thinking of "pre-modern" cultures.

In the late seventeenth century, pious natural philosophers, like Willis and Boyle, sought to eradicate one of the more egregious examples of this "horrible mishmash" by combating the pagan or heretical belief that humans and animals shared a soul. Versions of this belief could be found in Platonism, Pythagoreanism, animism, pantheism, ideas of transmigration, and different characterizations of *anima mundi*, or the World Soul. Boyle rejected all Eastern religions, partly on the grounds that they represent "a discouraging impediment to the empire of man over the inferior creatures."[43] For his part, Descartes was adamant: "There is none which sooner estrangeth feeble minds from the right way of vertue, then to imagine that the soul of beasts is of the same nature as ours."[44] Given his turn to Gassendi and a tripartite model of ensoulment, Willis has gone down in medical history as something of an animist, his concept of the corporeal soul "criticized as a retrograde animistic step, in contrast to Descartes' animal spirits which were thought to be entirely physical and part of a machine."[45] Willis' neuroanatomy resists a Cartesian impulse toward purification. William Bynum argues Willis's anatomical texts are characterized by two "sometimes conflicting views" of the human nervous system: on the one hand, it is a more "complicated and refined" version of the nervous system of all animals, and, on the other, it is so similar to the nervous system of the higher quadrupeds that "some immaterial principle . . . must be postulated to in order to account for the mental difference between man and animals."[46] If differences between human and animal nervous systems are foregrounded, then, humans can be seen as "purified" versions of animals on a continuum of physiological development; and if similarities between human and animal nervous systems are emphasized, then humans emerge as hybrid creatures, more-than-animal only because they are endowed, *deus ex machina corpore*, with an immortal, and a physiological, soul.

One can see both of these processes clearly in *De Anima Brutorum*, or *Two Discourses Concerning the Soul of Brutes*. In this text, Willis addresses directly and systematically the issues of animal immortality, and thus human exceptionalism, a subject "almost worn thread-bare," he concedes, by ancient and modern writers (*AB* 38). Willis explicitly rejects the idea that the "Soul of the Beast is an Incorporeal Substance, or Form," a belief he associates with the "*Platonick* Fiction, concerning the Soul of the World" (*AB* 4); he also cannot stomach the beliefs of Originists, a heretical Christian sect that believed in the preexistence of souls. Although admitting he can "be a little solicitious, for [the souls of] the almost infinite multitude of the more perfect Beasts, which have liv'd, and do live," Willis balks at the idea that vermin can lay claim to any kind of "Incorporeal" soul. In challenging this "Fiction," he asks:

> Yet where do many Myriads of Souls, even innumerable, of Insects and Fishes, which are daily produced, subsist, and what do they? The Bodies of very many of these serve only as Food to other Creatures. And for that the Souls to these Bodies, serve chiefly to preserve them only for a little time, and as it were pickle them to keep them from putrefaction, there is no need that these should be therefore immaterial and immortal. Besides, when of old, Egypt was infected by Divine Punishment, with Swarms of Fleas, Flyes, and other Various Kinds of innumerable Insects, and that the same also abounded every where, it is not easily to be Conceived, from whence so many Souls were so suddenly Called, and into what places, the same being by and by separated, could be placed. (*AB* 4)

Produced "daily," the insecta serve largely as "Food to other Creatures," even as they multiply and swarm in their roles as instruments of "Divine Punishment." They are purely instrumental beings, called into existence beyond the regimes of human counting and calculation. Because their sheer number boggles the mind, it is impossible "to be Conceived" how their souls could pre- or post-exist transitory lives. Countering the logic of metempsychosis, Willis points out so many freed or "separated" insect souls could not be housed or "placed" in the more finite number of more perfect creatures.

Even as Willis casts vermin beyond the pale of theological belief, his insistence that humans share with the "more perfect" creatures important neuroanatomical similarities makes him, at least in his own mind, vulnerable to charges of theological unorthodoxy. Published in English almost twenty years after *Cerebri Anatome*, his *Two Discourses Concerning the Souls of Brutes* makes clear the stakes in the constitution of the "human," perceived both in resemblances to the other creatures—as an embodied modification of a single animating energy—and in terms of profound differences. In "manifold and comparative anatomy," he explains at the beginning of *De Anima Brutorum*, the manifold and wonderful wisdom of the Creator is manifested; so are by the same discovered, even in the smallest and most despicable Animals, not only mouths and limbs, but also hearts, being as 'twere so many altars and hearths to perpetuate this vital flame. Here the reader will meet with very skillful and accurate Dissections of the Silk-worm, Oyster, Lobster, Earthworm; as also of divers Brains; and first, of that of a Sheep.... And secondly, of a new one of a Humane Brain.... That so by confronting these Brains, the vast difference of the Soul of a Brute and that of a Man may the better be shewn. (152)

Even the "most despicable Animals," those that presumably lack souls, wit, and therefore any kind of agential capability, are marshaled to demonstrate "the manifold and wonderful wisdom" manifested in living creatures. Tracing the animal spirits up the Great Chain of Being, from earthworms and crustaceans to humankind, Willis tries to offer incontrovertible evidence— "through very skillful and accurate dissections"—that humans, despite being theological "twins" to hot-blooded animals, are indeed God's chosen creatures on earth.

Throughout this text, Willis attempts to reinforce ideas of human exceptionalism not by Cartesian purification—by casting animals as mere "machines"—but by creating "double soul'd" humans who are characterized (unlike the brutes) by both a corporeal and rational soul. In other words, in Latour's terms, he re-creates the human as a hybrid. In a frequently cited passage, Willis writes:

truly it is most evidently plain, from what hath been said, That man is made, as it were, an Amphibious Animal, or of a middle Nature and Order, between Angels and the Brutes, and doth Communicate with both, with these by the Corporeal Soul, from the Vital Blood, and heap of Animal Spirits, and with those by an intelligent, immaterial, and immortal Soul. And Indeed, Reason persuades us plainly that 'tis so, to wit, for as much as we find in ourselves, as by and by shall be more fully shown, the Strifes and Dissensions of one Soul with another, sometimes this, and sometimes that getting the Rule, or being in Subjection. (AB 41)

Understandably, this characterization of the two souls in conflict has captured the imagination of historicist scholars looking to tie early studies in neuroanatomy to Restoration culture.[47] Elsewhere, Willis uses explicitly political language to describe the relationship between the corporeal and incorporeal souls: these two souls "differ among themselves, yea sometimes are wont to dissent, and move more than Civil Wars" (*AB* 38). In the aftermath of the English Civil War, and particularly during the Exclusion Crisis, any mention of civil strife had wide-ranging and usually destructive (or self-destructive) implications. In one respect, then, the "double soul'd" human fits conveniently into both a traditional Protestant rhetoric (the sinful body and immortal soul) and the mindset of late seventeenth-century politics. Yet, in another sense, this political imagery is only one of many metaphors Willis deploys to explain tensions between these two souls: besides a civil war within the human, the relationship between the corporeal and rational souls is figured as a solar eclipse (*AB* 11), a metamorphosis (*AB* 11, 32), a storm (*AB* 24), musical pipes (*AB* 34), an oxen overthrowing a yoke (*AB* 43), "a double Army" (*AB* 43), captivity (*AB* 43), "Twinns" in the "same Womb" (*AB* 43), a turbulent sea (*AB* 48), waterworks (*AB* 40), and a lute (*AB* 60). Employing a commonplace traceable to Epictetus and recently revived by Thomas Browne in *Religio Medici*, Willis describes "man" as an "Amphibious Animal," implicitly rejecting Cartesian and theological dualisms.[48] Willis seems to multiply these metaphors because none of them can be definitive: the human exists *only* in the disjunctions between the corporeal and rational souls. As his figurative language suggests, this conflict manifests (as it does for Freud) in internal dysfunction, strife, and dissension. Such dissension, in turn, is disclosed somatically in the pathologies that Willis describes in the second half of the book: insomnia, headaches, lethargy, nightmares, vertigo, apoplexy, palsie, delirium, melancholy, madness, stupidity, and (a malady that afflicted Shadwell) gout.

In addition to coining the term "neurologie," then, Willis offers the world a new "psychologia," or psychology, making important contributions to several disciplines, including pediatrics and etiology.[49] By psychology, writes Carl Zimmer, "Willis meant an account of the workings of the human soul as a compound of a rational, immaterial substance nested within a swarm of chemical spirits traveling along pathways through the brain and into the nerves."[50] Zimmer's use of "swarm" to characterize the unpredictable movement of the animal spirits hardly seems accidental. For Willis, the "human" is founded on the ability of the rational soul to manage the proliferation of impulses and thoughts that frequently, if not characteristically, are figured in animal form. In a revealing passage, he describes sleepwalking in terms of "fierce" and "unquiet" animal spirits that "will not lye down together, but . . .

some of them, more fierce than the rest, leap forth of their own accord, and enter into Motion, like as perhaps one or two Dogs, starting out without government, leave the company of the rest and fall to Hunting" (*AB* 18). As is often the case in his prose, Willis almost unleashes the vehicle of the metaphor from the tenor: the figurative dogs are granted an unruly agency ("of their own accord") that points to the lack of a controlling "government" as well as to their own refusal to act in concert with the "company." The conflicts within human "psychologia" that result in sleepwalking suggest the extent to which Willis's "double-soul'd" man remains imbricated in a world of animal populations that are subject, but only barely, to control or dominion. When control slips, humans experience the stings, pricks, passions, and swarms of corporeal life.

The greatest source of internal dissension for this "Amphibious Animal" is the conflict between lust and "Reason and Religion" that Willis explains biologically as the competing demands on the circulation of the blood and animal spirits. In this conflict, he writes, "may be most clearly discerned the distinct Strivings, and contrary Endeavors, of two Souls":

> because, whilst the Corporeal Soul being incited to Lust, inclines herself wholly towards the Genital Members, and compels thither greater floods of the Blood, and greater Store of the Animal Spirits, the Heart and Brain being left wanting of Provision; on the contrary, the Superior Mind, rising up, and shewing the Commands of Reason and Religion, shows a receipt to the other, and commands that the Animal Spirits return to their tasks, to be performed within the Brain. . . . Hence the flame of Lust being re-extinct for a time, and the Powers of the Inferior Soul being reduced into Order, the Acts of Sobriety, Prudence, and of other Science, and Discipline, may be exercised; but if the Reins of Reason be let loose, or new incentives of Lust are brought, the Corporeal Soul, shaking off the yoak, snatches her self again to the like Enormities. (*AB* 55)

Willis's version of the conflict between flesh and spirit differs from, say, Plato's account of the passions in its medico-physiological focus on the circulation of the blood and the role of the brain. In "Lust, even against the Mind," he writes, "the Blood boils up, the Marrow in the Back grows hot, the eyes are inflamed, the Genitals are inflated, so that there wants little (unless Reason coming between recalls her, and prohibits her from the Beastliness of it) but that the whole Corporeal Soul, on every occasion, should be dissolved in Lust" (*AB* 55). To overcome "Beastliness"—that is, the natural strivings of the corporeal soul towards what Willis calls "Propagation"—the brain must enlist a host of practices designed to alter the course of blood. Strong prayer, he maintains, can "call back the Blood towards the Praecordia," the part of the brain where animal spirits are "inkindled" and housed (*AB* 47). In addition to these spiritual exercises, purgatives and herbals—many of the former, not coincidentally, composed of animal parts—can help encourage, if not fully restore, something closer to proper distillation and circulation.

"LIFE" AND THE HUMAN

Based upon a sliding scale of differences, this new psychology, or doctrine of the soul, requires vermin play their part to shore up the argument from design. Willis's insistence that *insecta* or vermin can demonstrate more effectively than perfect creatures the nature of life was a commonplace in the seventeenth century, particularly in theological treatises directed against Lucretian atomism. In *The Darknes of Atheism Dispelled by the Light of Nature* (1652), the physician Walter Charleton, who knew Willis's work, asks us to imagine the principle—the organizing intelligence—that makes the bodies of all animals seemingly irrefutable evidence of a metaphysical agent at work in the design of living creatures:

> should we take a man, who had been born and bred up to maturity of years in some obscure cavern of the earth, and never lookt abroad upon the World, nor heard of more then what immediately concerned his aliment and other natural necessities; on a suddain educe him from his dungeon, and shew him an Animal cut in pieces, and all its dissimilar parts, as skin, muscles, fat, veins, arteries, nerves, tendons, ligaments, cartilages, bones, marrow, &c. laied together in a promiscuous heap: doubtless we could not quarrel at his incredulity, if he would not be perswaded, that any thing but Chance had a hand in that confusion. But should we instantly present him another Animal, feeding, walking, and performing all the comely functions of vitality; instruct him in the several uses and actions of all those parts, which he had formerly surveyed in the disorder of an heap; then kill that Animal also, and for his farther information, anatomzie its carcase; and exhibite to him the several parts, in all things

respondent to the former: tis conjectural that we should finde, that the rudeness of his education would not so totally have extinguished the Light of Nature in him, as not to have left some spark, by the glimmering whereof he might discover some more noble Principle then Fortune, to have been the Efficient of that more then ingenious machine.[51]

Charleton's argument turns on the ability of his illiterate man to perform a series of interpretive operations: he must witness an animal "cut in pieces," anatomized into "all its dissimilar parts"; observe another, live animal of the same species eating, drinking, and performing other functions; listen to a narrative about the relationship between form and function; witness the dissection of that second animal, accompanied by a second lecture that elucidates the relationships among these muscles, tendons, ligaments, organs, and the animal's earlier actions. Two dead animals and two lectures later, the uneducated man, insists Charleton, would "discover some more Noble principle than Fortune"—providential design—in the creation of "that more than ingenious machine."

As Charleton's thought-experiment suggests, the theological value of comparative anatomy turns on a tautological argument: sophistication of form in animate nature points to a higher intelligence as the agent of creation; the assumption of an intelligent creator demands the structure of all living things—perfect and imperfect—demonstrate a transcendental principle of providential design. Imperfect creatures are especially important to such arguments because they demonstrate, as Hooke's flea suggests, the aesthetic beauty and unity of form and function indicative of divine workmanship. For this reason, Charleton claims the "aedifice of a spontaneous *Animal*" (an animal born of putrefaction) has a structure "more difficult" and less given to "*Chance*" than a city, and then copiously piles example on example: "the *Heart* of a *Pismire*" has more "magisterial artifice" than the Eschurial monastery (which had just been built); "the proboscis or trunk of a Flea more industry in its delicate perforation" than the Roman aqueducts or the Arsenal of Venice; "the breast or laboratory of a *Bee*" contains more "anfractuous convolutions" than the St. Lawrence monastery, regarded as the eighth wonder of the world; and "the *skull* of a *Louse*" has more ventricles for the "numerous swarms of Animal Spirits" than the Roman amphitheater had seats for spectators.[52] No one, Charleton asserts, can "admit the managery of an Architect, or knowing principle, in the structure of a house, and yet determine the more magnificent Creation of the Universe upon the blind disposal of Fortune" (64). Once the question of life is framed in terms of agency—what "Architect, or knowing Principle" designed the flea?—then the answer is overdetermined: a Supreme Being. Atheism, as the title of his treatise suggests, is refuted.

The argument from design is especially important in an environment in which natural philosophers, like Willis and Charleton, readily admit that neither the corporeal nor incorporeal souls can be perceived by the senses. Brain and nerve structure may seem to make visible what were imagined as (al)chemical processes.[53] From his dissections of oysters, lobsters, earthworms, pikes, salmons, oxen, foxes, dogs, cats, and sheep, Willis tried to ascertain "not only the faculties and uses of every organ, but the "impressions, influences, and secret ways of the workings of the sensitive soul" (CA 6). In effect, this meant positing a vital principle, endowed by God and located in the blood, an animating energy differentially distributed across the animal kingdom. In De Anima Brutorum, following Gassendi (rather than Descartes), Willis argues the corporeal soul lies "hid in the Blood, or Vital Liquer" and can be described as a "certain fire of flame" (AB 5) whose sustenance is "supplied from sulphur or some other nitrous thing in the air" (AB 6). He finds historical precedents for this definition of life in Critias, Empedocles, and, significantly, in the Scriptures, where "eating of Blood is forbidden, because it is the Life, or the Soul" (AB 2). In chapter 5 of De Anima Brutorum, Willis considers the "proper essence" of the animal spirits, admitting this is a matter "hard to be unfolded" because "we can hardly meet with anything in Nature, to which they can be compared in all things. Wherefore, it is better . . . that we liken these Spirits sent from the Flame of the Blood, to the Rays of Light, at least to them Interwoven with the Element and the Air." Like the air, the animal spirits "can often break forth into meteors, viz. Winds, Hurricanes, and Horrid Thunder" (AB 23). These Galenic images of heat and fire were central to a number of scientific inquiries during the late seventeenth century, notably alchemy and its purifying flame that served not only as a means for (supposedly) separating gold from dross but as a potent image for natural philosophy more generally: to seek knowledge is to purify the soul.[54] Willis acknowledges that this commonplace metaphor of enkindling—"the Ancients did declare the Soul to be Fire, and the more modern Fire or Flame"—is merely a figure for the operations of the corporeal soul "which cannot be perceived by our Senses, but is only known by its Effects, and Operations" (AB 6). Heat comes closest to being an actual empirical phenomenon in the "more perfect creatures" where it appears as "a certain fire or flame": anyone witnessing the exhalations of a furry beast "may well believe," writes Willis, "that that the blood doth truly flame forth, and that Life is not so like to flame, but even flame itself" (AB 7).

The belief that "Life" is located in a corporeal soul that "cannot be perceived by our Senses" helps explain why imperfect creatures were essential to the early modern project. Latour argues modernity set itself the task of carving out two realms, one characterized by a free-thinking subject, the realm of humans and politics, and one inhabited by mute objects, the realm of "Nature"—that, through scientific investigation can be made to "speak the truth." These "nonhumans," writes Latour, "lacking souls but endowed with meaning, are even more reliable than mortals, to whom will is attributed but who lack the capacity to indicate phenomena in a reliable way."[55] On the one hand, as with Charleton, the sophisticated design of imperfect creatures can be held up as proof of divine authorship. "This little living creature," writes Willis of the worm, "though it be esteemed vile and contemptible, hath allotted to it vital organs, as also other viscera and members, made most admirably by a Divine Workmanship" (AB 13). As importantly, the nervous systems of imperfect creatures make visible the presence of animal spirits; vanishing "after life is extinct," he writes, animal spirits "leave no Foot-steps of themselves" (AB 6). Maimed reptiles also helped make the argument that a corporeal soul is spread throughout the entire body since, when worms, eels, and snakes are cut into pieces, they will "move themselves for a time" (AB 5).

Finally, worms, oysters, and lobsters "speak the truth" not by demonstrating their similarities to humans, as do dogs, cats, and foxes, but by manifesting their quiet, cold difference. Willis places living creatures into three classes according to the "Various Constitution of the Vital Humour": those without blood (insects, certain fishes, oysters, lobsters, and crabs); those with "less perfect" or frigid blood (earthworms, some fish, frogs, serpents, lizards); and those of "more perfect" or hot blood (fowls and four-footed beasts) (AB 7). Each class of animals has varying concentrations of the "vital" liquor, and thus different kinds of corporeal souls, with the soul of hot-blooded brutes being "a Rule or Square, by which others more inferior ought to be measured, and as the same actuating the humane body" (AB 18). The souls of "less perfect, or frigid animals," in contrast, are characterized by their *proximity* to a heat that is, and is not, metaphoric: "although we do not say the soul is properly flame," Willis writes, "yet (which is next to it) we say it is a most thin heap of subtil particles, and as it were, fiery, a certain spirituous breath" (AB 7). Even lower down the chain of being, earthworms, some fishes, frogs, serpents, and reptiles have a false fire, and therefore merely the appearance of life: "we suspect the Souls of these ["frigid" creatures, like worms], though of a fiery nature, to have not a flamy *Hypostatis*" but a breathy vapor "hardly or not at all inkindled, like an *ignis fatuus* or false fire, . . . destitute of sensible heat" (AB 13). In arguing for a "vast difference" between classes of animals based on the presence and motion of animal spirits in the blood—in making a cut between the hybrids—Willis creates a structural, neuroanatomical basis for the uneven distribution of "life" across species. What Willis's imperfect creatures "indicate," finally, is not simply complexity of design but proof of a system. The *chain of differences* that begins with worms and ends with humans can itself be figured only as a mode of hybridity, so that what distinguishes humans is the incorporation of the qualities of other beasts.[56]

Indeed, Willis's argument for human exceptionalism—for the existence of a rational, incorporeal soul—is also based primarily on effects, rather than causes, on function rather than form. In chapters 6 and 7 of *De Anima Brutorum*, Willis addresses differences between what he calls "the Science of Brutes" and the forms of knowledge peculiar to humans and their rational souls by emphasizing, first, that humans are capable of contemplating things beyond the realm of immediate sense, "Material or Immaterial, true or fictitious, real or Intentional" (AB 38), and second, that the rational soul "excels" the corporeal soul in the exercise of "Apprehension, Enunciation, and Discourse." A dog, for example, seeing a human in the distance, formulates a response to a sensible thing, based on memory and associations: he will fawn on a friend or bark at an enemy. The "humane Intellect," in contrast, judges objects of sense "whether they be true or false, Congruous or Incongruous," and is, moreover, capable of ordering and disposing such objects of sense into "Series of Notions, accommodated to speculation or practice" (AB 39). Sounding a bit like Descartes, Willis emphasizes the presumably unique human ability to deduce "many other thoughts unknown to the sense"; to conceive the "formal notions of Corporeal things, abstracted from all matter"; and to "understand axioms or first principles alone, and as it were by a proper Instinct, without regard to Corporeal Species" (AB 39). While the more perfect beasts do indeed exhibit acts of "Judgment and Discourse, or Ratiocination" (AB 39), compared to the "Scientifick Habits" of humans, such acts "will hardly seem greater than the drop of a Bucket to the Sea":

> For to say nothing of that natural Logick, by which anyone endowed with a free and perspicacious mind, probably and sometimes most certainly concludes, concerning all doubtfull things, or things sought after, if that we mind how much the humane mind being adorned by Learning, and having learnt the Sciences and the liberal Arts, is able to work, understand, and search out; it would be thought, tho in an Humane Body, to be rather living with Gods or Angels. For indeed here may be Considered, the whole *Encyclopedia* or Circle of Arts and Sciences, which (excepting Divinity) hath been the Product or Creature of the Humane Mind, and indeed argues the Workman if not divine at least to be a particle of the Divine Breath, to wit, a spiritual Substance, wonderfully intelligent, Immaterial, and which therefore for the future is Immortal. (*AB* 39–40)

In an argument for human uniqueness that Swift will later satirize in *Gulliver's Travels*, proof of the "Superior Soul" can be found, insists Willis, in "mathematicks, especially algebra, geometry, astronomy, and mechanics," and in the "artificial Smiths-Works wonderfully made" (*AB* 40).

Willis's "neurologie," then, culminates in an argument for culture and technology as all that distinguishes humans from other hot-blooded creatures. Animals, in contrast, are "altogether ignorant of the Causes of things, and know not Rights or laws of political Society; further, they make no Fires or Houses, nor find out any mechanical Arts, they put not on clothes, not dress their food, yet unless taught by Imitation, they know not how to number three" (*AB* 40). In emphasizing the obvious, Willis concludes with a second and equally tautological argument from design. The apparent sophistication of human learning—"the whole *Encyclopedia* or Circle of Arts and Sciences"—stands as proof that the "Workman" must at least embody "a particle of the divine breath" (*AB* 40). This proof of "divine breath," in turn, as we have seen, is manifest not so much in positive qualities as in humankind's metaphorically imagined differences from animals. Because hot-blooded humans serve as what Willis calls "a Rule or Square, by which others more inferior ought to be measured" (*AB* 18), the scale of hierarchical relations is never distinct from the physiology of minute differences that Willis documents in *Cerebri Anatome*.

"I AM A PERSON"

Shadwell's satire of Sir Nicholas Gimcrack depends, in part, on the audience's distaste for Gimcrack's verminous objects of attention—the mites, maggots, and flies about which his nieces complain. But it also turns on the ability of audience members literate enough in science to recognize that Sir Nicholas is an outrageous poseur. He repeatedly reveals himself to be altogether ignorant of what Willis calls "the Causes of things," finally admitting at the end of the play that he wished he had "studied mankind instead of spiders and insects" (V.vi.122–23). This comment is usually taken as a satire on natural philosophy as a whole, but natural philosophy, as we have seen in Willis's efforts to describe the corporeal and rational souls, always included the relations between things, human and more-than-human, material and immaterial. Gimcrack's problem, from this perspective, is not that he studies natural philosophy but that he does it badly—exaggerating his discoveries, misrepresenting his experiments, and failing (hilariously) to demonstrate that he is capable of distinguishing between "true or false, Congruous or Incongruous."[57] He is, in other words, incapable of rising to that uniquely human capacity of disposing phenomena "into Series of Notions, accommodated to speculation or practice" (*AB* 39).

Given that the ability to order nature is a mark of the rational soul, the spectacle of Sir Nicholas parading his presumed knowledge is as destabilizing to the pretense of human exceptionalism as is the transpecies blood transfusion he claims to have facilitated. In an allusion to Martin Lister, who had identified thirty-seven spider types in England, Sir Nicholas brags of having found out "more phenomena or appearances of nature in spiders than any man breathing" (III.iii.39–40).[58] He retains Lister's number, more or less, but confuses types of arachnids with breeds of dogs: "There's your hound, greyhound, lurcher, spaniel spider" (III.iii.40–43). When Longvil, egging him on, mentions the "tumbler spider"—the "tumbler," like the "lurcher," is a name for dogs trained to catch meat—Gimcrack enthusiastically takes the bait: "O sir. I am no stranger to't. It catches flies as tumblers do conies" (III.iii.45–46). The joke is not directed at Sir Nicholas' arcane knowledge, but at his foolishness in conflating two categories of creatures, perfect and imperfect, dogs and spiders. His inability to distinguish between "true or false, Congruous or Incongruous" even more outrageously leads him to elevate a "spaniel" spider to the status of a hunting dog. "I had called him

Nick," brags Sir Nicholas, "and he knew his name so well he would follow me all over the house. He was the best natur'd, best condition'd spider that ever I met with" (III.iii.73–76). Sir Nicholas's enthusiasm turns him into what Shadwell called in his Preface to *The Humorists* "a proper object of comedy" (4), a gentleman exhibiting "the artificial folly of those who are not coxcombs by nature but with great art and industry make themselves so" (4).

Throughout *The Virtuoso*, Gimcrack fails the Royal Society's test of the usefulness of experimental knowledge. Sir Formal (in a travesty of Boyle's argument from design) brags that there is "Not a creature so inanimate ... to which [Gimcrack] does not give a tongue, he makes the whole world vocal" (I.i.270–74). Yet in marked contrast to Charleton's anonymous anatomist explaining the relationship between a "promiscuous heap" of body parts and a live animal, the creatures in Gimcrack's laboratory reveal no universal principles of design and disclose nothing about the nature of physic, respiration, or locomotion. This is especially true of his swimming lesson. Instead of trying to understand kinetics, the relationship between form and function (which, according to Charleton, would have required at least one dead frog), Gimcrack tries to "outswim" the struggling amphibian and thereby to "exceed nature" (II.ii.25). As he says to Sir Formal, "I doubt not, sir, in a very little time to become amphibious. A man by art may appropriate any element to himself" (II.ii.26–30). Paradoxically, then, in a play that satirizes the Royal Society, Gimcrack is ridiculous not because he is too speculative, but because he is not speculative enough. Rather than investigating what Charleton calls "the comely functions of vitality" by demonstrating the unity between form and function, Gimcrack desires to "become amphibious"; far from speaking "Nature," Gimcrack's frog, tethered to a buffoon, is forced to swim for its life. From the perspective of physico-theology, Shadwell's attack on Gimcrack is not an attack on the Royal Society or its principles—Gresham College, after all, "refus'd" Gimcrack—but a send-up of the excesses to which such study can lead when it privileges the policing effects of Willis's "rational soul."

I emphasize this point not as an apology for the Royal Society and its experiments, some of which are clearly satirized in Shadwell's play, but by way of shifting critical emphasis from the value of experimental science, as a practice, to debates about the nature of ensoulment that, as we have seen, motivated a good number of Royal Society experiments. *The Virtuoso* satirizes the self-defeating delusion that the rational soul governs corporeal desire through repeated, often jarring, incongruities between characters' pretenses to what Willis calls "The Sciences and the Liberal Arts"—as proof of a "Superior Soul"—and their comic identifications with horses, dogs, lobsters, cockroaches, frogs, maggots, flies, and mites. Indeed, the play opens by foregrounding such an incongruity. Bruce delivers a paean to the "great Lucretius," who demonstrated, in his Epicureanism, that "poetry and good sense may go together" (I.i.5–6). "Good sense," as the scene soon makes clear, is based on atomistic philosophies and materialist accounts of the human-animal soul. But Bruce's rhapsody—and he quotes from Lucretius in the original Latin—is quickly corporealized by Longvil's entrance with this question for his friend: "What great author are thou chewing the cud upon?" (I.i.13–14). The random swerves of Lucretian "sense" almost immediately become entangled comically with the sexual desires that Willis laments cannot always be controlled by the rational soul. By turning Bruce into a ruminant, Longvil initiates a witty but perhaps too-anxious effort to distinguish himself and his friend from the usual butts of 1670s satire, a "race of gentlemen more degenerated than that of horses" (I.i.23). Their derision of what they term "over grown animals" (I.i.29–30) resonates ironically with Willis's characterization of the lustful corporeal soul: "gentlemen care not upon what strain they get their sons, nor how they breed 'em when they have got 'em" (I.i.25–27). By casting upper-class education and sociability in terms of animal husbandry ("breed"), Longvil underscores the *hybrid*, rather than satirically bestial, nature of Restoration society. Bruce and Longvil are implicated ironically in the very behavior they ostensibly mock: both have sex with Lady Gimcrack at the masquerade—a "temptation," says Bruce, "too strong to be resisted"—and, in Act 5, easily switch the objects of their desire when they find (by eavesdropping) that Miranda loves Bruce (not Longvil, who has been pursuing her) and Clarinda loves Longvil rather than Bruce (V.iv.80).

For Shadwell, then, struggles between the corporeal and incorporeal souls are the subject of sexual farce rather than moralistic philosophizing. Far from appearing to live "with Gods or Angels," the men and women in *The Virtuoso*, in pursuing a series of sexual assignations, end up cornered, like rats or mice, in a woodhole. In Act 4, Lady Gimcrack and Hazard turn the word "husband" into various species of noisome vermin or inanimate objects: as a "a clog" (IV.ii.43), a "dog in a manger" (IV.ii.44); "an insect, a drone, a dormouse" (IV.ii.48); "a cuckoo in winter" (IV.ii.50); and "a body without a soul" (IV.ii.52). This slide of cuckolded husbands down the Great Chain of Being ends with Sir Nicholas imagistically reduced to "a pitiful utensil," a thing good only for the veneer of legitimacy he provides (IV.ii.60). But

Lady Gimcrack and her lover have to cut their assignation short and hide in the woodhole when Sir Nicholas enters with his mistress, Mrs. Flirt. In a chaotic scene of comic discovery, husband and wife accuse each other of infidelity, and then, after they realize that Flirt and Hazard have been having an affair, turn on their lovers to excoriate them for betrayal,. The woodhole becomes a refuge for the very behavior that reduces the characters to vermin.

Every human pretension descends into corporeal degradation and sexual farce. The play's second-string "virtuoso," Sir Samuel Hearty (Miranda's "well-educated spaniel") imagines himself a "flashy wit"; yet his wit, according to Bruce, consists largely of "nonsensical bywords" (I.i.136) that mean "no more to him than breaking wind" (I.i.136). During the course of the play, dressed first as footman and then as a woman, Sir Samuel is "kick'd, beaten, pumped, and toss'd in a blanket" (V.vi.115–16) by Longvil, who refers to him as an "impudent dog" (II.i.102). Later, Sir Samuel escapes "naked" through a window but ends up the victim of mob punishment. Snarl, the play's would-be moralist, who complains about the lewdness of women and the "filthy lascivious beasts of this age" (IV.ii.188–89), joins Mrs. Figgup, who defends herself as "civil and virtuous" (IV.ii.185), in some sadomasochist jollies, while denouncing the "ranting rogues" of the "impudent vicious age" (IV.ii.4–5) Snarl wants to be whipped with rods. Indeed, he is the first to secure a key to the woodhole for his pleasure. One after another, Shadwell's pretenders to disembodied reason are confronted with their own hypocrisy. Most vulnerable, in this regard, is Sir Formal Trifle, who, trying to pacify the aptly named Snarl, offers moralizing advice on the dire effects of unregulated passions: "Sir, I have often intreated you to avoid passion, it drowns your parts, and obstructs the faculties of your mind, while a serene Soul, like that which I wear about me, operates clearly, notwithstanding the oppression of Clay, and the clog of my sordid humane Body" (II.i.226–30). Sir Formal's claim to "unbodi'd" desire—"I am all Rapture, all Extasie, my Soul, methinks, is fled from its corporeal clog"—turns to hash in Act 4 when, "inflam'd" by Sir Samuel in a woman's dress, Sir Formal tries to rape him. As Sir Formal's attempts to fondle the would-be wench threaten to reveal the "difference of the sexes," Sir Samuel fights back (literally), while calling his attacker "a libidinous goat" and a "lustful swine" (IV.i.69, 79). While the obvious satiric butt in this scene is Sir Formal, his pretensions to *subdue* the animal spirits— the goats and swine *within* the human that define the corporeal soul—mark him, as Snarl says, as a "fine, formal hypocrite." Caught with his whore, Sir Formal has to endure being outfaced by another's hypocrisy when Snarl asks mockingly, "Does your noble soul operate clearly without the clog of your sordid, formal body now?" (IV.iii.143–144).

In satirizing pretenders to scientific wit, Shadwell returns again and again to their denial of corporeal pleasures and material responsibilities. Early in the play, Gimcrack proudly declares that "I seldom bring anything to use; 'tis not my way. Knowledge is my ultimate end" (II.ii.84–86). This rejection of Boyle's usefulness of natural philosophy assumes comic form in Act 5 when a mob of ribbon weavers, under the impression that Sir Nicholas has invented a new weaver's loom, descends on his house clamoring for revenge.[59] These ribbon weavers—yet another clever allusion to spiders, worms, or vermin—are confronted by Sir Trifle Formal, who imagines he can quell their "rash outrage"—their intention to destroy "the engine and the rogues that invented it" (V.iii.14–15)—by his already discredited oratory. Before he even begins, the mob grabs him and debates whether to hang him or let him speak. While he begins in his familiar vein—"Englishmen, good commonwealth's men, and sober, discreet ribbon weavers," he declares, "should [not] be thus hurried by the rapid force of the too dangerous whirlwind or hurricane of passion" (V.iii.40–45)—his extended metaphor-making quickly exceeds their vocabulary, patience, and sense: "Of passion, I say, which with its sudden and, alas, too violent circumgyrations does too often shipwreck those that are agitated by it, while it turns them into such giddy confusion that they can no longer trim the sails of reason or steer by the compass of judgment" (V.iii.48–52). For his eloquence, Sir Formal is kicked, beaten, and pelted with oranges before he cries out—"All this I can bear, gentlemen. I am a person" (V.iii.62–63). The Weavers' response is significant precisely because it challenges Sir Formal's claim to personhood: "A person—a rogue, a villain, a damn'd vertoso! A person! . . . We'll use you like a dog, sir" (V.iii.64, 66). Not only is Sir Formal reduced to the level of a cur, his rhetoric of subduing the passions provokes only more fury. For his part, Sir Nicholas, cowering behind his door with a blunderbuss, tries to save himself by calling out, "I never invented an engine in my life . . . I never invented so much an engine to pare cream cheese with. We virtuosos never find out anything of use, 'tis not our way" (V.iii.76–79). Both of the "damn'd, lying vertoso[s]" have to be rescued by Longvil and Bruce, armed with pistols.

Both science and politics, then, descend into violence. The play's two wits treat the weavers as animals that, in Willis's formulation, "know not Rights or laws of political Society," even as Sir Nicholas, in declaring his mechanical ignorance, undercuts one of Willis's arguments for the rational soul: animals, we recall, remain "altogether ignorant of the Causes of things, . . . nor find out any mechanical Arts." Shadwell frames the conflict between the would-be virtuosi and the rioting weavers as a kind of street fight among different breeds of dogs. His refusal to condemn the weavers for their uprising—what one moralistic, anonymous writer called the "great Mischief and disorders [that] happened by the Insurrection of the Weavers"—differs from the responses of some of his contemporaries.[60] Instead, Shadwell uses the street scene as a way to make clear that the technological privileges of the upper-classes—the gentlemen who can afford and legally own guns—do not correlate unproblematically to moral superiority. Indeed, "civil society," one of Willis's tests for human difference, is absent from this play or, more precisely, is always and already represented in terms of more-than-human relations. Rather than lamenting the tendency of the incorporeal soul to slip the leash of reason, The Virtuoso, it seems to me, represents the pure, Cartesian rational soul as a kind of metaphysical superstructure that cannot be wished into existence; creatures who walk on two legs are no less governed by Willis's animal spirits than are the frogs and dogs that populate the play. Indeed, seventeenth-century neuroanatomy medicalizes and literalizes perceived tensions between the "human" and the "animal" in ways that put into motion what Laura Brown identifies as a "tendency either to alienation or to association," apparent not only in natural philosophy but in post-Darwinian behavioral animal studies.[61] Because we have always imagined animals as in some sense kin—whether happily or not—they offer us desired or despised models of social and political order. The next chapter explores this point of view by returning to Shadwell, this time in his tragic rather than comic mode. Focusing largely on dogs and parasites as contemporary models of sociosexual relations, I examine in Shadwell, Bernard Mandeville, Rochester, and John Gay the creaturely contours of disease and desire.

CHAPTER 4

Libertine Biopolitics
Dogs, Bitches, and Parasites in Shadwell, Rochester, and Gay

Companion comes from the Latin *cum panis*, "with bread."
—DONNA HARAWAY, *WHEN SPECIES MEET*

In Cowley's version of *The Plagues of Egypt*, dogs appear as the faithful, stricken companions of shepherds during the time of pestilence, the fifth plague. "The starving sheep refuse to feed," writes Cowley, "They bleat their innocent souls out into air; / The faithful dogs lie gasping by them there; / Th' astonish'd *Shepherd* weeps, and breaks his tuneful *Reed*" (240). In this heart-wrenching inversion of the pastoral, Cowley reinforces the role of dogs as economically valuable and blameless victims of a metaphysical catastrophe. Yet, in some versions of the ten plagues, dogs act as scourging agents rather than as humankind's suffering aides. The Hebrew term *arov* in the fourth plague refers, ambiguously, to a "swarm" or to some other kind of "mixing," whether of "flies" or "wild beasts"; the Haggadeh of Venice interprets these swarms as predatory dog-like creatures, rather than insects, and depicts them attacking citizens.[1] In *Journal of the Plague Year*, Defoe reports over 40,000 dogs were destroyed, an officer having been "appointed for the execution."[2] That dogs can be either the instruments of God's anger or the shared victims of his punishment reinforces the unstable differences between domestic creatures and vermin. Loyal companions can easily become scavenging or threatening packs.

I focus on dogs in this chapter because, of all the "more perfect" creatures, they are the ones who most frequently and characteristically cross and recross the lines between singular objects of affection—"man's best friend"—and dangerous populations. Even now, this is true: in 2014, Russian officials hired a pest control company to exterminate roaming dogs in Sochi's Olympic Village, while animal welfare advocates set up makeshift shelters and "adoption centers" on the outskirts of town. But in the seventeenth century, the potentially dangerous status of dogs was even more pronounced. In May 1636, London exterminated 3,720 dogs, roaming animals that, according to Mark Jenner, were perceived as "visible sources of disorder, out of control and unsanitary . . . without a master and not visibly and physically fixed in a social relationship."[3] Pet culture arose in the context of civic-minded extermination of canines, and Restoration writing bears many traces of the curs who offer a different and more dangerous kind of trans-species relationship than do the individuated lapdogs of eighteenth-century satire, as in Pope's *Rape of the Lock*. During this period, loose, wandering dogs—especially dogs in a pack—continued to be regarded as vermin because, like rats and flies, they were associated with filth, infection, and madness. In literary texts, correspondingly, dogs frequently serve as abjected surrogates for humans in dystopian versions of pastoral or civic order. This chapter examines works by Thomas Shadwell, John Wilmot, Earl of Rochester, and John Gay, all of which, in different ways, explore parasitism, disease, desire, and the wavering line between the domesticated and the verminous.

Precisely because of their radically unstable position, dogs are critical in thinking through seventeenth-century versions of biopolitical order. Although much has been written about the role of bees as a model for early eighteenth-century socioeconomic ideals—a tradition represented by the *The Grumbling Hive* and, later, *The Fable of the Bees*—Mandeville's 1705 argument that private vices lead to public benefits was itself a response to a prior and complementary discourse in which the polis was imagined not as a well-ordered hive but as a chain of parasites, one feeding on another. Populating Mandeville's hive are "Sharpers, Parasites, Pimps, Players,/Pickpockets, Coiners, Quacks, and South-sayers," along with the "Fools" who believe that an "Honest Hive" can prosper.[4] Seventeenth-century satire often depicts rivalrous socioeconomic and personal relationships as inherently parasitic, the city inhabited by real and metonymic dogs, fleas, and flatterers.[5] In Ben Jonson's *Volpone; or, The Fox*, Mosca (from the Latin *musca*, fly) vies against warm-blooded vermin—a Raven, a Vulture, a Crow, and a "she-*Wolfe*"—to be named Volpone's heir. The play opens with Mosca congratulating himself for raising the usual "*Court-dog-trickes*" of flattery and fawning to the level of an art. This art, in turn, reveals the underlying, if disavowed, principles of sociobiological relations. "O! Your *Parasite* / Is a most pretious thing," he declares:

> . . . dropt from above,
> Not bred 'mong'st clod, and clot-poules, here on earth.
> I muse, the *Mysterie* was not made a Science,
> It is so liberally profest! Almost,
> All the world is little else, in nature,
> But *Parasites*, or *Sub-parasites*.[6]

Mosca inverts the conventional medico-physiological view of vermin—parasites as the product of putrefaction, "bred 'mong'st clod, and clot-poules, here on earth"—to imagine himself as a "true" parasite of divine origin, "dropt from above." Mosca's comic claim to heavenly birth is troubled by the identification that he celebrates: "parasite" comes from the latinization of the Greek: *para* means "beside" or "by" and *sitos* means "wheat" or, more generally, "food." As *Volpone* demonstrates, the parasite is neither above nor below but "beside," operating in conjunction with host bodies and inevitably surrounded by other parasites.

Given their ubiquitous presence and proximity to sources of food, dogs are essential actors in the parasitical system.[7] (Indeed, it is worth remembering that Jonson's suppressed, politically provocative play was entitled *The Isle of Dogs*.) It is nearly impossible to find a portrait of an early modern dining hall that does not include at least one canine, looking longingly at a handful of meat, or waiting expectantly for a scrap to fall on the floor. Such postures make dogs vulnerable (like Jonson's Mosca) to charges of self-interested pandering. As Clifford Davidson has demonstrated, the "most important emblem of the deceptive language of flattery is the dog": Henry Peacham's *Minerva Brittanica* (1612) uses dogs as an emblem of flattery.[8] In Henry Hartflete's "The Hunting of the Fox: or, Flattery Displayed" (1632), flattery is described as a "fawning" and "dog-like vice": the flatterer uses his *"mouth as the dogge wags his tayle, the one to obtaine a boone from his friend, the other to gaine a bone from his Master."*[9] When Mosca refers to "the usual *Court-dog* tricks," then, he draws on this perception of domesticated canines as embodying a shameless flattery that drives socioeconomic relations in seventeenth-century society. Jacobean city comedy, like *Volpone*, is full of parasites, not only because the symbolic yoking of animals and flatterers offers a convenient means of inveighing against luxury and corruption but also because the city is already corrupted morally and ecologically by humans who draw dogs, flies, and other vermin—the whole cast of *Volpone's* animal symbolism—in their wake.

Outside the city, moreover, removed from a ready food source, packs of dogs could become dangerous. What Davidson calls dogs' "equivocal" status stems from the recognition that interspecies accord was largely situational; dogs could and would turn against humans if compelled by food scarcity.[10] Ripa's figure of Ingratitude tellingly includes the following words: "Feed dogs, until they eat you."[11] This characterization pervades the Restoration. "Dogs," writes Bernard Mandeville in *Fable of the Bees*, "tho' become Dome-stick Animals, are ravenous to a Proverb, and those of them that will fight being Carnivorous, would soon become Beasts of Prey, if not fed by us."[12] Sources of both affection and affliction, dogs are capable of moving, within a single generation, from domestic companions to wild beasts. This point was driven home to seventeenth-century readers by accounts of shipboard dogs turning feral and menacing once they got to overseas colonies, where they were abandoned. Dogs had accompanied European voyagers to the Americas since Columbus; cast aside on shore, they had reproduced with indigenous canine populations. Particularly in the Caribbean, these wild or feral dogs were exterminated en masse. In the 1670s, Alexandre Exqueme-lin, an official with the French West India Company, describes the situa-tion on Tortuga, an island off the coast of Venezuela, where colonists were confronted by packs of wild dogs. Fearing the dogs would eat all the wild boar, the "common sustenance of the Island," the island's governor set out a "great quantity of poison, to be brought from *France*, therewith to destroy the Wild-Mastives":

This was performed in the year 1668, by commanding certain horses to be kill'd and envenom'd, and laid open in the wood and fields, at certain places, where mostly Wild-Dogs use'd to resort. This being continued for six Months: there were kill'd an incredible number, in the said time. And yet all this industry was not sufficient to exterminate and destroy the race; yea, scarce to any diminution thereof, their number appearing almost as entire as before. These Wild-Dogs are easily rendered tame among people, even as tame as the ordinary dogs we breed in Houses. Moreover the Hunters of those Parts, whensoever they find a wild-bitch, with young whelps, do commonly take away the puppies and bring them to their houses, where they experiment them, being grown up, to hunt much better than other Dogs.[13]

Exquemelin's account underscores the status of wild dogs as markedly liminal animals, both vermin and hunters, competing with humans for food and helping them to procure it. The wildness of the domesticated dogs, their proximity to nature, is simultaneously the source of their ability to hunt and the reason they can revert to an atavistic state. In their complex role as vermin, predators, and companion animals, dogs represent better than any other creature the conditional nature of being vermin. They demonstrate how this status is mediated by a host of factors—including population numbers, food scarcity, and indigenous theories of disease.

By the time Jonson wrote *Volpone*, dogs, humans, and parasites (both biological and behavioral) were closely linked, their connections being reinforced through several interrelated discourses: the political, the medical, the agricultural, and the moral. A term originally applied to humans who fed at the tables of their human hosts, "parasite" had not yet been appropriated by the natural sciences as an exclusive descriptor of what Anders M. Gullestad calls "sponging animals and insects"[14]—that is, of nonhumans, mostly fleas and lice. Instead, much like "vermin," "parasite" names a subject position somehow related to feeding practices. What interests me here is what this classic social type can tell us about seventeenth-century literature and science as they struggled to articulate new sets of social relations, or to reform old ones. Canines are crucial to the depiction of the social not only for the reasons outlined above but also because, as we have seen, during this period biological differences between humans and dogs (like that between humans and apes) largely disappear under the pressures of comparative anatomy. Indeed, to the extent that late seventeenth-century neuroanatomy treated dogs and humans as "twin species," endowed with similar appetites and similar forms of intellection and affection, traditional typological connections among humans, dogs, and parasites are further intensified, feral dogs and packs of dogs providing for Shadwell and Rochester models of the social, sexual, and political order. The first section of this chapter focuses on Thomas Shadwell's adaptation of Shakespeare's *Timon of Athens*. Like *The Virtuoso*, this play is heavily populated by vermin; *Timon* casts dog-like humans in a tragic—and paradoxically satiric—system of socioeconomic relations, in what Serres calls "an endoparasitic cycle [of] mammalian reproduction" (230). Shadwell's dark, squirming vision of the collective challenges simple notions of affective ties and calls attention to the critical role of mimetic contagion in parasitical economies. Mimetic desire creates rivalries, and the proliferation of rivalries eventually leads to seizing on a scapegoat, who is excluded and sacrificed for the sake of the group. Rivalry, in this respect, is accompanied by an act of foundational violence, a disruption and reformation of the system itself.

Packs of dogs exemplify the violence at the heart of the parasitical order and what Serres calls its cycle of "mammalian reproduction"; like sexed and gendered humans—or so the argument goes—dogs turn on each other if pressed by either hunger or lust. Masculine rivalries threaten idealized visions of the polis. When their "Fury is provok'd by a Venereal Ferment," according to Mandeville, males "exert themselves chiefly against other Males of the same Species. They may do Mischief by chance to other Creatures; but the main Objects of their Hatred are their Rivals, and it is against them only that their Prowess and Fortitude are shewn."[15] In their violent relationships to one another dogs embody parasitical culture in a more profound and gendered way than contemporary scientific definitions of "the parasite" as living *in*, rather than *beside*, the host might suggest.

I trace the above set of relations in Rochester's poetry of the 1670s, especially his "A Ramble in St. James's Park"; here the mirrored cognitive and emotional structures of canines make them not only appropriate surrogates for humans but also ready scapegoats, capable of being kicked, beaten, and removed from "civilized" spaces. Both parasited and cast as parasites, dogs slink in and out of seventeenth-century literature, begging, stealing, barking, mating, flattering, eating, and fighting, so, at times, it is no longer possible to distinguish between human parasites and their canine twins. Such twinning is literalized in contemporary descriptions of rabies or *hydrophobia* in which dogs and humans manifest the same symptoms and the same desires. Focusing on signs of rabies in Rochester and John Gay, I conclude this chapter by exploring how, nested within these parasitical relationships are depictions of madness, figured in both gendered and canine terms.

DOGS AND FLATTERERS IN TIMON OF ATHENS

While *The Libertine* (1675) and *The Virtuoso* (1676) may be the best known of Thomas Shadwell's plays, his *Timon of Athens* was one of the most popular tragedies of the Restoration period, first produced in 1678 and regularly restaged for the next seventy-one years.[16] Like *Volpone*, *Timon* satirizes luxury and corruption, but instead of Jonson's sadistic miser, Shadwell's titular hero, like his Shakespearean progenitor, is an overly generous host, the foolish representative of a dying tradition of noblesse oblige. *Timon of Athens* begins with Demetrius greeting a Poet or, as he puts it, "a Fellow Horse-leech."[17] These two bloodsuckers quickly fall into a discussion about the stylistics of flattery, or how best to ingratiate themselves at the "Lord's Table," by considering which animal—lion, bull, fox, raven—is most suited to the "lofty and high sounding" verse of panegyric (2). Through this ironic meta-discussion about the appropriate use of animal metaphors in literary pandering, Shadwell depicts Timon's body as crawling with parasites, feeding on his lifeblood—his wealth. Like Jonson's fox and fly, Shadwell's parasites gorge on Timon, even as they violate the bond between word and intention. Apemantus, the honest but "snarling Cur" who stands in for the Cynic, makes this point very early in the play by warning Timon that "these smell-feasts" who "lye and fawn," flattering to feed on his "Mutton" and "Partridge," are mere "Flies, who at one cloud of winter-showers" will drop away (19). In commenting on Timon's feasts, mostly through a series of asides, Apemantus characterizes the host as the main course: "Ye Gods, what a number of men/ Eat *Timon*!"

> . . . and yet he sees 'em not.
> It grieves me to see so many dip their meat
> In one man's Bloud, and all the madness is
> He cheers 'em to't.
>
> (20)

Apemantus condemns both Timon and his flies and leeches, but the power of the image resides in the hero being cast as a kind of living gravy pot, encouraging his guests to "dip" in his "Bloud."

The nature of the parasite is to consume under the cover of a fiction of exchange. As Serres reminds us, the parasite never pays in kind for what he or she receives, instead offering words and noise in exchange for food and privilege. While there is no way to escape the play's parasitical economy, Apemantus occupies a different place within it; the word "cynic," after all, is derived from Ancient Greek *kynikos*, or "dog-like." Thou art "a thing," says Timon to Apemantus, "whom Fortunes tender arms/ With favor never claspt, but bred a Dog" (52). To be "bred a Dog" is, in Timon's view, to lack investment in the social order. Unlike the "smooth Parasites around him," Apemantus—the name means "without affect"—neither trades nor equivocates in affection; refusing to engage in a "Horse-Leech" style of flattery, he maintains a satiric distance from the economy of Timon's court. Patrolling the borders of the social order, Apemantus growls at the vermin who swarm about the house and threaten the gullible Timon; he travels back and forth between the house and the woods, following Timon, behaving not only as a Cynic but also as its prototype, the cur. As Thomas Nashe writes of cynic / dog figures, "for they will snarl and bite; / Right courtiers to flatter and to fawne; / Valiant to set upon the enemies / Most faithfull and most constant to their friends."[18] While his movements between the castle and the woods may evoke the scavenging habits of dogs, his refusal to join Timon's table, despite repeated invitations, removes him from the interspecies feeding frenzy that characterizes Timon's Athens. Instead, Apemantus consumes roots and berries in the woods. This vegetarian diet makes him less dog-like. As street scavengers during a time of comparative scarcity, dogs fed on feces and carrion.[19] In extreme cases, dogs would eat corpses, especially during plague years or in the aftermath of battles when bodies could be found putrefying on the streets of London and battlefields. Dozens of early modern writers use some variant of the term "foule-mouthed" to describe their distaste for dogs' feeding practices, a revulsion exacerbated by the canine tendency (as one writer puts it) to "feast on his own heave," or "to vomit up his shame again."[20] When Apemantus claims, "I devour no Lords," he clearly distinguishes himself from the pack (8).

By rejecting the rich food and luxury of Timon's feasts, Apemantus attempts to live outside a chain of mimetic desire, with its inevitable production of rivalry. In some sense, he serves as a model for Timon after misfortune and the discovery of his false friends turn the generous patron into a scavenger himself. Mimicking the behavior of Apemantus, Timon leaves the city for the woods and survives by digging for roots. At one point he addresses the earth itself, pleading with it to yield roots, not gold—to "Sear up thy fertile Womb to all things else"—because humans, he now recognizes, are little more than "ungrateful" sponges on the natural world (50). "Dry up thy marrow, thy Veins, thy Tilth and Pasture," Timon commands of the earth, "Whereof ungrateful man with liquorish draughts/ And unctuous morsels greases his pure mind, / That from it all consideration slips" (50). By "ungrateful man," Timon evokes a class of beings very close to what Serres calls "*Parasitus sapiens*," the thieving, greedy species that has managed to convince itself of its own claims to devour without bounds or limits (104). "History," Serres writes, "hides the fact that man is the universal parasite, that everything and everyone around him is a hospitable space":

> Plants and animals are always his hosts; man is always necessarily their guest. Always taking, never giving. He bends the logic of exchange and of giving in his favour when he is dealing with nature as a whole. (24)

Timon's injunction to Nature, then, exposes the continuities between the rhetoric of parasitism and Enlightenment critiques of excess and luxury: while it may be better to dig for roots ("unctuous morsels") than for the gold in nature's "Veins," humans are always in the position of feeding on an earth ravaged to supply their insatiable desires. Not even the Cynic can escape the one-way "logic of exchange" that characterizes parasitical relations.

Within the seventeenth-century version of this system, dogs and dog-like figures occupy equivocal positions; as figures of greed, lust, and rivalry, they typify its workings; but as figures of loyalty, obedience, and sacrifice, they seem to offer hope of escape. Several times in the play, Timon evokes dogs as an absent emblem of allegiance. "How much is a dog more generous than a Man," he laments after losing his wealth, "Oblige him once, hee'l keep you Company, / Ev'n in your utmost want and misery" (37). In Act 5, Timon declares to Alcibiades, "I am *misanthropos*! I hate Mankind: / And for thy part, I wish thou wer't a Dog / That I might love thee something" (59). In both cases, Timon seems to hold out the paradoxical possibility that canines, traditional emblems of either flattery or ferocity, transcend the system of one-way relations in which he is enmeshed. Dogs embody the (absent) virtues that ostensibly define humankind's better nature. Timon's mistress, the "constant" Evandra, similarly fulfills this fantasy canine function. Shadwell's most extensive revision of Shakespeare's play, as critics have noted, is the addition of a love plot in which Evandra and the jilt Melissa vie for Timon's attentions.[21] In Act 1, Evandra warns Timon that Melissa's love is "Most mercenary, base," mere "Marriage-Love"; she gives her body in "vile exchange" for his liberty (13). In contrast, after having witnessed Timon's humiliating demise and Melissa's flight, Evandra offers Timon her gold and professes her unconditional devotion: "I am no base Athenian Parasite / To fly from thy Calamities," she declares, "I'll help to bear 'em" (39). Abandoning the property that makes her human, Evandra joins Timon in his homeless scavenging. If Melissa's name associates her, however ironically, with flattery, with honeyed words that vanish in the light of Timon's poverty, Evandra's behavior links her to another group of animal images, the "generous" (or masochistic) spaniel who, while suffering kicks and rejection, follows her "master" in his hardship, even to the grave.[22]

As Apemantus exits in Act 4, Timon curses him off the stage with "Slave! Dog! Viper! Out of my sight" (53). Timon's unsettling linkage among chattel, curs, and poisonous vermin suggests how dogs, as the middle term in this chain of invectives, trouble the distinctions between useful companion and toxic threat. The Cynic often functions in classical tragedy as a scapegoat figure, an individual singled out as a collective object of contempt. Apemantus, however, is only one of several scapegoats in the play. In Serres' analysis, scapegoating is a function of rivalry: because "humans are parasites to one another," explains Steven Brown, "rivalry must occur, which is solved by sacrifice—the existing guests work together to expel the uninvited guests."[23] Scapegoating serves a useful but short-lived function; expulsion offers a temporary solution to the problem of rivalries, helping to "adapt social relations to subsequent acts of parasitism," thereby shifting "the basis of community towards new norms."[24] Both Timon, the philanthropical benefactor, and Alcibiades, the military hero in Shadwell's play, can be regarded as scapegoats, then. At more or less the same time Timon retreats to the woods, Alcibiades is exiled from the city, only to return, triumphantly. In Serres' reading of parasitical relations, the scapegoat once excluded, always returns. The play ends with Alcibiades being swept into power, promising a new freedom for the Athenians, the overthrow of "Tyrants" who have functioned as state-parasites, robbing and pillaging from the people to increase their own "private stores." When "the Government / Is in the Body of the People," he pronounces, "they / Will do themselves no harm" (68). This statement, written six months before the advent of the Popish Plot and the Exclusion Crisis, is in keeping with Shadwell's opposition political principles; it implies parasites are foreign or alien forces corrupting a body politic that otherwise would be self-regulating, autopoietic.[25] Commanding the people to return home, to repair to their "several Trades, their Business and Diversions," Alcibiades assures them he will protect the borders of the city and guard them "from [their] active Foes" (68). In this respect, *Timon* reinforces a critique of Charles II's court as a nest of flatterers and parasites, feeding, like Timon's poet and painter, on the body of the King as well as the nation.

The double suicides of Timon and Evandra seem to offer, in the end, a sentimental alternative to the feeding frenzies of city life, even as they under-score, in a grimly ironic way, the impossibility of escaping a parasitical econ-omy. Both Evandra and Timon succumb to an originary order of parasites, becoming food, as Prince Hal says over the body of Hotspur, "for worms." If *Timon* teaches anything, it is that parasites feed and breed within the body politic, confusing what one imagines to be distinct. Humans and flies eat at the table; men become dogs; gold turns to shit. Consequently, an absolute freedom, in the sense of a nonparasitical economy, is an illusion. Timon's epitaph reads, "*Here lies a wretched Corpse, of wretched Soul bereft / Timon my name, a Plague consume you Caitiffs left*" (68). While this parting shot im-plies that, unlike the living "Caitiffs" or slaves, Timon is now "free" from the plagues he wishes on others, the audience knows that, in their mingling and decaying bodies, Timon and Evandra have given themselves over to a sub-terranean world of feeding things, to the biological forces that, throughout the play, define the parasitical social and political world. However entombed and memorialized, their rotting, worm-ridden corpses call into question the confident assertions of Alcibiades that any government can "protect" the interspecies citizen-body from the self-consumption of "*Parasites* and *Sub-parasites.*" In this sense, writes Brown, the history of human relations, is "not the war of 'all against all' that Hobbes described. It is the war of all against one: the parasite who will become the scapegoat."[26]

IN PRAISE OF JOWLER: ROCHESTER ON PARASITES

The satiric overtones of Shadwell's reading of Shakespeare's text become full-blown strategies in other libertine writers, wit-laced condemnations of the hypocrisy and double dealing that define the social order. Rochester's "Satyre Against Reason and Mankind" offers a biting portrait of parasitical relations. In his best-known work, Rochester describes "natural" order in terms of feeding systems perversely corrupted by humans. What he regards as necessary violence in the animal world gives way to frenzied destruction and self-destruction among men:

> *Birds* feed on *birds, beasts,* on each other prey,
> But savage man alone does *man* betray,
> Pressed by necessity, they kill for food,
> *Man* undoes man to do himself no good.[27]

"Good," in the speaker's view, means whatever contributes to "life's happiness," a condition associated with bodily pleasure and health, with stalking, sex, and feasting. Instead of acting like dogs and other predators that "hunt / Nature's allowance" (l. 134), humans are motivated by fears that cannot be pinned down to specific agents or conditions. Humans' only recourse is to insinuate or force themselves into deceptive and self-deluding positions on a parasitical chain where they can feed on others. Although he does not use the word "parasite" here, Rochester describes man as inherently given to hypocrisy and flattery: man, "with smiles, embraces, friendship, praise / Inhumanly his fellow's life betrays" (ll.135–36). In contrast to animals who "fight and tear" for "hunger or for love," man is undone by an imagination that piles fear upon fear:

> wretched man is still in arms for fear.
> For fear he arms, and is of arms afraid
> By fear to fear successively betrayed;
>
> (ll. 140–42)

Because fear is "the source whence all his best passions came: / His boasted honor, and his dear-bought fame" (ll. 143–44), man, in effect, has internalized the parasitical economy; every move is motivated by his recognition that he himself is being, or is about to be, victimized. In such passages, Rochester adapts Hobbes, who similarly treated the "dominion" of men over the other creatures as a function of animal fear, rather than any natural authority. The "dominion of man consists in this . . . though a Lion or a Bear be stronger than a man, yet the strength, and art, and specially, the Leaguing and Societies of men, are a greater power, than the ungoverned strength of unruly Beasts."[28] If a "hungry Lion" were, however, to meet an "unarmed man" in the desert, the lion would have dominion. Human power over the other creatures, then, is situational rather than affixed to species being, and what we wrongly term human "dominion" over domestic animals, such as sheep and oxen, is in fact "hostility" on our parts rather than obeyance on theirs.[29] Rochester explicitly echoes this view: fear of parasitism or predation produces parasitical and predatory behavior. His skepticism about finding a man who, like Alcibiades, has apparently broken free from the parasitical chain, is manifest in the poem's final couplet: "If such there are then grant me this at least, / Man differs more from man than man from beast" (ll. 220–21).

The apparent distinction between "beast" and "man" in this iconic couplet, like Rochester's portrait with the monkey, has led critics to conclude that Rochester, following Boileau's version of Juvenal's fifteenth satire, rejects religious and philosophical arguments for humankind's superiority to animals. It is hard to deny the binary set up in Rochester's theriophilic opening. The speaker desires to exchange his human "case of flesh and blood" for the body of a "dog, a monkey, or a bear / . . . anything but that vain animal / Who is so proud of being rational" (II.4–7). Throughout the poem, Rochester redefines the traditional ideas of the Great Chain of Being to claim that "beasts are, in their degree / As wise at least, and far better than" a humankind wracked by fear, doubt, and duplicity (ll. 115–16). What is crucial, however, and requisite for his satiric critique, is that Rochester's *identification with* animals is bound up with his satiric *disidentification from* the *parasite* man—"the mite who thinks he's an image of the infinite." Both the "mite" and the "dog" allow Rochester to lay bare the parasitical order as a way to counter the false economy of reciprocal exchange:

> Those creatures are the wisest who attain,
> By surest means, the ends at which they aim.
> If therefore Jowler finds and kills his hares
> Better than Meres supplies committee chairs,
> Though one's a statesman, th' other but a hound,
> Jowler, in justice, would be wiser found.
>
> (ll. 117–22)

Poking fun at the frustrated ambitions of Sir Thomas Meres to ascend to the ranks of Parliamentarian forces eager to block the ascension of James II, the speaker makes Jowler an ironic standard for beings whose desires and accomplishments converge. Dogs, unlike human parasites, serve as models of "right reason" in action. Jowler's ability to locate, chase down, and catch hares demonstrates the success of creatures who follow their senses and are naturally suited to their environment, in contrast to "man" who conjures up a "sixth" sense—abstract reason divorced from "certain instinct"—to "contradict the other five" (ll. 9–10).

Despite this avowed identification with "more perfect" creatures, Rochester is no Jowler. Given his own dependence on Charles II and his position at the court (from which he was temporarily banished), Rochester occupies the ironic position of the *hyperparasite*, the courtier who feeds off the host who, in turn, feeds off others. Although I borrow the term from contemporary biology, one can find the concept of hyperparasites in Mosca's division of the world into *"Parasites and Sub-parasites"* or, more wittily, in Jonathan Swift's depiction in "On Poetry: A Rhapsody":

> So nat'ralists observe, a flea
> Hath smaller fleas that on him prey;
> And these have smaller fleas to bite 'em.
> And so proceeds *Ad Infinitum.*

(ll. 337–40)[30]

Ad infinitum—into infinity. Both in the "Satyre" and elsewhere, Rochester's poetry reveals the logic of reciprocal exchange, far from being the law of things, is an idealized exception, much like the ideal of the "good man" who gives as much as he takes. The default economy is instead a series of ill-disguised, one-way relations practiced cynically by persons who pretend to offer service or objects in return. As John Gay writes in "The Man and the Flea": "For thee! Made only for our need/That more important fleas may feed" (ll. 45–46).[31]

When Rochester turns to the figure of Timon in his poem "Timon" he recasts Shakespeare's and Shadwell's blasted idealist as a distrustful town wit, misled by parasites whom he does not trust but whom he cannot escape. The poem begins with a question by Apemantus to Timon:

> What, Timon! does old age begin t'approach
> That thus thou droop'st under a night's debauch?
> Hast thou lost deep to needy rogues on tick,
> Who ne'er could pay, and must be paid next week?

(ll. 1–4)

Apemantus's suggestion that Timon may have lost money to people who played with nothing—"on tick," or with the (empty) promise that money would be forthcoming if they lost—locates the poem in a credit rather than patronage economy. Intentionally or not, the colloquialism "on tick" also weaves together the biological and economic orders, conflating Timon's "needy rogues" with small arachnids that live off the blood of others. Apemantus's question, however, turns out be a mere prelude to another version of the parasitical relationship, whereby literary endeavor is figured as a form of unequal exchange.

Timon explains to Apemantus that a "dull dining sot" had "(s)eized" him in the Mall and bribed him to dinner with promise of witty companions: "Sedley, Buckhurst, and Savile" (l. 34). Because food, words, speaking, and eating are conjoined in parasitical economies, this dinner invitation should result in pleasure and even patronage for the speaker, whose literary reputation provoked it: "He knew my style, he swore, and 'twas in vain/ Thus to deny the issue of my brain" (l. 25–26). Instead, Timon reaches the would-be wit's home, only to discover his companions are not the elite circle of Restoration literary culture but Halfwit, Huff, Kickem, Dingboy, and a wife—the worst kind of pretenders to wit, taste, and learning. Like his namesake, then, Rochester's Timon is victimized, but in a sardonic mode, the results satirical rather than tragic. Half-bribed, half-coerced with flattery, Rochester's Timon is condemned to a bad beef dinner with ignorant, blustering would-be playwrights. The meal descends to chaos when Halfwit, Huff, Kickem, and Dingboy turn to violence, their disagreements about politics leading to fisticuffs, which become the night's entertainment: "we let them cuff / Till they, mine host, and I had all enough" (l. 173). Like the meals Serres invokes in *The Parasite*, from Plato's *Symposium* to the fables of La Fontaine, this one is interrupted, and Timon leaves vowing "nevermore / To drink beer-glass and hear the hectors roar" (ll. 176–77).

This poem, suggests Kirk Combe, satirizes Charles II and his court and displays how Rochester works as "an agent of chaos against order."[32] Extending Combe's point, I suggest that Rochester depicts an intrinsically rivalrous order, which must be shored up and remade; in a parasitical system, order is less the law of things than it is the ideal that must be disrupted: "By virtue of its power to perturb," write Serres' editors, "the parasite ultimately constitutes, like the *clinamen* and the demon, *the condition of possibility of the system*."[33] Rochester's "Timon" reveals that the contractual basis of parasitism—good words in exchange for good food—is always in the process of collapsing into violence, in part because it is the nature of the parasite to disrupt and redirect energies. If the parasite is a scapegoat, it is also what Serres calls "a conductor" (190), which, precisely because it disrupts, creates the very conditions that constitute the system. In this respect, the interrupted feast of Rochester's poem allows Timon to see through the social illusions of reciprocity and to acknowledge his own vulnerability to flattery. But Rochester's "Timon," the poem, allows the reader to see how the literary system is populated by "*Parasites* or *Sub-parasites*," the difference between them determined largely by one's proximity to Sedleys, Buckhurts, and Savilles, rather than Halfwits, Huffs, Kickums, and Dingboys. In both cases, flattery, rivalry, and violence define the system's operations.

SCENTS AND SENSIBILITY IN ST. JAMES'S PARK

In Rochester's and Shadwell's texts, dogs and other vermin function largely (although not exclusively) as metonymical figures typical of seventeenth-century satirical tradition. This tradition, in turn, is bound up in with discourses of disease, and especially zoonotic disease, in which infection and infestation travel in tandem. As beings who "shared human spaces, food, and names," dogs, according to Jenner, could "readily be imagined as the means by which infection was communicated."[34] Mullett reports on a "little book" reprinted in 1603 that advocates people "keep their houses, street, yards, sinks and ditches sweet and clean from all standing puddles, dunghills and corrupt moistures, and not let dogs 'which be a most apt cattle' to carry the infection, come running in to the house."[35] What interests me in Rochester's poetry is how sixteenth-century zoopolitics are rethought in the late seventeenth-century urban space. Before germ theory, the open spaces of London's parks provided sunlight and fresh air in a dirty and polluted city, and therefore, writes Nan Drehrer, "were believed to inhibit disease."[36] St. James's Park in particular, a former wetland drained at great expense by James I and redesigned by Charles II, represented for Londoners the triumph of art over nature, the miasmic conditions of an unhealthy swamp converted to playgrounds for fashionable humans, exotic animals, and domesticated creatures. The first keeper of St. James's Park, Moses Pitt, prided himself on having filled in all the low ground around "the Birdcages" and Storey's Gate, where water "stagnated" and "was the cause of fog and mist, so that thereby that part of the park was clear from fogs, and healthy."[37] Animals were an important part of the reclamation project. In his diaries, John Evelyn describes at length the creatures of Charles II's park, focusing on pelicans and other exotic birds, which he perceives as "great devourers"; a "Balearian crane" on a prosthetic leg; and "numerous flocks of ordinary and extraordinary wild fowl," which, he says, "for being near so great a city, and among such a concourse of soldiers and people, is a singular and diverting thing."[38] In addition, he continues, "There were also deer of several countries, white; spotted like leopards; antelopes, an elk, red deer, roebucks, stags, Guinea goats, Arabian sheep, etc."[39] Evelyn's description emphasizes the extent to which St. James's

Park offers a spectacle of the world's animals, many ripped from their natural habitats and restricted to specific areas in a kind of aestheticized display.

Although Evelyn does not focus on dogs in his description, we know dogs traditionally wandered freely throughout the park. L. R. Sadler (James Larwood), the major historian of London's parks, mentions that dogs chased the nearly tame, wild animals on exhibit in the park during the reign of Charles I.[40] Charles II, known by the nickname "King of the Curs," kept his dog kennel in St. James's Park and, according to Sadler, was "constantly losing [dogs] in the Park, and advertisements about these animals appear frequently in the newspapers during his reign."[41] In 1660, a humorous description of a "Black Dog, between a Greyhound and a Spaniel," "His Majesty's Own Dog," appeared in *Mercurious Politicus*. "It doubtless was stoln," reads the ad, "for the Dog was not born nor bred in England and never forsake his Master." [42] In 1671 *The London Gazette* reports a "Dog of His Majesty, full of blue spots, with a white cross on his forehead, and about the bigness of a tumbler" was lost in St. James's Park. Because other dogs were harassing his fowl, Charles at one point banned all hunting dogs, or dogs over a certain size, from the Park. Coincidentally or not, eighteenth-century paintings by Gainsborough, Ricci, Rowlandson, and Sandby that depict individuals and couples strolling down the avenue, "taking the air," feature small to medium dogs, usually frolicking, sometimes on scent. The dogs in these paintings in no way threaten either grazing animals or the humans around them.

Such airy pastoral versions of London's most famous public green differ radically from Rochester's "A Ramble in St. James's Park." In this satiric poem, "Strange woods spring from the teeming earth," the product of ancient kings masturbating on their "mother's face" (ll. 12–19). Men and women of all classes mingle with the dogs in an environment both venal and venereal, reminding its readers that St. James's Park was originally a miasmic swamp. These miasmic conditions and the disease and filth they represent return in the form of Corinna's "grace cup" (l. 122), her vagina "full gorgéd" with "nasty slime" (ll. 117–18). In Rochester's satire, the dogs, correspondingly, have at least as much in common with plague dogs as they do with the playful, companionate ones that are featured in eighteenth-century versions of the Park. William Austin's *Anatomie of a Pestilence* reads: "When *dogs* combine in numerous company/And arm themselves to make a mutiny, / They're such *presaging* heraulds make appear, / *Plague* is to follow *victor* in the *rear*."[43] Defoe's *Journal of the Plague Year* defends shutting up the infected because otherwise, like a "mad Dog" running through the streets and biting everyone "he meets," the sick would have "offer'd all sorts of Violence," wounding others who would, in turn, have become "incurably infected."[44] Even if Rochester's human-canine hybrids are not plague carriers, both Corinna and the speaker become associated through the poem with "frenzies" and related illnesses that reinforce the close relationships between dogs and humans in the parasitical economy.

Despite the striking examples of the monkey in Rochester's portrait, dogs are the most frequent partners in his species dysphoria, and crucial to his argument about their virtues and vices is their canid sense of smell. One could even argue that dogs' olfactory capacities help ground his materialist philosophy. Robert Boyle, in 1673, had deployed the hunting dog in his corpuscular philosophy to illustrate what he called "The Determinate Nature of Effluviums."[45] Boyle offers an anecdote about a Bloodhound capable of tracking real and decoy poachers for seven miles or more, and argues that a gentleman can determine whether his hounds chased a hare or a fox "by their way of running, and their holding their Nose higher than ordinary when they pursue a Fox, whose scent is more strong."[46] Boyle's argument, like Rochester's, is not simply that hounds are fine-nosed but that their behavior may be taken as proof of the physical nature of otherwise invisible phenomena: corpuscular philosophy, in Boyle's case, "right reason," in Rochester's "Satyre." The hunting dog thus offers Rochester and Boyle an alternative to the parasite and a ready source of identification or disidentification.

The dog pack serves a similar but more overtly corporate function, providing a model of political order suited to seventeenth century England. The pack's—or kingdom's—stability can never be taken for granted but must be policed, maintained, or "restored" through acts of exclusion or violence. Freed of their "masters," free-roaming hunting dogs, like Exquemelin's feral mastiffs on Tortuga, revert to rivalry and mimetic contagion, quickly returning, for distraught humans, to the status of vermin, canid "smell-feasts" competing with each other for food and sex. Under conditions of scarcity, hunting dogs resemble wolves more than hounds, and in early modern England, the wolf symbolizes the Hobbesian universe, always in a state of Nature at odds with humankind's efforts to domesticate animals and protect the agro-political order. The now-ubiquitous expression "son of a bitch" is based on the intense rivalry and violence of lupine procreation. What beast is it, asks one of Donne's Satyres, which his "own sire ne're knows" for "at th' engendring he his life doth lose?" The answer to this riddle is the "Bitch Wolf" who

... when she's proud with dogs do go
Raving and raging ever too and fro.
Where they a filthy coil about her keep,
Till wearied out, at last they fall asleep,
She wakes one, which her lines, & when each misses
His prey, they tear him limmally in pieces.[47]

This satire reinforces the biologically valid notion that a "proud" female, one in heat, will be followed by many dogs during her five-to-seven-day *oestrus*; right before she is ready to mate, she releases sex hormones to which all male members of the pack, including puppies, respond. Donne's description of the "Bitch Wolf" is coupled with the less-defensible idea, however, that the act of reproduction among wolves is always violent, since wolf packs usually have an established hierarchy in which the alpha male and female, determined long before, are the only ones who mate.[48] Nevertheless, because pack survival depends on successful procreation between powerful males and females, canine and lupine hierarchies are easily mapped onto seventeenth-century human categories of rank and gender.

Rochester's "A Ramble in St. James's Park" exploits this assumption about dogs, pressing it into the service of an extended satire on humanity's pretenses to reason.[49] His "Ramble" begins where "Timon" ends. The speaker, having just left a feast—a "diet at the Bear"—wanders drunkenly into St. James's Park, hoping, he says, "to cool my head and fire my heart" (l. 8). He sees his mistress Corinna, who, in "proud disdain" (l. 36) walks by him without acknowledgment, followed closely by three men who "with wriggling tails made up to her" (l. 44). The word "proud" rather than "disdain" initiates the canid imagery that structures the rest of the poem. This scenario is reminiscent of Henry Bulkely's complaint in a letter to Rochester: fops, he laments, "herd with one another" because their "Honour, Honesty, and Friendship is like the Consent of Hounds, who knowe not why thay runn together, but that they hunt the same sent."[50] "A Ramble in St. James's Park" dramatizes a similar ambivalence about hypergendered, heteronormative masculine behavior, and the homosocial rivalries accompanying it, through the four men who find themselves in a pack, pulled along by Corinna's invisible something. Three of these men are described metonymically as a trio of "wriggling tails" or "whiffling fools"; the fourth is the narrator, trying desperately to manage his rage after Corinna walks by him in her "proud disdain."

Within this misogynist fantasy of female desire and desirability, it is not immediately clear who or what the object of satire is: the parasitical fops who follow Corinna, Corinna for exercising such poor judgment in encouraging them, or the jilted speaker, who resorts to cursing the woman and her "lewd cunt" (l. 113). What is clear, however, is that Rochester is imagining human social order as comparable to that of canines, and that his vision of canine pack behavior is as uncertain and potentially destructive as the complex parasitic economy of Charles's court. The "Whitehall blade" in St. James Park cannot lay claim to being a first-order parasite but is himself a *hyperparasite* who boasts of being distantly related to a woman who procured him a place at the "Waiters' table" where he heard a story about the King's preference for "Banstead mutton" (ll. 47–50). The "Gray's Inn wit" lives by flattering his landlady, and the third, "an eldest son," pins his sexual fortune partly on the abilities of the first two. These men hunt instinctively after fashions in a chaos of mimetic desire that escapes any rational justification. In a parasitical economy, as Rochester writes of the first parasite he encounters, such scenting after fashion leads the fop to try "to do like the best"; lacking "common sense," however, he is capable only of converting "abortive imitation / To universal affectation" (ll. 54–58). The parasites, therefore, fail the Jowler test.

"A Ramble in St. James's Park" describes a male homosocial order gone awry. There are biblical precedents for Rochester's portrayal of Corinna, which would have been familiar to Rochester's audience. "Moses," writes John Trapp, "fitly compareth a whore to a *salt-bitch* that is followed after by all the dogs in a town."[51] Rochester's parasites/dogs are described as "humble curs" who "obsequiously . . . hunt / The savoury scent of salt-swol'n cunt" (ll. 85–86). These hangers-on blindly follow a salted, or "proud," bitch, hoping to be the one who will "line" her, or mate. And much to his horror, the speaker finds himself at the wrong end of this parasitical chain. A thorough-going Hobbesian, the speaker assumes he and Corinna had an agreement based on libertine principles: she would pursue sexual pleasure where she found it, as he would. But Corinna's structural position within the parasitical economy is more powerful than his. If Hobbes sees society as a state of nature mediated by self-interest and fear, for Serres, "sociality is neither an atomistic adding together of individuals, nor an abstract contractual arrangement. It is a collectivity assembled and held together by the circulation of an object" (21–22). In Rochester's poem, Corinna is that object, the salted bitch, functioning as the source of both order and disorder. What the speaker discovers in the park is not only the indifference of his mistress but also the secret of the parasitical economy: identity is conferred not by the subject but by the object. In actor-network theory, the quasi-object is that which accords a relational identity on the players of the game—in Charles II's favorite game of Pall-Mall, the ball bestows identity on the players not simply as a passive object, but as actant. Similarly, in coursing, the hare bestows identity on the greyhound, the greyhound on the master. The minute Corinna passes by the narrator without acknowledging him, she alters not only his position in the game, whose terms he thought he had created, but also his identity. Stripped of his fiction of libertine exchange—"Such naturals freedoms are but just: / There's something generous in mere lust"—he can now imagine what he calls "her treachery" only as a one-way movement—that is, only in parasitical terms (ll. 97–98). She becomes the verminous eater of men.

At this point, Rochester's speaker conflates the difference between sex and eating. He describes Corinna's "devouring cunt" in terms of its gluttony, taking into itself "the seed of half the town":

> My dram of sperm was supped up after
> For the digestive surfeit water.
> Full gorgéd at another time
> With a vast meal of nasty slime
> Which your devouring cunt had drawn
> From porters' backs and footman's brawn,
> I was content to serve you up
> My ballock-full for your grace cup.
>
>   (ll. 115–23)

While Corinna's "Full gorgéd" and "devouring cunt" has been perceived as a figure of the *vagina dentata*, the extended metaphor of the "vast meal" also serves a more complex function than mere misogyny. It allows Rochester's narrator to represent himself as the victim, much like Shakespeare's Timon, as the too-generous host of a voracious guest. That what he served Corinna was primarily a "ballock-full" of spermatic juices reflects a libertine ethos that translates parasitical consumption into sexual license. The "head" and "tail" are "interchangeable"; at "her mouth her cunt cries, 'Yes!'" (l. 78).

Because it collapses differences between female dogs and human women, "A Ramble" has been regarded as one of Rochester's most misogynist poems. It is worth pointing out, however, that what makes Corinna "vile" to the hyperparasite speaker is not her animality but her pretense to having been, like Mosca, "dropped from above": anyone witnessing her contempt for him would have "swore / She dropped from heaven that very hour/ For-saking the divine abode / In scorn of some despairing god" (ll. 38–40). The speaker revenges himself precisely on those pretensions; in a kind of onto-logical throwdown, inverting the image of sacred birth, the narrator claims he will plague Corinna until "Crab-louse, inspired with grace divine / From earthly cod to heaven shall climb" (ll. 147–48). This startling image of a para-site climbing out of human pubic hair into heaven introduces the rejected speaker's curse.

Returning to his familiar canid imagery, the speaker imagines Corinna alone and suffering under perpetual *oestrus*: "May your depravéd appetite / That could in such whiffling fools delight / Beget . . . frenzies in your mind" (ll. 135–37). Significantly, the English word for Latin *oestrus* is *frenzy*; the period between the female canine's two annual heats is called *anoestrus*, "without frenzy," and it lasts about five months. In effect, the speaker wish-es on Corinna painful and unrequited sexual desire; her "longing arse," he imagines, will be turned to "th' air" waiting for a north wind to "bluster" in her "cunt" (ll. 138–41). A dry north wind was thought to be most capable of carrying scent—the scent, according to the logic of the poem, of her salt-swollen genitals—but this time, no wind blows.[52] Nature conspires with the jilted narrator to punish Corinna, leaving her in a state that, in eighteenth-century humans, would be called *furor uterinus* or, in the nineteenth century, nymphomania.[53] The speaker intends to defer his "revenge," however, until the now-desperate Corinna is married and pregnant, or "limed"(l. 154), after which he will provoke jealousy in her "poor cur" (l. 158) until

> . . . I have torn him from her breech
> While she whines, like a dog-drawn bitch,
> Loathed and despised, kicked out of th' Town
> Into to some dirty hole alone
> To chew the cud of misery
> And know she owes it all to me.
>
> (ll. 159–64)

In this especially sadistic fantasy of *coitus interruptus*, Rochester's speaker takes advantage of his knowledge about canine reproduction to inflict pain on Corinna and provoke rage in the would-be father: a single litter can con-tain pups from different dogs.[54] In the speaker's own frenzied imagination, the alpha female is driven from the human pack—indeed, from the species, given that she is transformed into an cud-chewing ungulate—by "scandals, truth, or lies" (l. 157). Put another way, he has removed Corinna from the libertine game by imagining her pregnant and alone: "And may no woman better thrive / Who dares profane the cunt I swive" (165–66). The patrilineal imperative—to secure familial inheritance and identity through the virtue of the mother—becomes turned, in the bestial world of "A Ramble," into the speaker's fantasy position as the alpha male. At least in his imagination, his stories about Corinna's liaisons will result in a pup without a father, in a yet-to-be-born son of a bitch.

As the most sexualized, freely circulating, and scavenging inhabitants of London, dogs provide a ready source of libertine identification: through the dog, sex is naturalized and can be presented as a simple matter of appetite, a form of feeding. But those who feed too freely or too often are figured as sexual gluttons, as in the satire on the Duchess of Cleveland, also attributed to Rochester: "Full forty men a day provided for this whore / Yet like a bitch she wags her tail for more."[55] The reason "A Ramble in St. James's Park" remains powerful, then, is that it explores, through dogs, the mimetic contagion at the heart of Restoration sexual relations. Carole Fabricant points out that "Rochester's poetry is characterized, not by the exaltation of sexuality as commonly assumed, but by an unequivocal demonstration of the latter's transience and futility."[56] At stake in the performance of libertine frustration is less the *value of sex* than the *fragility and violence of intersubjective relations* that sex demystifies. The libertine recognizes that the mistress endows his subjectivity. She is the quasi-object who, in the words of Serres, "designates a subject who, without it, would not be a subject.... The quasi-object, when being passed, makes the collective," and "if it stops, it makes the individual" the "it" (225). To be without the quasi-object is to be part of an undifferentiated horde, and, in one sense, this is the threat haunting libertine wit: the fear of being socially indistinguishable, of being lost in what Bulkeley calls "the herd."

Libertine freedoms may promise to unleash desire and "free" the subject, but libertine men, as Rochester seems to recognize, find themselves embedded in a pack, chasing a predesignated object, pulled along by one or another invisible scent. Raging against the curs and the "vile" bitch they pursue does little to improve the speaker's lot and disqualifies him from the privileged, ostensibly affectless subject position of the Cynic. But because foaming at the mouth, rather than the pintle, is a sign of danger for Restoration readers, his misogynist curse offers the speaker only the illusory comfort of distinguishing himself from the "arrogant oafs" pursuing Corinna. The speaker embraces the ironic fate of having transformed himself into a more dangerous, because more furious, member of the breed.[57]

ANIMAL SPIRITS, WET WOMEN, AND ZOONOTIC DISEASE

In his "A Satyr Against Wit," Richard Blackmore lampoons fashionable wits in a stock character who descends, dog-like, into spewing fury: "He grins and snarles, and in his dogged Fit/ Froths at the Mouth, a certain Sign of Wit."[58] Rochester's speaker fares little better: he begins drunk and ends furious in a culture in which both states were legally-recognized departures from the supposedly normative state of being *compos mentis*.[59] John Brydall describes "Mad, or Distracted Persons" as suffering from "over heated" animal spirits: "When the Animal Spirits, by some Accident or other, are so over-heated, that they become unserviceable to cold and sedate Reasoning; and then Reason being thus laid aside, Fancy gets the Ascendent, and *Phaeton*-like, drives on furiously, and inconsistently."[60] "Madness," from this medico-poetic perspective, may have many causes—"Love, in Grief, in Jealousie, in Wrath, and Vexation."[61] A seventeenth-century physician, then, might diagnose Rochester's speaker rambling through St. James's Park as suffering from melancholic rage, his animal spirits coursing through a heated body and seething brain. "Spirits are set on fire," writes Brydall, "by the Violence of their own motion; and in that Rage are not to be governed by Reason."[62] So close are the connections among heat, agitation of the animal spirits, and madness that the term "Mad-man," in Brydall's text and elsewhere, is used interchangeably with the hybrid noun "Furor-Man"—or, more simply, "Fuiriosus."[63] Rochester's speaker, in this context, is the poetic counterpart of Mandeville's description of male dogs pursuing a bitch in heat: "When their "Fury is provok'd by a Venereal Ferment," Mandeville writes, males "exert themselves chiefly against other Males of the same Species."

In Rochester's poem, as we have seen, a good deal of the speaker's fury is directed towards "vile" and gluttonous Corinna; in other words, he projects the verminous qualities of feral dogs onto the figure of the bitch, herself a hybrid incarnation of "Venereal Ferment." This double displacement—men are mad dogs but bitch women are worse—is a cornerstone of eighteenth-century misogynist satire, particularly, if not exclusively, in "the lady and the lapdog" genre, explored by Laura Brown.[64] In Brown's view, the lapdog stands metaphorically, or almost metonymically, for female sexuality in "a dynamic that places the animal simultaneously within and outside the realm of the human, or—from another perspective—places the woman both within and outside the realm of the animal."[65] Corinna's status as a salted bitch demonstrates the extent to which the uncertain organic boundaries between dogs and humans could be exploited in seventeenth-century satire. Defining both male and female sexuality in canine terms, and explicitly connecting it to madness and fury, Rochester follows Gassendi and Willis (discussed in chapter 3), in promoting a nuanced, anti-Cartesian view of human and non-human animals. Humans and the "more perfect" creatures are "twin" and entwined species, capable of sharing memories, desires, and diseases.

Animal studies scholars have coined the term "transcorporeality" to insist the human body is porous, permeable, and deeply entangled with those of other species. In the seventeenth century, what we would now call transcorporeality (real and imagined) extended beyond the discourses of the plague (discussed in chapter 2) and the domain of comparative physiology (chapter 3) to include the realm of madness and fury that figures prominently in "A Ramble." Indeed, early modern biopolitics in general and libertine biopolitics in particular depended on a collective understanding that humans and the more perfect creatures shared affinities, dispositions, and vulnerabilities, including zoonotic disease. The most dramatic symptom of this organic and cultural entanglement was rabies. Before 1700, no clear distinction existed between the psychological state of being furious and the medical state of being rabid; indeed, the term rabies (based on the Latin *rabere* "be mad, rave") was applied primarily to humans and only secondarily to dogs. Rabies often was described as an "ungovernable fury."[66] I want to close this chapter by exploring, in a preliminary way, the relationships among an Enlightenment discourse on rabies, new views of the parasite, and libertine biopolitics, focusing on John Gay's "The Mad Dog" (1730). What is imagistic in Rochester's poem—the nexus of dogs, disease, and desire—becomes an explicit and sexualized aspect of Gay's poem.

By 1730, London was more than sixty years beyond its last major outbreak of the plague, if not beyond recurrent fears.[67] In its own way, rabies was equally terrifying and only slightly less mysterious. Dogs were widely agreed to be the most common source of infection, but why they acted as disease vectors was not understood. Popular theories during the seventeenth and early eighteenth centuries emphasize dogs' emotional susceptibility, eating habits, and biological makeup: dogs had a "more melancholy temper and nature" than other animals (thus the "Black Dog of Melancholy"); they ate carrion; and they were more susceptible to heat. Often these explanations overlap. Relying on classical writers, who sometimes identified melancholy with hydrophobia, Robert Burton describes the poisoned "Braine" of the mad dog as "so hote and dry, that it consumes all the moisture in the body."[68] In his *Tractatus de Venenis; or, a Discourse of Poysons* (1661), William Ramsay abdicates trying to solve the "Controversie" of why dogs, more than other creatures, turn rabid; he claims only that dogs "are more addicted and pro-pence unto this Delirium, then other Creatures; out of a peculiar inherent or innate property in themselves; which, in plain English, is as much as to say, I am ignorant of the cause."[69] Rabid dogs mark the limits of human knowledge.

Despite dissent about the etiology of rabies, physicians agreed about its symptoms: infected humans assumed the characteristics of canines. Men, women, and children barked, bit, foamed at the mouth, and otherwise dem-onstrated the collapse of human-animal difference. Daniel Peter Layard puts the matter succinctly: "A Person thus affected may be said in a Degree to have put on the *Canine* Nature."[70] Consequently, persons who died of ra-bies were sometimes denied sacrament. This was the case for James Corton, a London upholsterer, bitten by his neighbor's dog. Martin Lister—better known for his work on conchs and spiders than rabies—published *A Re-markable Relation of a Man Bitten with a Mad Dog, and Dying of a Disease called Hydrophobia*, which was presented to the Royal Society in 1683. It re-counts in considerable detail Corton's demise over an eight-week period: the pain in his bones, nausea, vomiting, and thirst, accompanied by an inability to drink—he "started and trembled at the approach" of any "fluids."[71] Much of the treatise rehearses what Lister took to be the victim's assumption of canine characteristics. Since "in the erect posture of a man," writes Lister, "he could not so much as endureth the approach of liquor," Corton was per-suaded to hang his head over the side of the bed:

> In this posture then of a Dog, he suffereth a large Bowl filled with small Beer to be brought under his head, and imbraceing it with raptures of joy, he declared he was infinitely refrest with the smell of it; that he now saw it with delight, and assured us he should be able soon to drink it all off . . . he endeavored with great earnestness to put down his head to it, but could not; his Stomach rose as often as he opened his Lips; at length

he put out his tongue and made towards it as tho he would lap; but ever as his tongue never so little touched the Surface of the beer, he started back affrighted.[72]

When his family members exchanged the beer for ale, Corton lapped in the air, but was unable to drink. Repositioning him, they tried to hydrate him through a quill, "but he could not manage it, nor such no more than a Dog" (166). Soon he fell into a convulsion, "bit and snarl'd and catch'd at every body, and foamed at the mouth" (165). Within two days, he was dead.

Lister draws two conclusions from this "remarkable" case. The first and most surprising is that Corton had metamorphosed physically: he "had some of the organic parts of his body transformed into, or affected after the nature of a Dog, especially the *Gula, Tongue &c;* so that what was offer'd him in the erect posture of a man was very frightful, as well as difficult for him to take, because against his *new nature,* as much as it would be for us to get a dog to drink standing upon his hinder legs."[73] Lister's second conclusion is that Corton is contagious—his *"spittle is envenomed"*—so that, having been bitten by a mad dog, Corton becomes one, adopting not only its "affect" but its bodily fluids. That the dog who bit the upholsterer was still alive, apparently well, and potentially wandering through the streets at the time of Corton's death creates a kind of panic in Corton's neighborhood. A mercer exhibits extreme concern about a "black Dog, which he verily believed to be the same"; it "came and bit a Whelp of his in his Shop. The next day the Whelp ran mad up and down the House, and bit both him and the Maid, him in the hand, and the Maid in the leg, and dyed that very day."[74] While there was no clear chain of contagion—the mercer fell ill and recovered but the maid was never affected—Lister's detailed description sheds light on how humans and dogs coexisted in seventeenth-century London. The doctor, the mercer, the upholsterer, his cousin, the whelp, the black dog, and the maid crossed paths in and out of households. Lister's account of the rabid upholsterer shows us how dogs, like other vermin, were entangled in attempts to control public health—in practices, knowledge, and forms of power that, after Foucault, go under the name of "biopower" and "biopolitics."

While as late as 1665, canines had been subjected to mass extermination in plague-ridden London, in the eighteenth century, the threat of rabies forced city dogs into regimes of hygiene, containment, and control. Both the feeding practices and the sexual habits of domesticated dogs were made more predictable, their real and imagined parasites minimized through regular baths and fresher meals. Indeed, by 1738, in *A Treatise on the Venereal Distemper*, the French physician Pierre-Joseph Desault argues, following Mathiolus, that rabies is caused by "little Worms"; "Dogs," in his view, "are more subject to Madness than any other Animals" not because they so are so hot-blooded, as Burton had suggested, but "because they eat Carrion; perhaps these rotten Carcases are proper Matrixes to hatch these mad Worms, which stick to the Dog's Spittle whilst he is feeding."[75] Desault cites as evidence for this "Conjecture" a specifc pattern of infection: even though the number of dogs in the towns surpasses those in the provinces, "mad Dogs are more frequent in the Country, because they meet there with more Carrion; whereas in Towns where they are better fed."[76] The relationship among worms and rabies, rabies and diet, and diet and disease, he argues, is "not built upon Supposition, for the Cause appears evidently even to the eye of an old Man without the help of Microscope or Spectacles."[77] He claims that his analysis, while still imperfect, at "least . . . has the Advantage of presenting the Hydrophobia under an Aspect susceptible of Cure."[78]

Desault's insistence that biological parasites can be a source of madness provides a medical context for reading John Gay's "The Mad Dog," an anti-Catholic, antifeminist, and almost pornographic satire that depends on the ambiguous nature of dogs as human companions and disease-ridden vermin for much of its libertine wit. The poem features a Catholic woman who, afflicted with an ardent desire for men, repeatedly sins, confesses, does penance, sins, then goes back to church where she "piously confes(ses) the same (l. 48)."[79] The priest exclaims that it is "strange" to find an otherwise devout "woman" so driven by sexual desire—"to one sin confin'd!"—and asks about the source of this strong "appetite" (l. 70–79). The woman blames her behavior on a "sad disaster" with her dog:

> That she a fav'rite lapdog had,
> Which, (as she strok'd and kiss'd) grew mad;
> And on her lip a wound indenting,
> First set her youthful blood fermenting.
>
> (ll. 87–90)[80]

This poem shares an allied set of images with Rochester's "A Ramble in St. James's Park": sexual desire, rage, contagion, insanity, aggression, and "heat." These behaviors are imagined as both as dog-like and, as in medical writing, illustrative of a more general principle of heightened "animal spirits," nervous fibers thought to be responsible for emotional and sexual states. In the image of the supposedly rabid lapdog, Gay conflates the sexual and the medical: it is not apparent whether the dog was already mad or was driven mad by the women's stroking and kissing. The "wound" left by the "mad" dog on her lip that "First set her youthful blood fermenting" can therefore be seen either as an effect of rabies or as a return of the woman's latent passions now enflamed by an interspecies, sexualized encounter. Her story in turn infects the priest with what Gay calls "zealous fury" (l. 91), and he blames her for not turning to doctors who "by various ways" can "Treat these distempers of the mind" (ll. 93–94).

The priest then recommends several "treatments" for her "venom'd bites" (l. 101) but focuses on the generally discredited practice of dunking: to "set the shatter'd thoughts arights; / They send you to the ocean's shore. / And plunge the patient o'er and o'er" (ll. 102–4). While this image may recall the trials for supposed witches, the practice of dipping rabies victims in seawater in order to cure them dates back to the Roman Cornelius Celsus. Writing in the mid-seventeenth century, the Dutch physician Herman van der Heyden describes the logic of dunking:

> [I]t is therefore still the Common use to throw such as are bitten by a Mad Dog, into the Sea, as well Men, as Beasts; or else into some River; and to do the same again for several times. By which repetition of the said practise, they suppose that the *Venom* will be the more easily suppressed, and the Party bitten will also be so much accustomed to the Water, that at length he will not be in any fear of it at all: Which Practise (say they further) having always continued, even to this very day, would never have been so held up, unless the speedy, and often repeated practise of the same had sometimes been found to doe some good.[81]

Dunking constituted a kind of coercive aversion therapy. Through it, the patient's phobic reaction to water—a rabies symptom—was countered through repeated exposure. But even fifty years before Gay's poem, this "cure" was contested, so that the priest's advice to the woman bitten by her lapdog signifies a credulous, even superstitious, gullibility at a time when physicians, such as Desault, concurred with Van der Heyden that water cannot counteract rabies, and that, indeed, dunking infected humans may actually corrupt the water. Writing about the rabies epidemic of 1730–31, Desault categorically denies the effectiveness of this ancient "cure": "Bathing in the

Sea, consecrated in a manner by the unanimous Consent of all Nations, and supported by publick Confidence as a Preservative, has been found fruitless, and many unhappy persons, who the Day after they had been bit went to dip in the Sea, which the Nearness of the Place made easy to them, have experienced the Uselessness of it, and died mad before the fortieth Day."[82] Gay's poem, published during this epidemic, consciously and satirically, associates the quack cure recommended by the priest with the superstitions of the Catholic Church.

The centerpiece of Gay's satire is an extended and prurient account of the young lady, a diseased Diana at her bath, being hauled to the seashore, stripped, and dunked:

> What virgin had not done as I did?
> My modest hand, by Nature guided,
> Debarr'd at once from human eyes
> The seat where female honour lies,
> And tho thrice dipt from top to toe,
> I still secur'd the post below,
> And guarded it with grasp so fast,
> Not one drop thro' my fingers past;
> Thus owe I to my bashful care
> That all the rage is settled there.

(ll. 110–18)

Gay, superimposing two versions of an antifeminist voyeurism, burlesques the idea of the shy virgin whose "modest hand" tries to cover her genitals from a crowd of onlookers by transforming the nude into a rabid young woman whose "zealous fury" compels her to seek sexual satisfaction.[83] Even the "cure" for her sin—dunking—turns into an erotic and perhaps autoerotic encounter: she guards her genitals "with grasp so fast" that "not one drop through [her] fingers past." The dunking treatment succeeds in firing the imagination of the onlookers and in focusing her "rage" in her genitals, the only part of her body to remain dry.

The idea of the woman protecting her much-visited vagina from the fluids intended to liberate her allows Gay to broaden his satire by suggesting that all men—the statesmen, the fop, and the wit—are similarly "bit" or mad, and similarly defend themselves against the cure by covering their most corruptible parts. "Plunge in a courtier," the speaker says, and he would

Direct his hands to stop his ears.
And now truth seems a grating noise,
He loves the sland'rer's whispering voice;
He hangs on flatt'ry with delight;
And thinks all fulsome praise is right.

(133–38)

This criticism of what Mosca calls "court-dog trickes" links Gay's poem to traditional satires of social parasitism and underscores the performative nature of fragile sexual and social identities. Yet, in "The Mad Dog" as in Rochester's "Ramble," what enables this satiric critique of corruption is the only real role available to women: the bitch in heat. Gay's dog-bite victim makes explicit the connection between rabies and female sexual desire and becomes an unusually overt example of the usually figurative tendency to conflate women and dogs. Like Corinna, Gay's young woman experiences her "disease" not as *canine furiosis* but as *furor uterinus*—as sexual hyperactivity, as desire that cannot be quenched. The woman's mouth and genitalia become virtually indistinguishable. Indeed, the genital "rage" driving her to men parallels a desire to confess that shores up a related economy of pleasure and prurience in which judges, priests, and readers benefit from her sexual transgression.

The judges (waked by wanton thought)
Dive to the bottom of her fault,
They leer, they simper at her shame,
And make her call all things by name.

(ll. 33–36)

In "calling all things by name," the woman stars in a voyeuristic heteronormative and masculinist fantasy. The simpering and leering male figures of legal and ecclesiastical authority "plunge" and "dive" to "the bottom of her fault" in a tautological exercise: they witness the sexual corruption they both seek and provoke. In the final lines of the poem, Gay generalizes from the behavior of this woman to the sex as a whole. Because "All women," he concludes, "dread a wat'ry death," they too will shut their lips when faced with dunking (l. 140). The surreal and obscure image with which the poem ends conflates the cure for rabies, the Catholic confessional, sexual titillation, and gossip:

And though you duck them ne'er so long,
Not one salt drop e'er wets their tongue:
'Tis hence they scandal have at will,
And that this member ne'er lies still.

(ll. 141–44)

To the extent that women preserve their ability to act as the subjects and authors of "scandal," Gay seems to suggest, they are agents in perpetuating a cycle of masculine rivalry and mimetic desire, proof of which is his wagging "member."

Libertine poetry, when read against the context of zoonotic illness, exposes the status of dogs as disease vectors that could release, in still-mysterious ways, the furious into the fashionable, unbridled desire into genteel society. Free-roaming dogs and their female counterparts, bitches, herald the return of atavistic qualities, primarily violence and madness. Even as it celebrates shared biological impulses between humans and canines, libertine writing tends to highlight the venereal qualities of dogs and thus the relationship between sex and violence, and between sex and madness. These satires showcase how rivalries, passion, and mimetic desire drive canid and human behavior in ways that reinforce the sentiment, traceable to Plautus, that *lupus est homo homini* or "Man is a wolf to [his fellow] man." If dogs are to become civilized companions, they must therefore (like the rake) be plucked from the pack like lapdogs. But females dogs, bitches, remain what Serres calls "the universal hostess," the "smooth space, the wax tablet, on which everything can be written"—a "matrix," as he says, "for thinking" (216). Given the gendered parasitical logic underwriting much Restoration literature, it is telling that what many people regard as the first English novel is therefore set outside the city. It contains no women and only a singular dog, rehabilitated, stripped of both canine companions and consorts, already domesticated as his master's best friend. Robinson Crusoe feeds his singular and loyal companion, and the dog guards the crops that ensure Crusoe's prosperity. In such an idealized and companionate relationship, rivalry and parasitism seem to disappear. But as we shall see in the next chapter, while it is possible to flee from the city and its women, the parasite returns in different guises as wolves, cannibals, birds, cats, and bears—and even in the form of Crusoe himself.

CHAPTER 5

What Happened to the Rats?
Hoarding, Hunger, and Storage
on Crusoe's Island

> Glory be to the verminous divine son of God.
>
> —MICHEL SERRES

In 2011, the Nature Conservancy began a two-phase project to eradicate nonnative animals that had been introduced in the seventeenth century to the Galapagos Islands and have been breeding ever since. After removing goats, cats, pigs, and burros, conservationists turned their attention to rats, whose population density had reportedly reached about one rat for every square foot on Pinzón, the main island.[1] In what one newspaper describes as the "biggest raticide in the history of South America," Ecuador began dumping twenty-two tons of poison, designed to kill eighteen million rats, eliminating (if all goes according to plan) the resident rat population by 2020. The ancestors of these doomed Galapagos rats, it is generally accepted, traveled from Europe and colonial South America on trading vessels and pirate ships, and there is strong evidence that, even in the early modern period, colonizing rats already were a significant problem. While there was considerable ambiguity, as we saw in the first chapter, about how rats were implicated in disease, their ability to destroy harvested grain and devastate food systems—especially aboard ships and on islands—was never in doubt. Indeed, European trading ventures and colonial aspirations depended, to a great extent, on (at least) battling vermin to a standstill. Not surprisingly, then, seventeenth- and eighteenth-century accounts dramatize these struggles, often restaging the metaphysical ravages of traditional plague literature, in a seemingly more secular key, as a series of biopolitical management crises. *Robinson Crusoe* similarly deploys vermin in this manner. Defoe transforms them from the ubiquitous threats that slither and crawl through seventeenth-century plague writing to difficult but controllable populations, human and nonhuman; rats, birds, wolves, and hostile indigenes become subject to many of the same disciplinary technologies: traps, toxicants, repellers, barriers, and exclusion.

In the early-modern voyage narratives on which Defoe drew for *Robinson Crusoe*, rats run rampant.[2] Garcilaso de la Vega, as I noted in chapter 1, describes "the incredible multitudes of Rats and Mice" brought to Peru by the Spaniards.[3] In a similar vein, Samuel Clarke recounts the history of a "great Plague" of rats that ravaged the first English plantation in Bermuda.[4] In William Dampier's accounts of his circumnavigations in the 1690s and early 1700s, rodents pose a dire threat to shipboard provisions. Leaving Cape Corrientes for the East Indies, Dampier describes the crew's fear at having their meager provisions ravaged by shipboard rats: "we had not 60 days Provision, at a little more than half a pint of Maiz a day for each man, and no other Provision except 3 Meals of salted *Jew-fish*; and we had a great many Rats aboard, which we could not hinder from eating part of our Maiz."[5] Dampier's fellow buccaneer, Woodes Rogers, who preyed on Spanish shipping along the coasts of Peru and Chile in 1708–9, found that even when he stole grain, it was quickly "much damag'd by the [shipboard] Rats."[6] After Rogers rescued the Scots sailor Alexander Selkirk, marooned for three years on the island of Juan Fernandez off the Chilean coast, he described Selkirk's living conditions. Selkirk was

> much pester'd with Cats and Rats, that had bred in great numbers from some of each Species which had got ashore from Ships that put in there to wood and water. The Rats gnaw'd his Feet and Clothes while asleep, which oblig'd him to cherish the Cats with his Goats-flesh; by which many of them became so tame, that they would lie about him in hundreds, and soon deliver'd him from the Rats.[7]

Before Selkirk semidomesticates the cats as a kind of feline Swiss Guard, rats—reproducing, like the cats, "in great numbers"—threaten to eat him alive. Richard Steele retells Selkirk's story but, in describing the rodent infestation, obscures the shipboard origins of both cats and rats: "His Habitation was extremely pester'd with Rats, which gnaw'd his Cloaths and Feet when sleeping. To defend himself against them, he fed and tamed Numbers of young Kitlings, who lay about his Bed, and preserved him from the En-

emy."[8] Particularly for Steele, a patriotic Englishman rather than a buccaneer, rats figure as "the Enemy" and mark the dark, even verminous side of
an emerging global economy. Transported to islands, vermin disrupt native
ecologies and become integral, if often threatening, components of a new
biopolitical order.

The colonial fantasy of Crusoe's island prosperity depends on the erasure of the threat posed by vermin: the rats that plagued Selkirk, marred
Rogers' pirated grain, and swarm, even three hundred years later, through
the indigenous ecology of the Galapagos. Defoe mentions rats only three
times in *Robinson Crusoe*, all of them in relation to a single bag of grain.
Scouring his shipwrecked vessel for provisions, he finds "a little Remainder
of *European* Corn which had been laid by for some Fowls which we brought
to Sea with us, but the Fowls were kill'd; there had been some Barly and
Wheat together, but, to my great Disappointment, I found afterwards that
the Rats had eaten or spoil'd it all."[9] The bag of grain is chicken-feed; the
shipboard fowl, intended as fresh food for sailors on transoceanic vessels,
have perished in the shipwreck, have already been eaten, or perhaps have
been killed by rats. It is only "afterwards," that Crusoe discovers the bag of
barley and wheat, then salvages the bag of corn that, he supposed, "was all
devour'd with the Rats" (114). Seeing "nothing in the Bag but Husks and
Dust," he shakes it out (114). A month later, miraculously, as he emphasizes, Crusoe sees "some few Stalks of something green, shooting out of the
Ground" (114). The providential preservation of grain against the threat of
hungry rats leads to a meditation on the nature of this agricultural miracle:

> for it was really the Work of Providence as to me, that should order or
> appoint, that 10 or 12 Grains of Corn should remain unspoil'd (when
> the Rats had destroy'd all the rest,) as if it had been dropt from Heaven;
> as also that I should throw it out in that Particular Place, where it be-
> ing in the Shade of a high Rock, it sprang up immediately; whereas, if
> I had thrown it anywhere else at that time, it had been burnt up and
> destroy'd. (115)

Because grain seeds quickly succumb to moisture, whether rain or rodent
urine, Crusoe attributes the fact that a few seeds remained "unspoil'd" to
divine intervention. That the "Work of Providence" secures a suitable ecological niche for the seeds, protected from the effects of the tropical sun,
reaffirms the values and assumptions of a colonial food system.[10] Strangely,

however, the rats that helped themselves to the poultry feed seem simply to have disappeared when the ship washed aground. Unlike Selkirk, then, Crusoe is not "pester'd with" rats.

The near-empty bag of grain reminds us that Crusoe depends on a food system—men grow grain, grain feeds fowl, fowl feed men—extremely vulnerable to rodents, before and after the shipwreck. But that the rats are present only in their absence—in the traces of food they leave behind—leaves unanswered the question posed in my chapter title: what happened to the rats? Other animals prosper on Crusoe's island, as they did on Juan Fernandez. Crusoe is surrounded by goats and cats, but unlike Selkirk, has no rats gnawing on his toes or, later, once he begins harvesting grain, eating his food supplies. This absence of rodents contrasts strikingly to other passages in his work, where Defoe cites historical accounts of rat infestations. In *A Tour thro' the Whole Island of Great Britain*, he characterizes the Island of Rona in the Hebrides, as having been "destroyed" forty years earlier by "first, a Swarm of Rats, none knows how, [that] came into the Island, and eat up all their Corn. In the next Place, some Seamen landed, and robbed them of what Provisions they had left. By this means they all died."[11] Indeed, given the 200 year history of rat infestations in European colonies, the seemingly deliberate erasure of rats on Crusoe's island is noteworthy, if not cognitively jarring. Even if one wanted to credit Defoe with finessing the rat problem by populating Crusoe's island with cats, the math is unconvincing. Cats produce two litters per year, with three to five surviving kittens per litter. At the end of Crusoe's first year on the island, the cat population has grown to between fifty and one hundred cats. Rats, in contrast, are incestuous and interbreed; they produce litters of between ten and twelve offspring; the gestation period lasts only twenty-two days; females can come back into heat an hour after birth; and (unlike cats) they stay in heat all year round. At the end of six months, then, two shipboard rats and their offspring could have produced 77,960 rodents, overrunning the island and wreaking ecological havoc—turning Crusoe's one-man colony into an eighteenth-century Galapagos. This difference in these reproductive rates is why Alexander Selkirk—while "preserved from the Enemy," as Steele writes, by half-feral cats—was miserable, and why, unlike Crusoe, he was starving and impoverished when rescued.[12] The agricultural economy of Crusoe's island depends, in other words, not simply on the providential *presence* of European corn but on the *absence* of the rats that plagued Selkirk and the millions of others across the early modern world, all struggling to protect their grain supplies against rodent infestation.

This point is crucial to understanding the ways that vermin figure in early eighteenth-century literature and its depictions of what we now would call ecology. As with Crusoe's near-empty bag of grain, vermin (real and imagined) are entangled in ecosystemic relationships, ecologies variously characterized as evidence of humankind's fallen nature—think back to Godfrey Goodman's *The Fall of Man, or the Corruption of Nature*—or as proof of God's benevolent design.[13] *Robinson Crusoe* does something a little different. Defoe "exorcises" the "pestiferous" rats (as the 1651 anathema terms them) and populates Crusoe's island with more perfect, more domesticable creatures: goats, a dog, cats, parrots, and human indigenes. Ultimately, the absence of rats reinforces John Bender's view of the novel as "apparitional." In producing a "coherent linguistic version of the real that never has been, is, or will be," Bender argues, the novel creates "a virtual reality possessed of the organic wholeness that the contingency of the lived empirical world cannot possess."[14] To put Bender's idea in ecological terms, the island's imagined environment is not an open, dynamic ecosystem but a closed, zoomorphic world in which Crusoe hunts, gathers, farms, and stores under metaphysically secured conditions.

Within this context, the near-empty bag of rat, chicken, and human food serves a double function: while its mostly consumed contents point in the direction of a food system partly dependent on grain, the bag itself gestures toward a crucial, if seemingly pedestrian, aspect of that food system: the problem of storage. Although tool use on Crusoe's island has received considerable attention, in the age before refrigeration proper food storage was often all that stood between a food-sufficient present and a harvestless future. Storage technology required the ability to imagine that future, to construct a calculus of future needs, and to protect against future shortages through managerial expertise. Because we live in a post-refrigeration culture, it is easy to "read over" the bag of corn in *Robinson Crusoe*; ideologically, we are trained not to perceive the threat of porous boundaries against vermin, moisture, and heat. The chewed-through bag of grain, though, for many eighteenth-century readers, underscores the vulnerability of food supplies. To reimagine that vulnerability, this chapter focuses on food insecurity in Defoe and how his ratless colony grows, through hoarding and proper storage, into an idealized system in which he defends his supplies from the vermin that threaten it.

PROVISIONING AND HOARDING ON CRUSOE'S ISLAND

Crusoe's island has no large predators. The goats and cats multiply without hindrance, and, despite his persistent fears, Crusoe finds himself alone at the top of the food chain. In reflecting on Providence and the "long series of miracles" that cast him on the island, he recognizes that while he "ha[s] no society," he, quite fortunately, encounters "no ravenous Beast, no furious Wolves or Tygers to threaten my Life, no venomous Creatures or poisonous, which I might feed on to my Hurt, no Savages to murther and devour me" (155). Given the absence of predators and "poisonous" creatures on the island, he can divide his efforts between animal husbandry and vermin control. The goats figure as a staple of his diet for twenty-eight years, but much of the novel's drama derives from Crusoe's culling the cats and fending off the birds that attack his grain.

One of the two female cats he rescued from the ship, having run away, returns with three kittens, engenders a population explosion; the cats multiply and annoy him until he "was forc'd to kill them like Vermine or wild Beasts" (133).[15] The fact that he exterminates them "like" vermin suggests how arbitrary boundaries are between different species of animals. Whereas Selkirk "cherish[ed]" his cats with goat meat to protect him from omnivorous rats, Crusoe's cats quickly lose their shipboard use-value—controlling rodent infestations that threaten grain supplies—once Crusoe brings them ashore.[16] Without rats to control, the cats themselves become a type of "Vermine" that stand in sharp contrast to the unnamed (and solitary) dog. Rather than pestering him, the dog, says Crusoe, "was a trusty Servant to me many Years; I wanted nothing that he could fetch me, nor any Company that he could make up to me, I only wanted to have him talk to me, but that would not do" (105). If the dog, in effect, is Friday's predecessor as a companion and servant, the proliferating cats exist outside of this kind of companionate interspecies relationship: they cannot hunt for Crusoe, as the dog does; they cannot fetch what he wants; and they do not provide him with domesticated "Company." Extraneous to the ratless island's economy, the cats may offer a form of resistance to Crusoe's "ideological superiority," as Rajani Sudan has argued, posing a "continual threat to the integrity" of his rule over the island.[17] In terms of his food supply, however, they are primarily a nuisance.

A more direct threat to the hero's sense of well-being comes from the birds indigenous to the island, which compel Crusoe to draw on familiar strategies of vermin control to protect his grain. Page after page in *Robinson Crusoe* deals with his efforts to turn the few seeds he salvaged from the ship into a sustainable crop that he can mill to produce a gustatory reminder of England—white bread. While growing barley and rice, Crusoe charts the advent and duration of the two rainy seasons each year, and he conducts ad hoc experiments to determine the best times to plant his grain crop (at the beginning of each of the rainy seasons).[18] These efforts make him, at least in his own mind, "Master of [his] Business"; he knows "exactly when the proper Season was to sow; and that I might expect two Seed Times, and two Harvests every Year" (135). Part of this mastery turns on his ability to keep devastating animals away from his delicate crop. Crusoe deploys the dog to protect the fledging shoots from goats and hares—"he would stand and bark all Night long" (143)—but the invading birds pose a greater menace, just as they did in England. Indeed, Crusoe's response to the birds recalls the kinds of policies against vermin still being enacted in his homeland. As Keith Thomas notes, vermin hunts mandated under the 1533 Acts of Parliament continued into the eighteenth century; in the late seventeenth century, the widespread use of guns replaced the use of nets and traps.[19] Crusoe's initial tactic of vermin control is to use his gun. Yet when he shoots at the birds in the trees, "there rose up a little Cloud of Fowls, which I had not seen at all, from among the Corn it self" (143). Alarmed, and with his crop already partly despoiled, Crusoe turns to a kind of a Foucauldian exercise, criminalizing the birds determined to invade his property. He deals with the dead birds "as we serve notorious Thieves in *England*": their bodies are "Hang'd . . . in Chains for a Terror to others" (143). This stratagem works so well that the birds "forsook all that Part of the Island, and I could never see a Bird near the Place as long as my Scare-Crows hung there" (143). Crusoe's juridico-political language underscores the extent to which the island's birds are imagined as a criminal threat to property rather than regarded as part of a complex ecological order. Not surprisingly, then, his solution is as much political as it is environmental.

While Crusoe's fear of wolves and cannibals understandably has attracted the lion's share of critical attention, it is worth considering in more detail what is at stake in his efforts to drive away the birds. Ostensibly, Crusoe takes such deadly measures because the birds "in a few Days . . . would devour all my Hopes, that I should be starv'd, and never be able to raise a Crop at all" (143). The image of (future) starvation harks back to Crusoe's initial fears when he was shipwrecked, and it serves as one of the hero's characteristic moments of writerly amnesia, seemingly contradicting what he had written a few pages earlier: "I had no Want of Food, and of that which was very good too; especially . . . Goats, Pidgeons, and Turtle or Tortoise; which, added to my Grapes, *Leaden-hall* Market could not have furnish'd a Table better" (138). Indeed, Crusoe's feasts of goat, pigeon, turtle, and grapes surpass what a Londoner of the middling sort might have considered a hearty meal. The corn crop, however, becomes precious for two reasons. First, it allows Crusoe to replicate more closely a kind of emblematic English meal of meat and bread—an ideological marker of his domestication of the island. Second, the grain (unlike meat and fruit) allows Crusoe to safeguard his food supply from contingencies and weather patterns; animal flesh and seasonal fruits offer a good deal of food security, but the grain can be stored for long periods of time. The corn crop therefore becomes a practical as well as talismanic safeguard against the hero's isolation and the uncertain future he faces.

Provisioning supplies to guard against real and imaginary food threats is an adaptive strategy common to human and nonhuman animals alike. Animal ethologists use the term "food hoarding" to describe the characteristic behaviors of secreting and storing food for future use.[20] As Stephen Vander Wall writes, "Food-hoarding animals have the capacity to control the availability of food in space and time. . . . By permitting animals a measure of control over their food supply, food hoarding has become an important element in adaptive strategies for circumventing problems of food limitation."[21] In the novel, Crusoe's hoarding signifies both the acknowledgement of food insecurity and the exercise of what seventeenth-century commentators would have regarded as an act of corporeal imagination. The root of provision is *providere*, Latin for "foresee"; as its etymology suggests, provisioning turns on acts of imagination, of vision.[22] In English, "provision" can serve as a verb (the act of supplying beforehand) or as a noun (that which is supplied). Outside the Cartesian tradition, various animals were described as capable of anticipating future needs and responding appropriately through acts of embodied imagination. Bacon invokes this faculty in *Sylva Sylvarum* to explain how bees can find their way back to a hive located two or three miles away, and both Thomas Willis and John Locke make analogous arguments for other creatures. While Willis identifies imagination in "less perfect" beings as instinctive, he argues that a corporeal imagination—closely related to memory—operates in higher mammals: it drives a "hungry Horse" from "place to place, till he has found our imagined Pasture, and indeed enjoys that good the Image of which was painted on his brain."[23] For his part, Locke acknowledges that in terms of memory—"the faculty of laying up and retaining the ideas that are brought into the mind"—other "Animals seem to have to a great degree [of that capacity] as well as man."[24] Put simply, (human) "provisioning" is (animal) "hoarding" resituated from an ecological to an economic discourse.

The close relationships among provisioning, hoarding, food insecurity, and imagination perhaps help explain why in Defoe's fiction, from *Robinson Crusoe* on, the accumulation of food against future contingencies seems, at once, prudent, nearly compulsive, and almost totemic, a strategic warding off of psychological distress and channeling deep-seated fears into seemingly productive activities.[25] In popular language, North Americans use the word "hoarding" to describe the pack-rat behaviors of humans who refuse to take for granted an (ostensibly) always-available supply of food, who store up excessive supplies against an imagined future dearth. Whether or not one is a hoarder is determined, in part, by whether or not others agree on whether one's provisioning is timely and measured. At stake in the behavior is never a simple economic principle of accumulation, stripped from any context, but a mixed set of social, psychological, and biological strategies of adaptation to an unpredictable environment. Many of Defoe's works, before and after *Robinson Crusoe*, contain extended accounts of elaborately designed and executed strategies of food storage, and these may attest to differences between our food system and his. In *Due Preparations for the Plague*, for example, Defoe describes the survival of a family in Marseilles during the devastating plague of 1665 when two-thirds of the city's population succumbed to infection. The head of the family, a merchant, furnished himself "with Stores of all sorts of Provisions," including "three Thousand Pound Weight of Biscuit Bread such as is Bak'd for Ships going to Sea, and had it put up in Hogsheads, as if going to be shipp'd off."[26] In addition to bread, wine, and herbs, the magazine also included the "Flesh" of "three Fat Bullocks," "Pickl'd and Barrel'd up, as if done for a Ship going on a long voyage; likewise six barrels of Pork for the same pretended Occasion" (68–69). The merchant and his family survive by treating their predicament as though they were pressed to endure the isolation and dietary self-sufficiency of an extended sea voyage. They eat what sailors in the early eighteenth-century ate—hardtack and pickled meat, both provisions that have incredibly long shelf-lives. Defoe presents the merchant's preparations as an emblem of both his foresight and his moral virtue.

The strategies that allow the Marseilles family to survive the plague are a staple of Defoe's fiction in which different degrees of food insecurity are part of the human condition. In *Robinson Crusoe*, the hero describes his chief employment as curing his raisins, then planting barley and rice, his goal being to have a "good Quantity" of bread "for Store, and to secure a constant Supply" (144). After a while, he devotes himself almost exclusively to bread making, employing all his "Study" and "Hours of Working" in creating the fences, instruments, and utensils required for bread making and seed storage, by which Crusoe imagines he can control an always uncertain future.[27] Crusoe's compulsive food-hoarding and the merchant's plague preparations reappear in different guises elsewhere in Defoe's work, often in relation to severe climatic conditions. In *Farther Adventures of Robinson Crusoe*, Crusoe describes long-term planning as a necessary strategy to cope with the Siberian winter: "Our Food was chiefly the Flesh of Deer dry'd and cured in the Season; good Bread enough, but bak'd as Biskets; dry'd Fish of several Sorts. . . . All the Stores of Provision for the Winter are laid up in the Summer, and well cur'd" (208). Salting and drying meat become a mark of prudence and, almost invariably in Defoe, an occasion for economic moralizing. In his final novel, *A New Voyage Round the World*, Defoe's sailors spend thirteen days on Juan Fernandez—Selkirk's island—to supply the ship for a cruising (or really privateering) voyage along the coasts of Chile before sailing south and east around Cape Horn and into the Atlantic. During their stay on the island, they "kill'd three hundred and seventy goats"; and the unnamed narrator tells us, "our Men who were on Board [the ships] were very merrily'd employ'd," and "did very little but *roast* and *stew*, and *broil* and *fry* from Morning to Night."[28] During the voyage proper, sailors kill cows, goats, deer, seals, and penguins, then salt the meat in order to season and preserve it. These preparations turn necessary fare into, as the narrator says of salted penguin, "a very wholesome Diet" (226). Food production for the voyage requires what Defoe calls "an exceeding Supply" (142) of all kinds of provisions, provisions that serve as insurance against the hardships that befell ships on transoceanic voyages. At sea and on land, such provisioning is a measure of moral probity and economic utility extending far beyond Crusoe's island.

"Reason" is the name Defoe gives to the economic logic behind his high-level food-hoarding activities, and he takes great pains to distinguish his responses to food insecurity from the presumably instinctual behavior of other species. While both humans and animals, as we have seen, can defer pleasure for the sake of a perceived future safety, Defoe declares that without the supplementary capacity of reason, humans would perish in a postlapsarian world of scarcity and Hobbesian aggression. "MAN," he writes in *Essays upon Several Projects*, "is the worst of all God's Creatures to shift for himself":

> no other Animal is ever starv'd to death; Nature, without, has provided them both with Food and Cloaths; and Nature within, has plac'd an Instinct that never fails to direct them to proper means for a supply; but Man must either *Work or Starve, Slave or Dye*; he has indeed Reason given to direct him, and few who follow the dictates of that Reason come to such unhappy Exigencies.[29]

While Defoe presses this presumed contrast between humans and other animals into the service of an argument about the importance of savings and pensions, it also describes the situation in which Crusoe finds himself: even with the benefit of an environmentally hospitable and rodent-free island, Crusoe must "*Work or Starve.*" While he may share hoarding behaviors with rats, the *complexity* of Crusoe's food-hoarding behaviors is, according to the logic of the novel, animated by the dictates of God-given reason and evidence, as Willis might put it, of a rational, rather than merely sensitive, soul.

The role of technology in distinguishing human reason from animalistic instinct is underscored in *Mere Nature Delineated; or, a Body Without a Soul*. Unlike other predators, Defoe writes, a human has no teeth or claws to "tear and devour."[30] Instead, says Defoe, God, "to supply all these by the Authority of his Person," provides man with a techno-physiological advantage: "an Awe of him is placed upon the Beasts and he has Hands given him, first to make, and then to make Use of, Weapons, both to rule [animals] for his Safety, and to destroy them for his Food." In such instances, Defoe sounds very much like Willis, for whom human difference is defined almost exclusively in terms of some presumably intrinsic Crusoean ingenuity: "Brutes know not Rights or Laws of Political Society," Willis asserts, "they make no Fires or Houses, nor find out any Mechanical Arts, they put not on Clothes, nor dress their food, yea unless taught by Imitation."[31] Defoe's version of this argument in *Mere Nature Delineated* is that human exceptionalism rests in tool use, without which, he insists, humans "will either be torn with wild Beasts (even Dogs would devour [them]) or [they] would be frozen to Death with Cold, or drench'd to Death with Water and Rain" (7). Indeed, the morphology of the human body—its *lack* of the sharp teeth and claws of predators—demonstrates that humans are superior to other creatures;

human anatomy "denies them the Honour of being Beasts in Form," he continues, "and in the ordinary Functions of sensitive Life, whatever they will be in practice" (12). From this perspective, Crusoe's gun and knife, in particular, are crucial to his efforts to establish and maintain his species identity as well as his sense of a civilized selfhood. Echoing a sentiment in *Mere Nature Delineated*, Crusoe insists on the importance of the knife in distinguishing him from "savages" and "beasts": "I should have liv'd, if I had not perish'd, like a meer Savage. That if I had kill'd a Goat, or a Fowl, by any Contrivance, I had no way to flea or open them, or part the Flesh from the Skin and the Bowels, or to cut it up; but must gnaw it with my Teeth, and pull it with my Claws, like a Beast" (53). In this imagined scene, cutting, as Derek Hughes claims, "divides man from the beast."[32]

And yet, this presumed difference—like that between "hoarding" and "provisioning"—is notoriously unstable. From a broader perspective, Defoe's human is more properly defined, in Michel Serres's phrase, as "the master of mediations," using traps, nets, guns, spears, horses, dogs, and "Scare-crows" to assert dominance over other species.[33] Being "Master of every Mechanick Art" also means transforming the food supply so that what one eats no longer resembles the food of beasts. Defoe argues in *A General History of Trade* that animals are "not to be Devoured, as one Wild Beast Devour[s] and Prey[s] upon another, but to be Kill'd, separated from the Filth, Blood, Hide, and Uneatable Parts, and then Prepar'd, Drest, and made Palatable."[34] According to Defoe, the "meer Savage" and the "Beast" are incapable of separating the edible "flesh" from the inedible "skin" and "bowels" of their prey. Whereas they take their food as they find it—bleeding and raw—civilized "man," in Defoe's writing, eats animal flesh only after it has been cooked or "dressed."[35] Cutting, then, occupies a place along a spectrum of other transformations: fish are dried and salted; cows are pickled; and goats, deer, and even penguins, are salted and preserved. At times, Defoe turns these dietary practices into an admonition. In *Due Preparations*, Defoe insists civilized humans must avoid eating meat that is "almost Raw," a predilection he associates with "*Tartars*," cannibals, and dogs (44). He tries to shame his fellow Britons about their less than civilized tastes:

[I]f we were but to be seen by the People of any other Country how we Eat, especially our Wild Fowl, the Flesh scarce warm thro', and all the undigested Impurities of the Entrails and Inside of them serving for our sauce. I say, when Strangers see us feeding thus, they must be allowed to take us, as they do, to be, if not Canibals, yet a sort of people that have a canine Appetite; and it was the modestest Thing I could expect of them, when in Foreign Countries I have heard them describe our way of Feeding in *England*, and tell us that we *Devour* our meat, but do not Eat it; *viz*. Devour it as the Beasts of Prey do their Meat with the Blood running between their Teeth. (44-45)

Such passages about feeding practices have a double function in Defoe's works: they scold his countrymen and women for their brutish, "canine" appetites and they try to reinforce distinctions between the "raw" and the "cooked," between "savage" and "civilized" behavior. Ethnic distinctions—Englishmen versus cannibals—are entangled in the logic of species differentiation.[36]

Much of *Robinson Crusoe*, correspondingly, is concerned with a range of domestic duties: planting, harvesting, drying, curing, weaving, roasting, and baking (157). So central is provisioning to Defoe's psycho-economics that Crusoe builds up supplies despite the God-given sustenance that the island provides: "I had great Cause for Thankfulness, that I was not driven to any Extremities for Food; but rather Plenty, even to Dainties" (138). Having secured his grain against goats, hares, and birds, Crusoe is able to produce "forty Bushels of Barley and Rice" at each harvest, "much more than I could consume in a Year." Yet this surplus is treated as an unmitigated good, a sign of his prosperity and security. Forecasting the likely return for his labor, Crusoe decides "to sow just the same Quantity every Year, that I sow'd the last, in Hopes that such a Quantity would fully provide me with Bread, &c." (148). The "&c." is suggestive; if we take Crusoe at his word, he is harvesting each year "much more" than he eats, and his supplies, therefore, are increasing annually. His grain stores become emblematic of the rationalized status of food hoarding on the island; overproduction is not only a mark of prudence but of providential favor, particularly in the years before Friday's appearance.

For us, Crusoe's planting, provisioning, and hoarding may verge on a compulsive set of behaviors; J. M. Coetzee's redaction of the hero in *Foe* (1986) focuses on the less-productive but just as obsessive terrace building. But these practices allow Crusoe to solve—at least fictionally—a critical problem in early eighteenth-century England. The provisioning of grain was, in the words of one historian, "among the most serious of problems faced by local and state government in preindustrial England."[37] Because a bad harvest or difficult winter could cause prices to double within a matter of months, grain storage was a hotly contested political issue that often pitted grain merchants against the poor, artisans living in towns, and those, in general, who did not grow their own food.[38] Grain prices and bad weather were problems intermittently throughout the seventeenth century. As Defoe's contemporary, Charles Davenant, wrote, "in England, in a plentiful years, there is not above five months stock of grain at the time of the succeeding harvest, and not above four months in an indifferent year, which is but a slender provision against any evil accident."[39] Compounding this problem of "slender provision" was wastage: an estimated twenty to thirty percent of grain supplies, even during a good year, were lost to smutting and rodents.[40] On Crusoe's island, however, provisioning against an "evil accident" seems to lessen the prospect of disaster each year because the hero's supplies show net increases that ensure his prosperous, if isolated, future.

While Crusoe's penchant for storing more than he can consume carries Reason to ecological and economic extremes, it exhibits the paradoxical logic of food-hoarding underwriting mercantile capitalism: *through excess, moderation.* Even as Crusoe continues to grow his food reserves, he admits his "thoughts run many times upon the Prospect of Land, which [he] had seen from the other Side of the Island" (148–49). The surplus Crusoe builds year after year attests to the animal foresight that Defoe depicts as uniquely human. In this regard, provisioning constitutes the precondition, means, and ends under which "the human" fully, if tautologically, emerges. Through hoarding, Crusoe arrives at a humanity denied to vermin, predators, and the savages who invade his island.

"HUNGER KNOWS NO FRIEND"

Robinson Crusoe's adventures do not end when he leaves the island. Several months after Defoe published the *Strange Surprizing Adventures*, the sequel, *The Farther Adventures of Robinson Crusoe* (1719) appeared. Through the end of the nineteenth century, the *Farther Adventures* was reprinted regularly with the first volume and had a significant publication history in its own right.[41] After seven years in England, Crusoe and his nephew board a merchant ship bound for the East Indies, with the intention to stop at his "Colony" off the coast of northern South America on the way and resupply it with skilled tradesmen and provisions.[42] En route, they encounter an English ship, driven from Barbados "a few Days before she was ready to sail, by a terrible Hurricane" (21), so before it was fully staffed and provisioned. With its masts severely damaged and its captain and first mate on shore, the ship's skeletal crew has no way to navigate. By the time Crusoe finds them, the crew and their passengers have had no "Bread and Flesh" for at least eleven days. Hearing this tale from the second mate and six sailors who make their way to his vessel, Crusoe resolves to visit the stricken ship and see the "Scene of Misery" for himself. There he encounters a tableau out of seventeenth-century famine literature. The three passengers, a "Youth and his Mother and a Maid-Servant," having been left for dead in their cabin, are in a "Condition that their Misery is very hard to describe" (22). Nonetheless, Crusoe's relation goes on at some length and furnishes his readers with a gruesome object lesson in what happens when provisions are destroyed.

The "poor Mother," a woman of sense and "good Breeding," sits on the floor, her back to the wall and her "Head sunk in between her shoulders, like a Corpse, tho' not quite dead" (24). She revives briefly when she is given some broth, but only to indicate by "Signs" that they should minister to her starving child instead. Her son, who "was preserv'd at the Price of his most affectionate Mother's Life," lies in a bed with a piece of old glove in his mouth, "having eaten up the rest of it" (24). The starving maid sprawls on the deck beside her mistress "like one in the last Agonies of Death" (25); terrified by the prospect of her demise, the maid is nevertheless "brokenhearted for her Mistress, who she saw dying two or three Days before, and who she lov'd most tenderly" (25). Such graphic images of starvation, as we have seen in plague literature, were often deployed theologically to remind humans of their intrinsic corruption and the prospect of eternal suffering.[43] Here, in contrast, the passengers and crew on the foundering ship are victims of misfortune rather than perpetrators of excess or evil. In fact, emphasizing the contingent, even arbitrary, nature of their suffering, Crusoe describes the victims as the most "innocent" creatures on the ship: a "poor Mother" willing to die for her son, a "well-bred Modest and sensible Youth," and a "poor Maid" (24, 25).

Even before Crusoe returns to the island, then, this horrific scene emphasizes the fundamental truth of shipboard travel and even everyday life: that food supplies are always contingent, subject to spoilage, bad luck, bad weather, and vermin. And because the maid and mother are "innocents," Defoe reintroduces, in a different context, the moral function of proper provisioning: to preserve the fragile boundary between savage and civilized behavior.

Under the conditions that Crusoe finds on the stricken ship, the characters' humanity, rather than their faith, is put to the question. The mother demonstrates her willingness to preserve her son by her own deprivation, but for Defoe, such self-sacrifice cannot be taken for granted. Indeed, much later in the narrative, the maid provides an extended account of her struggles with starvation and her powerful impulse towards self-preservation. Right before he leaves the island for good in the middle of *Farther Adventures*, Crusoe interrupts his narrative to allow Susan, the maid, to tell "one Story more" about her ordeal (115). Deprived of broth, bread, or even an old glove, Susan relates in horrifying specificity the suffering that culminates in an impulse to eat human flesh and drink human blood. During five days without food, she descended through "very great Hunger," through "the extremity of Famine," and to a grim cycle of affliction: "sick, sleepy, eagerly hungry, Pain in the Stomach, then ravenous again, then sick again, then lunatick, then crying, then ravenous again" (117). Describing herself as "twice raging mad as any Creature in *Bedlam*," she falls down, striking her nose against a bed; some of her blood is captured in a nearby basin. The next day, in a fit of "violent Hunger," she almost turns cannibal: "I got up ravenous and, in a most dreadful Condition. Had my Mistress been dead, as much as I loved her, I am certain, I should have eaten a Piece of her Flesh, with as much Relish, and as unconcerned, as ever I did the Flesh of any Creature appointed for Food; and once or twice I was going to bite my own Arm" (117). Instead, however, of declining into the "savagery," Susan catches sight of the basin with her blood in it: "I ran to it, and swallow'd it with such Haste, and such a greedy Appetite, as if I had wonder'd no Body had taken it before, and afraid it should be taken from me now" (117). Although soon the thought of drinking her blood "fill'd [her] with Horror," she admits that "it check'd the Fit of Hunger, and I drank a Draught of fair Water, and was compos'd and refresh'd for some Hours after it" (117).

Although Willis and others argued that blood (and especially blood of the "more perfect creatures") was a valuable source of nutrition, Susan's compulsion to drink her own blood both preserves her life and marks her descent into bestial behavior.[44] One moral of her gruesome story seems to be that the exogamous, highly mediated eating practices that characterize civilized behavior are themselves partially dependent on food security having been ensured. Defoe repeatedly stages, in different and often empathetic ways, dramatic scenes of near-starvation, the extreme and difficult choices they provoke, and how "ravenous" eating must be modulated through what he sometimes calls "self-command." In this case, the starving sailors are described as "ravenous": the men "rather devour'd than eat [the food]; they were so exceedingly hungry, that they were in a kind ravenous, and had no Command of themselves; and two of them eat with so much Greediness, that they were in Danger of their Lives the next Morning" (22). But the mother, her son, Susan, and the starving crew also illustrate a lesson about the nature of compassion. The "Sight of these Peoples Distress," Crusoe writes, "was very moving to me, and brought to Mind what I had a terrible Prospect of at my first coming on Shore in the Island, where I had neither the least Mouthful of Food, or any Prospect of procuring any; besides the hourly Apprehension I had of being made the Food of other Creatures" (23). Now, however, his own ship properly provisioned, Crusoe characterizes the foundering boat as a "Subject for our Humanity to work upon"; it offers an opportunity for him to exhibit his fellow-feeling and generosity, sharing with the passengers a substantial portion of his well-stocked magazine without expectation of profit or reward (21).[45]

Indeed, food insecurity, whether through bad luck or bad judgment, undermines one's ability to sympathize or empathize with the suffering of others. Several times during the voyage back to his island, Crusoe absolves the famished sailors of blame for having abandoned the three passengers to starvation or at least tries to justify their actions by emphasizing their equivalent "Distress": "The Seamen being reduced to such an extreme Necessity themselves had no Compassion, we may be sure, for the poor Passengers" (22). A few paragraphs later, he reports the Mate's confession that the crew had "wholly neglected" the passengers only because "their own Extremities [were] so great" (23). This qualified absolution establishes a causal relationship between a lack of compassion and a lack of food. Crusoe again reinforces the point when, at the end of the scene, the seventeen-year-old son begs to be taken aboard Crusoe's ship, claiming that the "cruel Fellows had murther'd his Mother" (25). Crusoe agrees with him, but mitigates any sense of moral culpability on the part of these "cruel Fellows":

And indeed so they had [murdered the mother], that is to say, *passively*; for they might ha' spar'd a small Sustenance to the poor helpless Widow, that might have preserv'd her Life, tho it had been but just to keep her alive. But Hunger knows no Friend, no Relation, no Justice, no Right, and therefore is remorseless, and capable of no Compassion. (25)

In one respect, Crusoe's generalization about the nature of hunger is contra-
dicted by what he finds on board the ship: the mother, after all, had sacrificed
her own life to preserve her son's. But his grim observation—"Hunger knows
no Friend"— also underscores, in dramatic fashion, his view that there is
often a gap opened by the demands of the corporeal soul for food and the
desires of the incorporeal one to embrace humane and civil virtues: kinship,
justice, and compassion. One's "humanity" is determined by the choices one
makes within a world sometimes, if not usually, characterized by the break-
down of sociopolitical, technological, and cultural relations that themselves
depend on the cultivation, proper storage, and distribution of food.

PREDATORS, BEES, AND PLANTATION POLITICS

For Defoe, as for his contemporary Bernard Mandeville, all creatures are
driven by appetite, although the force and quality of that drive is species
specific. The "fiercest Appetite that Nature has given [animals] is Hunger,"
Mandeville asserts. "Nature" has endowed "Beasts of Prey" with a "much
keener Appetite" than herbivores—a fierce desire (akin to sex) leading them
to "crave, trace, and discover" "good Food," along with an instinct "that teaches them to shun, conceal themselves, and run away from those that hunt after them."[46] Competing needs for food and safety mean that predators often
go about with "empty Bellies"—with an appetite that "becomes a constant
fuel to their Anger" (cv). Mandeville's ravenous predators, driven by their
"piercing" hunger and forced to "fatigue, harass and expose [themselves] to
Danger" (civ) for every bite, have much in common with the "beasts of prey"
appearing throughout the Crusoe trilogy. At the end of *Robinson Crusoe*,
Friday wrestles a bear in the Pyrenees, after which he and Crusoe drive off
a pack of wolves. In both episodes, Defoe emphasizes the predators' hunger: although men are rarely the "proper Prey" of bears, their behavior is
unpredictable when driven by hunger (275); the wolves come down from
snow-covered mountains into bordering forests and towns when their empty stomachs require them to hunt for prey. Being "excessively hungry and
raging on that account," "furious" wolves, incited by the smell of the horses,
have become "sensless of Danger" and are only with difficulty killed or driven
off by volleys of gunfire. Crusoe, in contrast, says, "I was never so sensible
of Danger in my Life": "seeing above three hundred Devils come roaring and

open-mouth'd to devour us, and having nothing to shelter us, or retreat to, I gave myself over for lost" (282). After escaping the wolves, he vows never to return to those mountains, claiming that he had rather "go a thousand Leagues by Sea, though I was sure to meet with a Storm once a Week" (282). What Crusoe describes in the Pyrenees is a weather-sensitive system populated by opportunistic carnivores sometimes driven by uncontrollable appetites. The violence of encounters between hot-blooded creatures (human or otherwise) is precisely what his colony, with its nascent infrastructure of agriculture and storage, is intended to prevent.

In *Farther Adventures*, Defoe recasts the dynamics of hunger, predation, and vermin control under the ideological shadow of a colonialist enterprise.[47] At the end of the first volume of the trilogy, Crusoe had left behind on the island seventeen Spaniards, five Englishmen, Friday's father, six slaves, some women, and a few firearms. In his absence, this fledgling colony is forced to deal with the arrival of two hundred and fifty Indians. Defoe's lengthy description of this encounter (as it is described to him) emphasizes the ways in which these "invaders" threaten fragile food systems and supplies. In the first two counterattacks, the colonists kill or wound about 180, then burn the canoes, fearing that the survivors (much like shipboard rats) would return with "multitudes" to "desolate the Island, and starve" the Europeans (69). Even after their victories, the colonists remain confronted by seventy or so fearful, desperate, and hungry men roaming the island, "like wild Beasts," damaging crops and property (70): they "trod all the Corn under-foot; tore up the Vines and Grapes, being just then almost ripe, and did to our Men inestimable Damage" (70). The colonists, with "their Provision . . . destroy'd, and their Harvest spoile'd," find themselves in "very bad Circumstances," with no idea "what to do, or which Way to turn themselves" (71). Drawing an explicit parallel between the scavenging Indians and the vermin that threatened him and his first grain crops more than thirty years earlier, Crusoe recasts the plight of the colonists in terms of both infestation and predation: "I look'd upon their Case to have been worse, at this Time, than mine was at any Time, after I first discover'd the Grains of Barley and Rice, and got into the Manner of planting and raising my Corn, and my tame Cattle; for now they had, as I may say, a hundred Wolves upon the Island, which would devour every Thing they could come at, yet could hardly be come at themselves" (71). Significantly, although Crusoe's language recalls his encounters with wolves, carnivorous predators, at the end of *Strange Surpriz-*

ing Adventures, the strategies the hero subsequently describes are designed less to exterminate the indigenes en masse than to reduce their potentially lupine-like violence to a problem of pest containment.

Linking the Indians to vermin, Crusoe's struggling colonists recast agricultural and ecological threats—in this case, crop destruction—as a military problem with a two-step solution: violence to terrorize and starve the surviving Indians, and subsequent managerial control to produce docile dependents. Having "daily hunt[ed] and harass[ed]" the Indians, killing as many as "they could come at, till they had reduced their Number" (71), the colonists drive the survivors to the island's "hollow Places" where they live hungry and miserable: "they reduced them to the utmost Misery for want of Food, and many were afterwards found dead in the Woods, without any Hurt, but merely starv'd to Death" (71). The second-generation colonists treat the Indians much as Crusoe treated the goats and cats during his first stay on the island, subjecting them through controlled starvation and tactical reward. Thus, with their lives and food supplies no longer threatened, the colonists, moved by pity, offer the remaining Indians a part of the island to inhabit, corn to plant, and some bread to keep them alive until they can harvest their first crop. In return, the Indians are forced to "keep in their own Bounds" and "not come beyond it to injure or prejudice others" (72). Coerced into becoming primitive agriculturists, supplied with bread, rice cakes, three live goats, and later knives and other tools, the thirty-seven remaining "Wretches," "confin'd to a Neck of Land, surrounded with high Rocks behind them" (172) lived as "the most subjected innocent Creatures that were ever heard of" (73). Crusoe banished the rats, culled the cats, drove off the crows, and tamed the goats in the first volume; employing similar strategies in the second, the colonists humble and make "tractable" potentially verminous humans, eventually teaching them, as he says, "how to plant and live upon their daily Labour" (172)—that is, how to accept integration into the plantation economy.[48]

Crusoe's insistence that the formerly verminous Indians have achieved, through farming, a kind of innocence is in keeping with seventeenth-century agricultural treatises that characteristically invoked an entire bestiary to describe the significance, naturalness, and moral superiority of farmers' labors. Abraham Cowley, in his influential essay, "On Agriculture," declares that farmers "live upon an estate given them by their mother . . . like sheep and kine," in contrast to "others" (presumably city dwellers and civil servants) who live on resources "cheated from their brethren . . . like wolves and foxes, by the acquisitions of rapine."[49] Cowley's imagery anticipates the logic of Crusoe's colony, where the major structuring difference between producers and consumers is figured in animal terms; indeed, Cowley's distinction between "useful" and "pernicious" members of the human-animal kingdom operated as a familiar—almost clichéd—basis for seventeenth-century writers to imagine an efficient and self-regulating agricultural economy. The theologian and mathematician Isaac Barrow linked predators and vermin in his posthumously published work, *Of Industry*, declaring that "a noble heart will disdain to subsist like a drone upon the hony gathered by others labour; like a vermine to filtch its food out of the publick granary; or like a shark to prey on the lesser fry; but will, one way or other earn his subsistence; for he that doth not earn, can hardly own his bread."[50] For Barrow, drones, vermin, and sharks are alike in their apparently willful refusal to "earn" their "bread' by working willingly for a communal good as well as for personal benefit; Defoe simply provides a primer for how, on a global scale, human vermin can be transformed in ways that make possible the colonial ideal of "innocent" and beneficial labor.[51]

And here one finally encounters bees. Whereas the teeming, thronging, and swarming movements of hungry crows, cannibals, and wolves threaten Crusoe's well-being, bees and their spatially organized hives helped to define, for him as for others, a cultural ideal of provisioning, prosperity, and political order. Impressed by the design and construction of the now-pacified Indians' highly efficient basket houses, the colonists, before Crusoe returns to the island, "got the wild Savages to come and do the like for them" (73). Crusoe reports on his arrival that the "two *English* Mens Colonies . . . look'd, at a Distance, as if they liv'd all like Bees in a Hive" (73). This simile draws upon the long tradition of georgic literature, going back to Hesiod, in which bees were cast as Nature's artificers, capable of producing their own government. As Danielle Allen has argued, "in all periods, the bees' hive was used to exemplify perfect political order, whether that was taken to be monarchic (Virgil), communitarian (Christian writers), or egalitarian (some French revolutionaries)."[52] Pliny, Aristotle, and Virgil had sung the praises of the bees for their sense of government in subordinating individual desire to the common good. Their "love of flowers, and glory in creating honey," as Virgil put it, is the foundation for the hive's prosperity: although individual bees have short lives, "the species remains immortal, and the fortune of the hive/ is good for many years, and grandfathers' grandfathers are counted."[53] In *Henry V*, the war-mongering Canterbury articulates the political lessons that bees embody. They are defined by their "Obedience" as "Creatures that by a rule in nature teach/ The act of order to a peopled kingdom."[54]

In anthropomorphizing bees as magistrates, merchants, masons, soldiers, citizens, and porters, Canterbury describes a hierarchical order that descends from a supposedly male monarch to "the lazy yawning drone" (I.ii.203). "Order," writes Allen, "consists precisely of functional differentiation" determined in relation to the all-important task of the hive: to produce and store sufficient food for the winter (88). Later in the seventeenth century, the Cambridge Neoplatonist Henry More singles out bees (along with elephants) to further his argument that there is "no *Evil* but *Good* in the *Animal* Life" because each species exhibits in its nature the wisdom of a Divine creator: peacocks exhibit a love of praise, storks natural affection for their offspring, and domesticated dogs a principle of altruism. The "Political order and government in the Commonwealth of Bees," More continues,

> is not only noted by great naturalists . . . but vulgarly known to every Countreyman that has Hives in his garden; where he may observe, how some one Bee by his humming, as by the sound of a Trumpet, awakes the rest to their work; how fitly the whole Company distribute the several tasks of *Mellification* amongst themselves; how severe punishers they are of *Drones*, ejecting them out of their Hives; how loyal they are to their King or Captain, moving as he moves, and sustaining him with their own bodies when he is weary with flying.[55]

For More, like Shakespeare, the "Commonwealth of Bees" depends on both the "loyalty" of worker bees to their "King or Captain," but also on the shared project of "*Mellification*," or producing the honey that sustains the colony.[56] Bees are a model of social order and government, then, precisely because they are highly efficient hoarders, mobilizing to sustain a polity defined in terms of the production, storage, and defense of a vulnerable food supply.[57] As Virgil puts it, "They alone . . . in summer, remembering the winter to come, / Undergo labour, storing their gains for all."[58] For More and his contemporaries, humans can learn from bees, these masters of corporeal imagination and foresight, that cooperative food production and storage are the primary means of self- and species-preservation.

Crusoe's commitment to the Georgic tradition is embodied in his admiring and lengthy description of the colony's architecture, which resembles a human apiary: catching sight of the Englishmen's houses, he remarks "at a Distance," it looked "as if they liv'd all like Bees in a Hive."[59] The form of the colonists' housing mirrors its primary function—to protect and preserve their fragile food stores. The Indians made both the houses and fences, "raddling or working" the dried plants "up like Basket-work all the way round, which was a very extraordinary Piece of Ingenuity" (73). The "Basket-work" of native materials underscores the bee-like self-sufficiency of these enclosures, and while the human apiary "look'd very odd," Crusoe remarks, the basket-work houses constituted "an exceeding good Fence, as well against Heat, as against all Sorts of Vermine" (73). Together the houses demonstrate that the colonists have escaped their former statuses as vermin, predators, or scavengers and have transitioned, collectively, into a working polis, a human instantiation of More's "Commonwealth of Bees."

Similarly, the house inhabited by Will Atkins—who, we are told, has become "a very industrious necessary and sober fellow" (73)—stands as the architectural apotheosis of the agro-colonial ideal. Defoe provides far more detail about this "Great Bee Hive" than does about the cave-like habitation in which he dwelled for over twenty years:

> [The house] was 120 Paces round in the out-side, as I measur'd by my Steps; the Walls were as close work'd as a Basket in Pannels, or Squares of 32 in Number, and very strong, standing about seven Foot high; in the middle was another, not above 22 Paces round, but built stronger, being Eight-square in its Form, and in the eight Corners stood eight very strong Posts, round the top of which he laid strong Pieces pinn'd together with wooden Pins, from which he rais'd a Piramid for the Roof of eight Rafters, very handsome I assure you, and join'd together very well, tho' he had no Nails, and only a few Iron Spikes. . . . after he had pitch'd the Roof of his inner-most Tent, he work'd it up between the Rafters with Basket-work, so firm, and thatch'd that over again so ingeniously with Rice-Straw, and over that a large Leaf of a Tree, which cover'd the Top, that his house was as dry as if it had been til'd or slated. Indeed he own'd that the Savages made the Basket-work for him.
>
> The outer Circuit was cover'd, as a Lean too, all round this inner Appartment, and long Rafters lay from the two and thirty Angles to the top Posts of the inner House, being about 20 Foot Distant, so that there was Space like a Walk within the outer Wicker-Wall, and without the inner, near 20 Foot wide.
>
> The inner Place he partition'd off with the same Wicker-work, but

much fairer, and divided it into six Appartments, so that he had six Rooms on a Floor; and out of every one of these there was a Door, first into the Entry or Coming into the Main-tent, and another Door into the Space or Walk that was round it; so that Walk was also divided into six equal Parts, which serv'd not only for Retreat, but to store up any Necessaries which the Family had Occasion for. These six Spaces not taking up the whole Circumference, what other Appartments the outer Circle had, were thus order'd: As soon as you were in at the Door of the outer Circle, you had a short Passage straight before you to the Door of the inner House, but on either Side was a wicker Partition, and a Door in it, by which you went, first, into a large Room or Store-house, 20 Foot wide, and about 30 Foot long, and thro' that into another not quite so long; so that in the outer Circle was ten handsome Rooms, six of which were only to be come at thro' the Apartments of the inner Tent, and serv'd as Closets or retiring Rooms to the respective Chambers of the inner Circle, and four large Warehouses or Barns, or what you please to call them, which went in thro' one another, two on either Hand of the Passage, that led thro' the outer Door to the inner Tent.

Such a piece of Basket-Work, I believe, was never seen in the World, nor a House or Tent, so neatly contriv'd, much less, so built. In this great Beehive liv'd the three Families. (73–75)

Although a beehive is composed of a series of regular hexagons and Will Atkins' house is an octagon subdivided into large and small apartments, both structures adhere to a strict geometric architecture. Hives protect bees and their food supplies from heat and moisture, while channeling movement into and from the hive and the outside world. In his account of the beehive later in the eighteenth century, Oliver Goldsmith anthropomorphizes apid architecture and the putative architects: "These lodgings have spaces, like streets, between them, large enough to give the bees a free passage in and out; and yet narrow enough to preserve the necessary heat. The mouth of every cell is defended by a border, which makes the door a little less than the inside of the cell, which serves to strengthen the whole."[60] Images such as this one naturalize an extended analogy between the biopolitics of bees and humans. The multifunctional and hyperefficient internal structure of the hive becomes a kind of disciplinary mechanism: according to Goldsmith, the "cells serve for different purposes: for laying up their young; for their wax, which in winter becomes a part of their food; and for their honey, which makes their principal subsistence" (71). With its living quarters, storerooms, antechambers, and passageways, Atkins' "Great Beehive" exhibits a similar kind of multifaceted order that, in its efficient procurement and storing of provisions, embodies and reinscribes the principles of an ordered state.[61]

The precondition of the apid state is hunger: its solution, industry; its outcome, morality. In his commentary on Aesop's *Fables*, John Trusler claims "the hive is a significant emblem of industry, it being the store-house, where the bees lay up their provision for the winter." Trusler then turns "industry," intensive labor, into a kind of trans-species ideal. "Industry," he continues, "is the straight line to retirement, for the diligent man maketh rich."[62] In *The Grumbling Hive*, Mandeville's argument about industry is more complex, but he begins by describing it as a response to "Hunger": "a dreadful Plague no doubt / Yet who digests or thrives without?" In his poem, "Insects" who "lived like Men" demonstrate how private vices lead to public good. Although Mandeville's poem is sometimes read satirically, within the context of early modern bestiaries, any comparison between men and bees signaled an attempt to define humans and their political relations in ways outside of, or tangential to, a Hobbesian zoography, dominated by predators and prey. If, the logic goes, all animals are driven by hunger and compete with each for food, and if hot-blooded animals (like dogs, wolves, and humans) are especially destructive in this regard, humans might do well to take a lesson from bees who, in their ability to convert natural resources, nonviolently, into food that sustains rather than destroys the hive, are not so much *anti-vermin* as *non-vermin*. By virtue of functional differentiation as workers, drones, and queens directed towards the shared goal of thoughtful provision, bees demonstrate how to arrive at communal plenty: through excess of industry, bees arrive at moderation.

Atkins's beehive house, then, is proof, presumably, of progress, of how far the colonists have come since Crusoe's first efforts, decades earlier, to lay up a store of raisins to "furnish" himself "for the wet Season" (131), only to find that they they had either rotted ("spoil'd") or had otherwise been made inedible by "wild Creatures thereabouts" (131). The colonists' mimicry of bees demonstrates their (admittedly shaky) claim to having escaped the less-desirable society of parasites and predators described in cringeworthy detail by Jonson, Rochester, and Shadwell. The plantation's "Barns" and "Warehouses" are offered as a sign that the Europeans' efforts are directed by a God who, from the beginning, has guided Crusoe into exhibiting his divine reason (125). As I have suggested, however, the materials and workmanship of Atkins's "Great Hive" are not really—or not solely—artifacts of European techno-superiority. Instead, the Europeans constructed their colony by appropriating the labor of men formerly described as "a hundred Wolves upon the Island." The "Great Hive," in other words, is built on a great violence. Mandeville defines "society" as "a Body Politick, in which Man either subdued by Superior Force or by Persuasion drawn from his Savage State is become a Disciplin'd Creature, that can find his own Ends in Labouring for others, and where under one Head or other Form of Government each Member is render'd Subservient to the Whole and all of them by cunning Management are made to Act as one" (ccxiv). From this perspective, Crusoe's multicultural island exhibits a kind of Mandevillian logic: both the Indians and the formerly "wild" colonists, like Will Atkins, have been "Disciplin'd" through a "Superior Force" or "Persuasion"—including near-starvation—to work together with supposedly hive-like efficiency. Solutions to the characteristic problems that confronted island colonies—deforestation, soil exhaustion, disease, dependency on foreign goods and supplies—can be managed, Defoe suggests, only through moral reformation and the careful appropriation of indigenous materials, know-how, and technologies.[63] It appears from his works that some may be starved to procure food for the many, and that food security constitutes one of the most important goals of the modern state.

COLONY COLLAPSE AND THE DEATH OF DRONES

Midway through *Farther Adventures*, Crusoe decides to leave the island for good and, now in his sixties, embark on a career as a merchant in Asia. Robert Markley calls attention to the vehemence of Crusoe's language in abandoning the colony: "I have now done with my Island, and all Manner of Discourse about it; and whoever reads the rest of my Memorandum's would do well to turn his Thoughts entirely from it" (125).[64] In Crusoe's absence, the beehive settlement seems to undergo a kind of colony collapse that is only partially explained in the novel.[65] "The last Letters I had from any of [the colonists]," Crusoe writes, "was by my Partners means; who afterwards sent another Sloop to the Place, and who sent me Word, tho' I had not the Letter till five Years after it was written; that they went on but poorly, were Male-content with their long Stay there: that *Will. Atkins* was dead; that five of the *Spaniards* were come away, and that tho' they had not been much molested by the Savages, yet they had had some Skirmishes with them; and that they begg'd of him to write to me, to think of the Promise I had made to fetch them away, that they might see their own Country again before they dy'd" (126). Without its "Patron" the leaderless colony, especially after Atkins's death, reverts to entropic disorder. The "People under no Discipline or Government but my own" (126), posits Crusoe, might have "done well enough," but without his "cunning Management," as Mandeville calls it, the colony becomes a failing backwater. Because it operated as a fantasy of collective zoopolitical structure rather than as a colony per se, Crusoe's island had never been attached to a state. Crusoe admits that he "never so much as pretended to plant in the Name of any Government or Nation, or to acknowledge any Prince, or to call [his] People Subjects to any one Nation more than another; nay, [he] never so much as gave the Place a Name" (125). Now, as the nameless colony collapses, the beehive metaphor crumples, too, reappearing in the context of stasis and idleness. "The whole World is in Motion," says an English merchant who persuades Crusoe to outfit a trading expedition to China, "rouling round and round; all the Creatures of God, heavenly Bodies and earthly are busy and diligent, Why should we be idle? There are no Drones in the World but Men, Why should we be of that Number?" (144).

For the merchant, drones are associated with a sedentary, land-based existence, the kind of life Crusoe compulsively seeks to escape in order to return to the sea. This analogy is worth exploring in more detail. At least since Virgil, as Allen argues, "the laboring bee is the picture of perfection, superior to the imperfect and lazy drone" (94). Imagined as females until the late 16th century—until the "king" bee was recognized as a queen—the "stay-at-home drones," neither gathering nectar nor building hives, were perceived as emblems of waste and luxury, as drains on the hive's food supplies.[66] The discovery that drones were male "came with a flood of anxieties," Allen continues, "about the relative value of male and female work" (96) along with, I would add, more animated discussion about the well-known phenomenon of drone sacrifice. Writing in 1637, Richard Remnant explains in *Discourse or Histories of Bees* how female bees kill the drones "for necessity": "for the males are exceedingly great eaters and wasters of the winter provision, therefore the females kill them, and had rather be without their sweet companie, than starve in their winter."[67] More than 100 years after Remnant, in *The Deserted Village*, Goldsmith describes this selective extermination as a "cruel policy," but one that attests to Nature's refusal of luxury: "The drone bees . . .

are marked for slaughter. These, which had hitherto led a life of indolence and pleasure, whose only employment was in impregnating the queen, and rioting upon the labours of the hive, without aiding in the general toil, now share the fate of most voluptuaries, and fall a sacrifice to the general resentment of society."[68] When Crusoe's merchant exhorts him to leave the hive—there are no "Drones in the World but Men"—he appeals to a similar moral and economic logic: as a male, he can either stay at home, like the drone, and be idle, or can join the ranks of the worker bee, "rouling round and round," "busy and diligent."

While Crusoe's "Great Hive" houses no drones—indeed, no queen, and very few females—the analogy nevertheless strikes me as being ontologically constitutive. If the Enlightenment state is built on the beehive, that state, like the beehive, contains within it and promotes a sacrificial economy. The famed efficiency of the hive, its legendary industry, depends (according to seventeenth- and eighteenth-century naturalists) on the systematic extermination of hungry members whose use-value has been expended. In this sense, the industrious beehive generates its own vermin, those who provoke "resentment" for their "rioting" on food for which they have not worked. Regarded as part of a sacrificial economy, then, the powerful bee analogy continues the impulse to extermination that we have seen in previous chapters populated by fleas, witches, rats, Jews, dogs, and other "imperfect creatures." Such "imperfection" may be variously associated, as we have seen, with a perceived lack of sexual development, with sexual or gender ambiguity, with simple because cold-blooded neuroanatomy, with rapid reproduction, and with an excess of appetite. Hungry, horny, effeminate, and luxurious drones fulfill several of these criteria. The important point is that drones, like these other vermin, are necessary to the "well-ordered" human hive, threatening but decidedly constitutive agents within its religious, sexual, medical, economical, and moral systems.

What Defoe's rats, wolves, cannibals, and drones make explicit—and what *Imperfect Creatures* has, I hope, conveyed—is how much those second-order systems depend on something many Anglo-European scholars take for granted: food. Mosca's observation on a corrupt Venice in Ben Jonson's *Volpone* holds true, it turns out, not only for Rochester's London but for Crusoe's island: "All the world is little else, in nature, / But *Parasites*, or *Sub-parasites*."[69] Crusoe, often taken as an embodiment of modern economic values, appears iconically in the eighteenth century in illustrations that show him, as Richard Nash puts it, "swallowed up in his goatskins."[70] These skins derive from the same goats that serve as his food, clothing, and, if Alexander Selkirk is any indication, perhaps his sometimes consorts. (Selkirk may have "cherished" his cats to ward off rats, but he had sex with the island's female goats, notching their ears as a sign that they had been "had.") In some sense, Crusoe's parasitic relationship to Nature mirrors our own. We too live "in the animal we eat," or, as Serres puts it, "We live within tents of skin like the gods within their tabernacles."[71] Defoe's hero struggles mightily to avoid descending to the level of scavenging or ravenous beasts, but his adventures are haunted by the half-realized knowledge that the lines between species, like those between "perfect" and "imperfect" creatures, are porous, and easily exposed. That rats, the primary material threat to his food supply, were banished in advance demonstrates the extent to which Defoe's metaphysical guarantees of species identity and providential fortune are themselves, as Serres suggests, always idealizations, ones that deny the force and historicity of nature. Complex ecologies function in and through the very parasites that an edenic nature must ignore. As English literature's most famous "verminous son of God," Robinson Crusoe signifies both the struggle and the failure to escape the entangled feeding practices of the more-than-human world.

AFTERWORD

We Have Never Been Perfect

"If there is one thing a literary education is good for it is to fill
you with a sense of doom."

—SAM SAVAGE, *FIRMIN: ADVENTURES OF A
METROPOLITAN LOW LIFE*

Reading beneath the grain encourages us to consider how engrained English
literary history is in food systems, in how and what to eat. Feeding practices
cut across and unite medical, moral, economic, and political histories in ways
that demand multidisciplinary work.[1] Animal studies, food studies, environmental studies, and agricultural studies are all points of emphasis in a much
larger network of biopolitical relations. The "question of the animal," then,
can be abstracted neither from matters of environmental stress nor from the
role of specific animals, including humans, within equally specific food systems. We survive (or not) with other creatures in living ecologies on which
we exert considerable pressure; as Serres puts it, we are "not separated, but
plunged, immersed in the Biogea, in cousin company."[2] In *Biogea*, Serres' goal
is to "think like that company, in it, by it, with it, for it" (107). *Imperfect Creatures* shares his sentiment if not his method; I have sought throughout this
study to treat insects, rodents, and occasional vermin as subjects of a shared
world. Vermin, I have argued, provide a point of entry to this living ecology,
not because they are constitutively different from other animals but because
they make explicit what we all have in common. In Serres' words, because
our behavior "resembles that of other insects, other rodents or poisonous
plants," neither scientifically nor morally can "we . . . claim to be subjects in
the midst of a world of objects" (107).

Indeed, one might argue, the reinforcement and obstinate staying power
of the subject/object, human/animal distinction in early modern culture,
symptomized in Descartes, is partially a byproduct of periodic food insecurity and correspondent feeding practices. By the seventeenth century, as

we have seen, humans lived, struggled, and died within a complex system of dietary habits and moral choices about which protein pools, in different circumstances, were deemed suitable, or unsuitable, for human consumption. Rapidly-reproducing creatures—frogs, mice, locusts, lice, snails, lobsters, and other "imperfect" beings—are treated by English writers as disgusting animals, fit for consumption only during dearth or famine. In natural philosophy, correspondingly, Willis refines and naturalizes this dietary practice in neuroanatomical arguments that the corporeal soul, which lies "hid in the Blood, or Vital Liquer," is distributed unequally across the animal kingdom.[3] He places living creatures into three classes according to "The Various Constitution of the Vital Humour": those without blood (insects, certain fishes, oysters, lobsters, and crab); those with "less perfect" or frigid blood (earthworms, some fishes, frogs, serpents, and lizards); and those with "more perfect" or hot blood (fowls and four-footed beasts) (7). From his perspective, to eat meat, or animal flesh, is to partake of food in its most nutritive because most complex or "perfect" form.

Eighteenth-century attacks on the eating of flesh similarly replicate the neo-Aristotelian division between perfect and imperfect animals but challenge the values inherent in these categories. Bernard Mandeville's 1732 statement against eating flesh, for example, often taken as a touchstone for "modern" vegetarianism, follows Willis in organizing edible animals into "more" and "less perfect" beings, but replaces the former's emphasis on "nutritive value" with "affective value." Writing after Willis, Richard Lower, Edward Tyson, and other comparative anatomists, Mandeville argues the anatomical similarities between "such perfect Animals as Sheep and Oxen" imply analogous emotional structures—an innate, automatic sympathy.[4] The "Heart, the Brain and Nerves differ so little from ours," he writes, sounding much like Willis in his account of the brute or sensitive soul, that ". . . the Separation of the Spirits from the Blood, the Organs of Sense, and consequently Feeling itself, are the same as they are in Human Creatures" (173). In contrast to Willis, however, Mandeville assumes such structural and emotional equivalencies make the "more perfect" not ideal but unfit for human consumption: "I can't imagine," he continues, "how a Man not hardened in Blood and Massacre, is able to see a violent Death, and the Pangs of it, without concern" (174). For him, a seemingly natural reluctance to kill perfect creatures, or to eat familiar ones, is proof of biological kinship from which the aversion emanates. Not only are most people averse to the idea of being a butcher, they are reluctant to "taste of any Creatures they have daily seen and been acquainted with, whilst they were alive" (174). Both reactions, he claims, suggest "a consciousness of Guilt" (174).

What makes Mandeville's argument for vegetarianism possible is not simply a discourse of sensibility or compassion but a prior recognition of biological kinship. Mandeville deploys a rhetorical shorthand, sidestepping the kind of neuroanatomical language that Willis had used in the 1660s, but preserving its logic. In his mind, sea creatures exist, for most people, beyond the affective realm that perfect creatures share. "Reason excites our Compassion but faintly," he argues, "and therefore I would not wonder how Men should so little commiserate such imperfect Creatures as Cray fish, Oysters, Cockles, and indeed all Fish in general: As they are mute, and their inward Formation, as well as outward Figure, vastly different from ours, they express themselves unintelligibly to us, and therefore 'tis not strange that their Grief should not affect our Understanding, which it cannot reach" (174). Because nothing "stirs us to Pity so effectually, as when the Symptoms of Misery strike immediately upon our Senses," some people, at least, are "mov'd" at the "Noise" of a "live Lobster upon the Spit"; despite being unintelligible to reason, lobsters and other arthropods have sensitive souls and therefore are not banished irrevocably from community and moral vision (174). Mandeville's argument for compassionate consumption, then, replicates the tendency of seventeenth-century natural philosophy to reject absolute differences between humans and animals. Instead, difference gives way to a *continuum of perfection*, to a series of distinctions imagined in terms of capacities and practices—not only "reason," abstractly considered, but "compassion," "benevolism," "imagination," and "mechanical art."

In his insistence that feeding practices are, or should be, tethered to one's capacity for fellow feeling, Mandeville promotes what, in his *Care of the Self*, Foucault calls a discourse of *epimeleia*, ancient regimens of self-discipline practiced in the name of "life."[5] Foucault attends to such modes of ethical self-fashioning primarily as a means of thinking about the individual organization of pleasure, whether health or sex, but refusing to offer a blueprint for society. In contrast, Mandeville's question to the epicurean—"what animal have you spared to satisfy the caprices of a languid appetite?"—implies that humans, by virtue of their species being, have an obligation to reject promiscuous consumption. In effect, Mandeville's argument is a purifying gesture typical of modernity; coming after Gassendi, Willis, Tyson, and others had challenged, if not swept away, human-animal difference, Mandeville restores the place of humans at the upper end of the scale by insisting on their innate moral sensibility. "As in all Animals that are not too imperfect to discover Pride," he writes, "we find, that the finest and such as are the most beautiful and valuable of their kind, have general the greatest Share of it; so in Man, the most perfect of Animals, [pride] is so inseparable from his very Essence . . . that without it the Compound he is made of would want one of the chiefest ingredients" (18). Although not peculiar to the human "Compound," the experience of pride in humans is sign and symptom of their status as the "most perfect of Animals," which in this case means the ones most subject to their complex biology: they should reason more rigorously, feel more strongly, and empathize more deeply. Humans are biological hybrids whose species identity depends on their ability to articulate distinctions between themselves and other perfect creatures. That may seem to be a surprising stance from the writer who promoted a satiric identification with insects in *Fable of the Bees*. But Mandeville's vegetarian ethos depends simultaneously on an identification *with* other creatures, who share our corporeal soul, and a disidentification *from* them because, being less perfect, they are not perfect enough.

Given his fascination with parasites and other vermin, Serres sometimes looks like a contemporary Mandeville; working both within and against the Enlightenment continuum of perfection, his writing, like Mandeville's, rests uncomfortably on the knife-edge between science and satire. Like Rochester, Pope, and Shadwell, Serres could be said to deploy rats, insects, and other less perfect creatures primarily as a means of satirical deflation, as in Rochester's sneer against the "mite" who thinks "he's an image of the Infinite." "We have made the louse in our image," Serres writes in *The Parasite*, "Let us see ourselves in his" (7). From this perspective, his task is largely deconstructive, its goal to make explicit and invert the value of the terms that anchor the Great Chain of Being. From the beginning, Serres insists, humans are "immersed" in the bios and occupy no God-given superiority within it; we are "on the same level as the other living things," he insists, "neither more or less than ants, seaweed or rats" (107). Indeed, *Biogea* describes humans as one of many "invasive species": "our hunting, gathering, cultivations, breedings, cities, industries and transportations," writes Serres, "continually disrupt vital local balances by favoring . . . the disembarkation of other species, just as invasive as we are" (107). In this posthumanist version of plague literature, Serres encourages us to acknowledge our status as the plagues from which other animals flee; like frogs, locusts, rats, lice, and other "imperfect" creatures, we overrun the Biogea, we spoil food systems, and we spread diseases whose origins are only less slightly mysterious than they were in the seventeenth century. "Sailors, rats, fleas microbes" move in great populations; they "flood the world" and encounter, on the way, other similarly "uncontrollable" species with whom they engage in "fierce competition" (106). At best, humans battle against other species in a constant, near-Hobbesian state of interspecies war.

The futility of such competition, however, seems to be the point of a story Serres, or his character Monsieur Arhan, a lighthouse keeper, tells midway through *Biogea* about a "ghost ship" of rats who, having triumphed over the crews' "attempt to reason" with them, and having "feasted on the organs and bones of all the sailors," were left the ship's "sole masters" (97). When the rats no longer had any food supplies to gnaw on—"hawser, barrel, dried cod, biscuits, or sailors"—they turned on one another like, Arhan says, "cursed shipwrecked people" (98). Eventually, the ship washes up on an Italian island, where "tens of thousands of animals, fasting since forever and a day" disembark and "galloped at the heels" of the lighthouse keeper "to devour him, peacoat included" (99). Arhan's colleague makes it to the lantern room but realizes the "entire islet" is now covered with swarming rats. He hears "the enormous rumbling of the rodents attempting to climb the tower, covering almost all of it":

> Was the door of the lantern going to hold? Howling and sticky, a mass was pushing against it, and behind that fragile panel, my colleague panting. That, madam, is the entire story: all of a sudden, without warning, alone against an army. You think you're calm, cleaning your things with a nanny-goat skin, and, suddenly, the downpour of rats. . . . Who'd believe it? (100)

Eventually, humans entice the rats away by loading a ship with rotting meat and then, once the rats are on board, setting the ship on fire.

For Serres, the eventually incinerated rodents are not antagonists in a tale of human progress. Instead, as in *The Parasite*, homologies between their feeding practices and our own underscore the need for humans to realize that fierce and destructive competition for food "in this island" he calls the Biogea will never stop. His tale about rat-inhabited ships both recalls the struggles on Crusoe's island and empties Crusoe's wars against birds, goats, and Indians of their theological power. While no less allegorical than *Robinson Crusoe*, *Biogea* has the polemical and empirical advantage of treating the world as an open system from which rats (human or otherwise) cannot and should not be excluded a priori. In contrast to the Garden of Eden, the Biogea was not created for the sons of God; indeed, its history thwarts even our claims to thanatological superiority: "In spite of our boasting," Serres writes, "even directed towards our most vile acts of violence, despite our sublime talents as murderers, we're not as good as the rats and the fleas, nor the bacteria and viruses" (105). This wry argument makes a crucial point: the politics of purity tend towards mutual and collective destruction. Crusoe attempts to "secure" his island and supplies through extermination and containment, prayer and conjuring—much in the same way that the Lord Mayor, Alderman, and people of London in *Journal of the Plague Year* sought to secure themselves from contamination: in addition to killing the "forty thousand Dogs" and "five times as many Cats," all "possible Endeavors were us'd . . . to destroy the Mice and Rats, especially the latter; by laying Rats Bane and other Poisons for them, and a prodigious multitude of them were also destroy'd."[6] Such efforts, whether applied to humans or nonhumans, are doomed in advance, claims Serres, because they imply a zero-sum game among matched participants. And when, or if, we have "destroyed every other living species" on this "ghost planet," Serres asks in the person of Arhan, will we turn on each other, as the shipbound rats do? Will we "drink the blood of our cousins"? (98–99)[7] This question, the dystopian version of Mandeville's challenge to the epicurean, similarly insists that moral and political relations cannot be species specific.

If we are to avoid the fate of cannibal rats adrift on a dead planet, according to Serres, we must negotiate what he calls "a mutual aid benefit pact" (171) that differs markedly from the violent, onto-theologic practices of Crusoe. In a powerfully constitutive metaphor, Serres argues that a precondition for such negotiation is "listening" to the languages, the signals, the sounds of the presumed objects against which (or whom) we define ourselves. While the Biogea includes the entire physical world, such sound "bursts forth better" from the "maws" of animals than from "floods, storms, and volcanoes" (109). Serres' parasite, then, his "noise," his "third man," turns out to be neither "man" nor "human" at all, but a collection of flocks, broods, colonies, swarms, packs, plagues, nests, and companies.[8] Vermin occupy a foundational place in Serres' ecozoography, not only because they share with humans invasive, infesting, infecting behaviors but also because they are physically, cognitively, morally, and theologically excluded from our idealized, still theologically inflected worlds.

Following Serres' lead, *Imperfect Creatures* has turned away from the pairs of perfect creatures ambling off of Noah's Ark and has listened, instead, to the noises of those excluded ones who intrude on our material and imagined fields and gardens, giving them shape. The vermin who cavort through Ben Jonson's *Volpone*, the locusts massing as armies in Abraham Cowley's poem, and the dogs rambling in St. James's Park encourage us to remain open to ontical and ontological skirmishes in seventeenth- and eighteenth-century literature, to examine Latour's nature/culture before "nature" has been dis-articulated, dressed, plated, and brought to the table. In this context, Serres' spiritual predecessor, Mandeville, reminds us that, if we have never been perfect, we have never stopped looking for humane and responsible ways to live in the world we share with swarms, packs, prides, herds, and flocks. If we have never been perfect, we have also never been entirely identical with the parasitical monsters that emerge as symptoms of our bloody diets and fermented imaginations.

Notes

Introduction

1. Aristotle, *The Treatises of Aristotle, Translated from the Greek*, trans. Thomas Taylor (London: Printed for Thomas Taylor by Robert Wilks), 1818. In *On the Generation of Animals*, Aristotle argues the scale of development is closely tethered to clearly marked sexual dimorphism. An animal is "perfect," he writes, when the "foetus is either male or female," and the "first" animal among the viviparous "is man" (305). Within that context, uniparous (single egg) creatures (like humans and elephants) have a greater chance of producing fully developed beings than either biparous (dogs, wolves) or polyparous ones. Reptiles and other "less perfect" creatures, one of whose characteristics is sexual hermaphroditism, occupy the lower end of Aristotle's scale of development, even as, I would argue, they ground the system itself.

2. Relevant early modern texts include Athanasius Kircher, *Scrutinium physico-medicum contagiosæ luis* [*Physico-Medical Studies on a Contagious Disease Called Pest*] Romæ: Typis Mascardi, 1658; and William Harvey, "Anatomical Exercises in the Generation of Animals," in *The Works of William Harvey*, trans. Robert Willis (London: printed for the Sydenham Society, 1847). Harvey wrote about disease as *contagium*, and van Leeuwenhoek wrote to the Royal Society about animacules, including what was later called *giardia*, found in his own feces. He was the first to realize that fleas have fleas. Francesco Redi's *Esperienze Intorno all Generazione Degl'insetti* (*Experiments on the Generation of Insects*) [Firenze: Nella Stamperis di Piero Matini, 1688] is significant for refuting theories of spontaneous generation. Malpighi may have been the first to see capillaries under a microscope. See Marcello Malpighi, *Anatome Plantarum* (London: Impensis Johannes Martyn, 1675). Swammerdam further reinforced theories of epigenesis in his posthumously published *The Book of Nature; or, the History of Insects*, trans. Thomas Flloyd (London: C.G. Seyffert, 1758). William Ramsay studied parasitical worms. See William Ramsay (Ramesey), *Helminthologia; or, Some Physical Consider-*

ations of the Matter, Origination, and Several Species of Wormes Macerating and Direfully Cruciating every Part of the Bodies of Mankind (London: John Streater for George Sawbridge, 1668). In the eighteenth century, Eleazar Albin published several books about insects, including *A Natural History of Spiders, and Other Curious Insects* (London: John Tilly, for R. Montagu; J. Brindley; O. Payne; J. Worrall; T. Worrall, and T. Boreman, 1736). The classic historical text on vermin and disease, especially typhus, is Hans Zinsser, *Rats, Lice and History* (1935; rpt. New Brunswick: Transaction Press, 2008). See also Walter Pagel, *New Light on William Harvey* (Basel and New York: Karger, 1976), 42–61.

3. On the relationship between worms and cosmogony, see Carlo Ginzburg, *The Cheese and the Worms: The Cosmos of a Sixteenth-Century Miller*, trans. John and Anne Tedeschi (Baltimore: Johns Hopkins University Press, 1980).

4. Athanasius Kircher, *Scrutinium Physic-medicum contagiosae luis, quae dicitur pestis* (*Physico-Medical Studies on a Contagious Disease Called Pest*), 1658. Quoted in Frank N. Egerton, *Roots of Ecology: Antiquity to Haeckel* (Berkeley and Los Angeles: University of California Press, 2012), 58.

5. Ramsay, *Helminthologia*, 2, 10.

6. See Jonathan Gil Harris, *Foreign Bodies and the Body Politic: Discourses of Social Pathology in Early Modern England* (Cambridge: Cambridge University Press, 1998). See also Rebecca Totaro, *Suffering in Paradise: The Bubonic Plague from More to Milton* (Pittsburgh: Dusquene University Press, 2005).

7. On early modern animal trials, see E. P. Evans, *The Criminal Prosecution and Capital Punishment of Animals* (London: William Heinemann, 1906); Walter W. Hyde, "The Prosecution and Punishment of Animals and Lifeless Things in the Middle Ages and Modern Times," *University of Pennsylvania Law Review* 64 (1916): 696–730; Piers Beirne, "The Law is an Ass: Reading E. P. Evans' The Medieval Prosecution and Capital Punishment of Animals," *Society & Animals* 2 (1994): 27–46; and Jen Girgen, "The Historical and Contemporary Prosecution and Punishment of Animals," *Animal Law Review* 9 (2003), 97–134.

8. Nicholas Humphrey, *The Mind Made Flesh: Essays from the Frontier of Psychology and Evolution* (Oxford: Oxford University Press, 2002), 239–40.

9. On animal trials in Great Britain, see Piers Beirne, "A Note on the Facticity of Animal Trials in Early Modern Britain; or, the Curious Prosecution of Farmer Carter's Dog for Murder," *Crime, Law, and Social Change* 55 (2011): 359–74.

10. On vermin-killing strategies, see Karl H. Dannenfeldt, "The Control of Vertebrate Pests in Renaissance Agriculture," *Agricultural History* 56 (1982): 542–59. Vermin-killing treatises abound in the early modern period, though most refer implicitly or explicitly to Mascall's *Book of Engines: Sundrie Engines and Trapps to take Polecats, Buzards, Rattes, Mice and all other Kinded of Vermin and Beasts Whatsoever* (London: Printed by John Wolfe and sold by Edward White, 1590).

11. On the role of rat populations and climate, population, grain transport, and dis-

ease in the late ancient and medieval periods, see Michael McCormick, "Rats, Communication, and Plague: Towards an Ecological History," *Journal of Interdisciplinary History* 34 (2003): 1–25. A general study making explicit the connection between vermin and ecological concerns is Egerton, *Roots of Ecology: Antiquity to Haeckel*. An important essay on early modern food systems and vermin is Mary Fissell, "Imagining Vermin in the Early Modern Period," *History Workshop Journal* 47 (1999): 1–29. See also Lisa Sarasohn, "'That Nauseous Venomous Insect': Bedbugs in Early Modern England," *Eighteenth Century Studies* 46 (2013): 513–30.

12. On the Little Ice Age, see Brian Fagan, *The Little Ice Age: How Climate Made History* (New York: Basic Books, 2000), especially 101–12. On the relationship between climate change and disease, see Paul Reiter, "Climate Change and Mosquito-Borne Disease," in *Environmental Health Perspectives* 109, Supplement 1 (2001): 141–61.

13. Dannenfeldt, "The Control of Vertebrate Pests in Renaissance Agriculture," 553–54.

14. Dannenfeldt, 551.

15. Hyde, "Prosecution and Punishment of Animals and Lifeless Things in the Middle Ages and Modern Times," 709. His summary is based on C.P. Evans's tables.

16. Francis Bacon, *Sylva Sylvarum: Or, The Natural History in Ten Centuries*, in *The Works of Francis Bacon*, ed. James Spedding, Robert L. Ellis, and Douglas D. Heath (rpt. New York: Garrett Press, 1968), 2: 554–55.

17. Quoted in Reiter, "Climate Change and Mosquito-Borne Disease," 145.

18. John Ovington, *A Voyage to Surat in the Year 1689*, ed. H.G. Rawlinson (London: Oxford University Press, 1929), 145.

19. Richard Walter, *A Voyage Round the World in the Years MDCCXL, I, I, III, IV* (London: Printed for the Author by John and Paul Knapton, 1748), 42.

20. Glyn Williams, *The Prize of All the Oceans: The Dramatic True Story of Commodore Anson's Voyage Round the World and How He Seized the Spanish Treasure Galleon* (New York: Viking, 1999).

21. Within early modern studies, that tendency is less pronounced. Foundational historical studies include Keith Thomas, *Man and the Natural World: Changing Attitudes in England, 1500–1800* (London: Allen Lane, 1983); Erica Fudge, Ruth Gilbert, and Susan Wiseman, eds., *At the Borders of the Human: Beasts, Bodies, and Natural Philosophy in the Early Modern Period* (New York: St. Martin's Press, 1999); Erica Fudge, *Perceiving Animals: Humans and Beasts in Early Modern Culture* (Urbana: University of Illinois Press, 2002); Bruce Boehrer, *Shakespeare Among the Animals: Nature and Society in the Drama of Early Modern England* (New York: Palgrave, 2002); Karen Raber and Treva J. Tucker, eds., *The Culture of the Horse: Status, Discipline, and Identity in Early Modern World* (New York: Palgrave, 2005); Richard Nash, *Wild Enlightenment: The Borders of Human Identity in the Eighteenth Century* (Charlottesville: University of Virginia Press, 2003); Erica Fudge, *Brutal Reasoning: Animals, Rationality, and Humanity in Early Modern England* (Ithaca: Cornell University Press, 2006); Nathaniel Wolloch, *Subjugated Animals: Animals and Anthropocentrism in Early Modern European Culture* (Amherst,

NY: Humanity Books, 2006); Frank Palmierei, ed., *Humans and Other Animals in Eighteenth-Century British Culture: Representation, Hybridity, Ethics* (Burlington, VT: Ashgate, 2006). Second-wave animal studies in the early modern period include Anne Milne, *"Lactilla Tends her Fav'rite Cow": Ecocritical Readings of Animals and Women in Eighteenth-Century British Labouring-Class Poetry* (Lewisburg: Bucknell University Press, 2008); Donna Landry, *Noble Brutes: How Eastern Horses Transformed English Culture* (Baltimore, Johns Hopkins University Press, 2009); Laura Brown, *Homeless Dogs and Melancholy Apes: Humans and Other Animals in the Modern Literary Imagination* (Ithaca: Cornell University Press, 2010); Laurie Shannon, *The Accommodated Animal: Cosmopolity in Shakespearean Locales* (Chicago: University of Chicago Press, 2013) and, most recently, Karen Raber, *Animal Bodies, Renaissance Culture* (Philadelphia: University of Pennsylvania Press, 2013). Both Shannon and Raber attend in passing to moles and others animals traditionally regarded as vermin.

22. Cary Wolfe, *Animal Rites: American Culture, the Discourse of Species, and Posthumanist Theory* (Chicago: University of Chicago Press, 2003), 7.

23. John Donne, *Poems, by J. D. With Elegies on the Authors Death* (London: Printed by [M]iles [F]lesher for John Marriot, 1633), 230–31.

24. On the tradition of the flea searcher painting, see Crissy Bergeron, "George de La Tour's Flea-Catcher and the Iconography of the Flea Hunt in Seventeenth-Century Baroque Art" (master's thesis, Louisiana State University, 2007), and Philip Conisbee, "An Introduction to the Life and Art of Georges de La Tour," in *Georges de La Tour and his World* (New Haven: Yale University Press, 1996), 13–148. See especially 94–97.

25. Peter Woodhouse, "The Flea" (London: Printed by Edward Allde for John Smethwick, 1605).

26. *The Autobiography of a Flea, Told in a Hop, Skip and Jump* (London: Edward Avery, 1887). Published in a run of 150 copies.

27. On the parts of this tradition often identified as "posthumanist" that are most relevant to animal studies, see Cary Wolfe, *What Is Posthumanism?* (Minneapolis: University of Minnesota Press, 2009); and Donna Haraway, *When Species Meet* (Minneapolis: University of Minnesota Press, 2008). In different ways, both Wolfe and Haraway emphasize the roles of Michel Serres and Bruno Latour, especially Serres' *The Parasite* (Minneapolis: University of Minnesota Press, 2007) and Latour's *We Have Never Been Modern*, trans. Catherine Porter (Cambridge: Harvard University Press, 1993). Posthumanism deconstructs the idea of distinctions between subjects and objects, and nature and culture, that traditionally are central to Western ideas of self and science.

28. Bruno Latour, *Politics of Nature: How to Bring the Sciences into Democracy*, trans. Catherine Porter (Cambridge: Harvard University Press, 2004), 75.

29. Erica Fudge, *Brutal Reasoning*, 188.

30. Elizabeth Graham, "Metaphors and Metaphorism: Some Thoughts on Environmental Metahistory," in *Advances in Historical Ecology*, ed. William L. Balée (New York: Columbia University Press, 1998), 124.

31. Mira Pajes Merriman, "Comedy, Reality, and the Development of Genre Painting in Italy," in *Giusseppei Maria Crespi and the Emergence of Genre Painting in Italy*, ed. John T. Spike (Fort Worth: Kimball Art Museum, 1986), 52.

32. Merriman, 52.

33. Aristotle, 408.

34. On women as imperfect creatures, see Londa Schiebinger, *Nature's Body: Gender in the Making of Modern Science* (New Brunswick, NJ: Rutgers University Press, 2004), especially 41–74; and Thomas Walter Laquer, *Making Sex: Body and Gender from the Greeks to Freud* (Cambridge: Harvard University Press, 1990), 35.

35. Contrast Agrippa: "Since then, Woman is the ultimate end of creation, the most perfect accomplishment of all the works of God, and the perfection of the universe itselfe, who will deny that she posseses honor surpassing every other creature? . . . For it is unreasonable and absurd to think that God would have finished so great a work with something imperfect." Henricus Cornelius Agrippa, *On the Nobility and Pre-eminence of the Female Sex*, trans. Albert Rabil, Jr. (Chicago: University of Chicago Press, 1996), 47–48.

36. Nicolas Andry de Bois-Regard, *An Account of the Breeding of Worms in Human Bodies* (London: H. Rhodes and A. Bell, 1701), 5.

37. *Health's Preservative: Being a Dissertation on Diet, Air, and Down-beds. And of the Cause and Cure of Bugs* (London: Printed for F. Cogan, 1750), 23.

38. *Microscopic Observations; or, Dr. Hooke's Wonderful Discoveries by the Microscope, Illustrated by Thirty-three Copper-Plates, Curiously Engraved* (Cornhill: Robert Wilkinson, 1780), 62.

39. See Ann Finch's poem, "Man Bitten by Fleas": "Go sweep, and wash, and strew thy Floor / As all good Housewives teach /And do not thus for Thunders roar, / To make some fatal Breach." In *Miscellany Poems, on Several Occasions: Written by the Honble Anne, Countess of Winchilsea* (London: Benj. Tooke, William Taylor, James Round, 1713), 226.

40. Londa Schiebinger, *Nature's Body*, 40–74. Schiebinger argues the scientific "fascination with the female breast helped to buttress the sexual division of labor in European society by emphasizing how natural it was for females—both human and nonhuman—to suckle and rear their own children" (41–42). Whereas in the Aristotelian tradition, "the female had been seen as a misbegotten male, a monster or error of nature," Linnaeus assigned a new role to the female, centered on her "unique role in reproduction" (53).

41. M. M., *A Short Historical Account of the Several Kinds of Worms Breeding in Human Bodies* (London: J. Baker and T. Warner, 1716).

42. Terry Eagleton, *Against the Grain: Essays 1975–1985* (London: Verso, 1986).

43. In extending the word to include mammals, Serres realizes he uses the term parasite in what he calls an "unusual" way (6). His point, however, is that parasitologists originally borrowed the word from "ancient and common customs and habits," so the

scientific vocabulary "bears several traces of anthropomorphism" (6). Something similar might be said of the term "imperfect creature," in which the social and the biological really are indistinguishable.

44. Serres' assumption is all systems are in disequilibrium; systems "work" because "they do not work" (13). The argument from design, the idea of a "balance of nature," makes sense in the seventeenth century, not despite but *because of* the parasites, vermin, and imperfect creatures that disrupt the smooth, harmonious, or perfect system. See Cary Wolfe's introduction, "Bring the Noise: The Parasite and the Multiple Genealogies of Posthumanism," in Serres, *The Parasite*, xi–xxviii.

45. Latour, "The Enlightenment Without the Critique: An Introduction to Michel Serres' Philosophy," in *Contemporary French Philosophy*, ed. J. Griffith (Cambridge, Cambridge University Press, 1988), 85.

46. Karen Raber, "Vermin and Parasites: Shakespeare's Animal Architectures," in *Ecocritical Shakespeare*, ed. Linda Bruckner and Daniel Brayton (Burlington, VT: Ashgate Press, 2011), 31. From Raber's perspective, vermin and parasites are both "part of the physical environment" and "fundamental to the ideological construction of nearly all conceptual categories" that structure physical and fictional worlds. She expands this argument in *Animal Bodies, Renaissance Culture*, 103–50.

47. Shannon, *Accommodated Animal*, 2.

48. Alexander Ross, *An Exposition on the Fourteene First Chapters of Genesis* (London: Printed by B[ernard] A[lsop] and T[homas]F[awcett], 1626), 18.

49. Kircher does include snakes and mice. See Olaf Breidbach and Michael T. Ghislen, "Athanasius Kircher (1602–1680) on Noah's Ark: Baroque 'Intelligent Design' Theory," *Proceedings of the California Academy of Sciences* 57 (2006): 991–1002. On Wilkins, see also Shannon, *Accommodated Animal*, 270–83.

50. Zinsser addresses this problem in *Rats, Lice, and History*, 182.

51. McCormick, "Rats, Communication, and Plague: Towards an Ecological History," 4.

52. On how early modern literature frustrates representational schema, see Laurie Shannon, "The Eight Animals in Shakespeare; or, Before the Human," *PMLA* 124 (2009): 472–79. This article is incorporated in *Accommodated Animal*, 1–28.

53. Janelle A. Schwartz, *Worm Work: Recasting Romanticism* (Minneapolis: University of Minnesota Press, 2012), 11.

54. Heinrich Kramer and James Sprenger, *The Malleus Maleficarum of Heinrich Kramer and James Sprenger*, trans. Montague Summers (New York: Dover, 1971), 109.

55. James I, *Daemonologie* (San Diego: Book Tree, 2002), 49–50.

56. Noah Webster, *A Brief History of Epidemic and Pestilential Diseases* (Hartford, CT: Hudson and Goodwin, 1799), 16.

57. Graham Hammill, "Miracles and Plagues: Plague Discourse as Political Thought," *Journal of Early Modern Cultural Studies* 10 (2010): 85–104, 85. This argument is extended in *The Mosaic Constitution: Political Theology and Imagination from Machiavelli to Milton* (Chicago: University of Chicago Press, 2010).

58. Robert Hooke, *Micrographia* (London: Printed by Jo. Martyn and Ja. Allestree, 1665), 210.

59. William Harvey, *Anatomical Exercises on the Generation of Animals,* trans. Robert Willis (London: The Sydenham Society, 1847), 165.

60. Thomas Willis, *Two Discourses Concerning the Soul of Brutes Which is that of the Vital and Sensitive of Man* (London: Thomas Dringe, 1683), 152.

61. Latour, *We Have Never Been Modern,* 10–11.

62. Haraway, *When Species Meet,* 45.

63. Daniel Defoe, *Journal of the Plague Year* (1722), ed. John Mullan (London: Pickering and Chatto, 2009), 58.

64. For more contemporary analyses of this subject, see the excellent essays in *Trash Animals: How We Live With Nature's Filthy, Feral, Invasive, and Unwanted Species,* eds. Kelsi Nagy and Phillip David Johnson, II (Minneapolis and London: University of Minnesota Press, 2013).

Chapter 1

1. Brian Fagan, *The Little Ice Age: How Climate Made History 1300–1850* (New York: Basic Books, 2000), 216. On plague and climate change, see John Kelly, *The Great Mortality: An Intimate History of the Black Death, the Most Devastating Plague of All Time* (New York: Harper Perennial, 2006), 17–38, 42–43, 58–77. On the Little Ice Age, see Robert Markley, "Summer's Lease: Shakespeare in the Little Ice Age," in *Early Modern Ecostudies: From the Florentine Codex to Shakespeare,* ed. Thomas Hallock, Ivo Kamps, and Karen L. Raber (New York: Palgrave Macmillan, 2008), 131–42.

2. Emily Oster, "Witchcraft, Weather and Economic Growth in Renaissance Europe," *Journal of Economic Perspectives* 18 (2004): 215–28.

3. Beginning in the 1980s, critics tended to read witchcraft primarily in terms of gender relations. See, in this regard, Brian Easlea, *Witch Hunting, Magic, and the New Philosophy: An Introduction to the Debates of the Scientific Revolution 1450–1750* (Brighton: Harvester, 1980); Deborah Willis, *Malevolent Nurture: Witch-Hunting and Maternal Power in Early Modern England* (Ithaca: Cornell University Press, 1995); Frances E. Dolan, *Dangerous Familiars: Representations of Domestic Crime in England, 1550–1700* (Ithaca: Cornell University Press, 1994); and Mary Floyd Wilson, *Occult Knowledge, Gender, and Science on the Shakespearean Stage* (Cambridge: Cambridge University Press, 2013). My reading builds on these feminist interpretations by examining vermin in the context of previous scholarship on women, witches, and disease.

4. On miasmic theory, see Anita Guerrini, "The Pathological Environment," *The Eighteenth Century: Theory and Interpretation* 31 (1990): 173–79.

5. See René Girard, "The Plague in Literature and Myth," *Texas Studies in Language and Literature* 15 (1974), 833–50, and Girard, *I See Satan Fall Like Lightening* (Maryknoll, NY: Orbis, 2001), 154–60. Girard argues, in contrast to other anthropologists,

that because there is no real break between the archaic and the modern, the phenomenon of scapegoating "is far from being a dead letter in our society" (160).

6. Kelly, *The Great Mortality*, 19.

7. The pioneering study of the plague by Wu Lien-teh, published in 1936 in China, includes articles by scholars from many different disciplines. See Wu Lien-teh, J. W. H. Chun, R. Pollitzer, and C. Y. Wu, *Plague: A Manual for Medical and Public Health Workers* (Shanghai Station, China: National Quarantine Service, 1936). See also the valuable studies of plague by David Herlihy, *The Black Death and the Transformation of the West*, ed. Samuel K. Cohn, Jr. (Cambridge: Harvard University Press, 1997), and William H. McNeill, *Plagues and Peoples* (Garden City: Anchor, 1976). On the complex relationships between plague and famine, see the essays in John Walter and Roger Schofield, ed., *Famine, Disease, and Social Order in Early Modern Society* (Cambridge: Cambridge University Press, 1989). Especially useful is their introduction, "Famine, Disease, and Crisis Mortality in Early Modern Society," 1–73. On plague and literature, see F. P. Wilson, *The Plague in Shakespeare's London* (Oxford: Clarendon Press, 1927); Leeds Barroll, *Politics, Plague, and Shakespeare's Theater: The Stuart Years* (Ithaca: Cornell University Press, 1991); Paul Slack, *The Impact of the Plague in Tudor and Stuart England* (New York and Oxford: Oxford University Press, 1991); Jonathan Gil Harris, *Foreign Bodies and the Body Politic: Discourses of Social Pathology in Early Modern England* (Cambridge: Cambridge University Press, 1998); Rebecca Totaro, *Suffering In Paradise: The Bubonic Plague in English Literature from More to Milton* (Pittsburgh, PA: Duquesne University Press, 2005); Ernest B. Gilman, *Plague Writing in Early Modern England* (Chicago: University of Chicago Press, 2009); and the special issue of *Journal of Early Modern Cultural Studies* 10 (2010), ed. Richard Barney and Helene P. Scheck on "Rhetorics of Plague."

8. George Wither, *Britain's Remembrancer* (1628; rpt. Manchester: Charles Simms, Printed for the Spenser Society, 1880), 104. All subsequent references, cited parenthetically, are to this edition.

9. Guerrini, "The Pathological Environment," 174.

10. Shelia Barker, "Poussin, Plague, and Early Modern Medicine, " *Art Bulletin* 86 (2004), 664.

11. William Austin, *Epiloimia Epe. Or The Anatomie of a Pestilence. A Poem in three Parts. Describing The Deplorable Conditions of the City of London under its Merciless Dominion* (London: Nathaniel Brooke, 1666), 57. Subsequent references are to this edition. On the different classical traditions of interpreting the plague, see Gilman, *Plague Writing in Early Modern England*, and Totaro, *Suffering in Paradise*.

12. Austin, 53.

13. Austin, 54.

14. Austin, 55.

15. Austin, 55.

16. Austin, 55.

17. Jean Bodin, *On the Demon-Mania of Witches* (1580), trans. Randy A. Scott (To-

ronto: Centre for Reformation and Renaissance Studies, 1995), 136. All subsequent references are to this edition. On Bodin's significant influence in England, see James Sharpe, *Instruments of Darkness: Witchcraft in Early Modern England* (Philadelphia: University of Pennsylvania Press, 1996), 22.

18. As Stuart Clarke notes, it was "the unanimous opinion," at least among the educated, "that devils, and a fortiori, witches, not merely existed in nature but acted according to its laws." Clarke, *Thinking With Demons: The Idea of Witchcraft in Early Modern Europe* (Oxford: Oxford University Press, 1999), 152.

19. Guerrini, 173.

20. Thomas Lodge, *A Treatise of the Plague* (London: Valentime Si[mmes], 1603). All subsequent references are to this edition. Pages unnumbered; sig. B2v.

21. Giambattista Della Porta, *Natural Magick* (London: Printed for Thomas Young and Samuel Speed, 1658), 28.

22. Henry Cornelius Agrippa, *Three Books of Occult Philosophy*, trans. J[ohn] F[rench] (London: R.W. for Gregory Poule, 1651), 55.

23. Edward Topsell, *The Historie of Foure-Footed Beastes* (London: William Iaggard, 1607), 506. The imperfect creature, writes Topsell, may "be engendered by seed and putrifying matter and afterwards beget more of his owne kind" (542).

24. Edward C. Green, *Indigenous Theories of Contagious Disease* (London: AltaMira, 1999), 18.

25. Henri Bouget, *An Examen of Witches* (*Discours des Sorciers*) (rpt. New York: Barnes and Noble, 1971), xxxii.

26. See Diane Purkiss, *The Witch in History: Early Modern and Twentieth-Century Representations* (London: Routledge, 1996), for a cogent argument against progressivist interpretations of "empiricism's triumph over the supernatural" (201).

27. Sheila Barker, "Poussin, Plague, and Early Modern Medicine," 665. See also Otto Neustatter, "Mice in Plague Pictures," *The Journal of the Walters Art Gallery* 4 (1941): 104–13. An important source for both Neustatter and Hans Zinsser, *Rats, Lice, and History* (1935; rpt. New Brunswick: Transaction Press, 2008) is Georg Sticker, *Die Pest in Berichten der Laien und in Werken der Künstler* (1898). Zinsser writes that Sticker collected many instances of what he takes (rightly or wrongly) to be indigenous understandings of the relationship between rats and plague. Ancient Jews considered all seven varieties of mice unclean and unsuited as food; Zoroastrians believed the killing of rats was "a service to God"; the god Apollo Smintheus, protector against disease, was also "a killer of mice"; and in the fifteenth century, Jews in the city of Frankfurt were taxed with the "annual delivery of five thousand rat tails" to officials (191–92). See also David E. Davis, "The Scarcity of Rats and the Black Death," *Journal of Interdisciplinary History* 16 (1986): 455–70.

28. Topsell, *The Historie of Foure-Footed Beastes*, 543.

29. Elizabeth Stiles, for example, was associated with a rat familiar (Purkiss, 137), and in Ben Jonson's *Masque of Queens*, twelve witches appear "all differently attir'd," some

with "Rats on the Head; some on their shoulders." *The Masque of Queens*, in *The Workes of Benjamin Jonson* (London: W. Stansby, 1616), 946.

30. Claudia Swan, *Art, Science, and Witchcraft in Early Modern Holland: Jacques de Gheyn II (1565–1629)* (Cambridge: Cambridge University Press, 2005), 144, 142.

31. Swan, *Art, Science, and Witchcraft*, 132.

32. Swan, 152.

33. Cited in Swan, 23.

34. Agrippa, *Three Books of Occult Philosophy*, 74.

35. Karen Barad, *Meeting the Universe Halfway: Quantum Physics and the Entanglement of Matter and Meaning* (Durham and London: Duke University Press, 2007). Barad's account is grounded in quantum theory, where representation and reality are never distinct.

36. Heinrich Kramer and James Sprenger, *The Malleus Malificarum of Heinrich Kramer and James Spranger*, trans. Montague Summers (1486; rpt. New York: Dover, 1971), 109. See also Michael Cole, "The Demonic Arts and the Origin of the Medium," *The Art Bulletin* 84 (2002): 627.

37. Kramer and Sprenger, *Malleus Malificarum*, 109.

38. According to Swan, de Gheyn's witchcraft works "reflect postclassical conceptions of the imagination as the locus of mental images" (123)—the kind of dysfunctional imagination associated with melancholy and other psychological diseases.

39. See Bruno Latour, *We Have Never Been Modern*, trans. Catherine Porter (Cambridge: Harvard University Press, 1993), 105–9.

40. Topsell, 506.

41. On the rat's tail as a vascular system, see N. J. Dawson and A. W. Keber, "Physiology of Heat Loss from an Extremity: The Tail of the Rat," *Clinical and Experimental Pharmacology and Physiology* 6 (1979): 69–80.

42. I follow Leeds Barroll's argument that apparent references to the Gunpowder Plot in *Macbeth*, traditionally used to date the play, must be reconsidered in light of what we know about theater closing during the plague years. See Barroll, *Politics, Plague, and Shakespeare's Theatre*, 133–47.

43. Wilson, *Plague in Shakespeare's London*, 98.

44. William Shakespeare, *The Tragedy of Macbeth* in *The Norton Shakespeare*, ed. Stephen Greenblatt, Walter Cohen, Jean E. Howard, and Katherine Maus (New York: Norton, 2008). Hereafter cited parenthetically in the text.

45. Markley, "Summer's Lease: Shakespeare in the Little Ice Age," 131–42.

46. On James I and Shakespeare, see Willis, *Malevolent Nature*, 116–58, and Purkiss, *Witch in History*, 199–230.

47. James I, 49–50.

48. Stephen Greenblatt, "Shakespeare Bewitched," *New Historical Literary Study: Essays on Reproducing Texts, Representing History*, ed. Jeffrey N. Cox and Larry I. Reynolds (Princeton: Princeton University Press, 1993), 108–35.

49. Purkiss, 130.

50. William Shakespeare, *Complete Works of William Shakespeare*, eds. Edmund Malone, George Steevens, et al. (Philadelphia: David McKay, 1887), 705.

51. Topsell, 506.

52. Topsell, 520.

53. Topsell, 506; Kelly, *The Great Mortality*, 66.

54. Walter and Schofield, "Famine, Disease, and Crisis Mortality in Early Modern Society," 7.

55. Garcilaso de la Vega, *The Royal Commentaries of Peru*, trans. Sir Paul Rycault (London: M. Flesher for J. Tonson, 1688), 385.

56. Samuel Clarke, *A True And Faithful Account of the Four Cheifest Plantations of the English in America* (London: Printed for R. Clavel, T. Passenger, W. Cadman, W. Whitwood, T. Sawbridge, and W. Birch, 1670), 27–28.

57. Willis, *Malevolent Nurture*, 215.

58. Robert Basset, *Curiosities: or The Cabinet of Nature. Containing Phylosophicall, Naturall, and Morall Questions Answered*, trans. R. B. Gent. (London, 1637), 211–12.

59. Kramer and Sprenger, *Malleus Mallificarum*, 23.

60. William Drage, *Daimonomageia. A Small Treatise of Sicknesses and Disease from Witchcraft and Supernatural Causes* (London: J. Dover, 1665), 15–16.

61. John Barrow, *The Lord's Arm Stretched Out in an Answer of Prayer, or A true Relation of the Wonderful Deliverance of James Barrow, the Son of John Barrow of Olaves Southwark* (London, [s.n.] 1664), 60. Barrow's story evidences what James Sharpe calls "practical demonology," his attempt to describe a hybrid phenomenon erased in many discussions of witchcraft (101). Unlike "Continental versions" of witchcraft (presumably characterized by witches' Sabbaths and Satanic pacts, reported by learned texts) or "English" ones (presumably associated with *maleficium* or village bewitchings), folk demonology, Sharpe argues, "did not lay too great emphasis on the devil, yet saw witches as his agents and placed them in the great struggle between good and evil, between God and Satan, which was central to the learned demonologists" (101).

62. Kramer and Sprenger, *Malleus Malificarum*, 113.

63. Thomas Ady, *A Perfect Discovery of Witches. Shewing the Divine Cause of the Distractions of this Kingdome, and also of the Christian World* (London: H. Broome, 1661), 135.

64. Ady, 135.

65. Mary Fissell, "Imagining Vermin in the Early Modern Period," *History Workshop Journal* 47 (1999): 21, 2.

66. McCormick, "Rats, Communication, Plague," 3.

67. Karl H. Dannenfeldt, "The Control of Vertebrate Pests in Renaissance Agriculture," *Agricultural History* 56 (1982): 555.

68. Quoted in Dannenfeldt, 557. Translated from the Latin found in Olaus Wormius, *Museum Wormianum* (Lugdunum Batavorum, 1651), 332.

69. On mice and the mousetrap scene in *Hamlet*, see Ruth Stevenson, "Hamlet's Mice, Motes, Moles, and Mincing Malech," *New Literary History* 33 (2002): 435–59; and Karen Raber, *Animal Bodies, Renaissance Culture* (Philadelphia: University of Pennsylvania Press, 2013), 109–23.

70. On early modern traps, see David Drummond, "Unmasking Mascall's Mousetraps," *Proceedings of the Fifteenth Vertebrates Pest Conference 1992*, ed. J. E. Borrecco and R. E. Marsh, paper 23, (Davis: University of California Press), 220–35. In his description of the African Mouse in *Historie of Four-Footed Beasts*, Topsell also raises the widely held belief that mice die as soon as they drink: "it shoulde seeme their temperament, or constitution is so moyst that nature can endure no addition" (506).

71. "An Eminent Poulterer," *The Compleat French and English Vermin Killer* (London: Printed for G. Conyers, [1710?]).

72. Robert Darnton, *The Great Cat Massacre and Other Episodes in French Cultural History* (New York: Basic Books, 1984).

73. Girard, *I See Satan Fall Like Lightening*, 159.

74. See Claude Rawson, *God, Gulliver, and Genocide: Barbarism and the European Imagination, 1492–1945* (Oxford: Oxford University Press, 2001).

75. Girard, "The Plague in Literature and Myth," 84.

Chapter 2

1. Godfrey Goodman, *The Fall of Man, or the Corruption of Nature* (London: Felix Kyngston for Richard Lee, 1616), 219.

2. George Wither seems to have been imprisoned three times. See J. Milton French, "George Wither in Prison," *PMLA* 45 (1930): 959–966.

3. Essays on Wither's politics include Allan Pritchard, "George Wither: The Poet as Prophet," *Studies in Philology* 59 (1962): 211–30; Jeffery S. Shoulson, "'Propertie in this Hebrew poesy': George Wither, Judaism, and the Formation of English National Identity," *Journal of English and Germanic Philology* 98 (1999): 353–72; and David Norbrook, "Levelling Poetry: George Wither and the English Revolution, 1642–1649," *English Literary Renaissance* 21 (1991): 217–56. On the politics of Cowley's poem, see Stella R. Revard, "Cowley's 'Pindarique Odes' and the Politics of the Interregnum," *Criticism* 35 (1993): 391–418.

4. John Walter discusses the "psychic hold [that] harvest failure had" on early moderns in "The Social Economy of Dearth in Early Modern England," in *Famine, Disease, and the Social Order in Early Modern Society*, ed. John Walter and Roger Schofield (Cambridge: Cambridge University Press, 1989), 75–128. On the question of whether rising and falling grain prices are accurate measures of crop shortages and dearth, see, in the same volume, Walter and Schofield, "Famine, Disease, and Crisis Mortality in Early Modern Society," 1–73, esp. 6–10.

5. On the relationship between hunger and disease, see John D. Post, *Food Shortage,*

Climatic Variability and Epidemic Disease in Pre-Industrial Europe: The Mortality Peak in the 1740s (Ithaca and London: Cornell University Press, 1985); Massimo Livi Bacci, *Population and Nutrition: An Essay on European Demographic History*, trans. Tania Croft-Murray and Carl Ipsen (Cambridge: Cambridge University Press, 1990). "Hunger and starvation," according to Livi Bacci, are "linked to increased mortality," not only because nutritional stress makes individuals susceptible to infections, but because hunger is associated with disruptions in the social order that create conditions for the transmission of disease (46–47). See also Andrew B. Appleby, "Epidemics and Famine in the Little Ice Age," *Journal of Interdisciplinary History* 10 (1980): 643–63.

6. Karl H. Dannenfeldt, "The Control of Vertebrate Pests in Renaissance Agriculture," *Agricultural History* 56 (1982): 553–54.

7. Michael McCormick, "Rats, Communication, and Plague: Towards an Ecological History," *Journal of Interdisciplinary History* 34 (2006): 22.

8. E. P. Evans, *The Criminal Prosecution and Capital Punishment of Animals* (London: William Heinemann, 1906), 3.

9. Evans, 2.

10. Evans, 4.

11. Evans, 5.

12. Michel Foucault, *Security, Territory, Population: Lectures at the College de France, 1977–1978*, trans. Graham Burchell (New York: Palgrave, 2004), 1.

13. Foucault, *Security, Territory, Population*, 31.

14. Foucault, 31.

15. Wendy Orent, *Plague: The Mysterious Past and Terrifying Future of the World's Most Dangerous Disease* (New York: Free Press, 2004), 150.

16. Wither, *Britain's Remembrancer*, "To the Kings Most Excellent Majestie," 7b.

17. Michael Drayton, *The Muses Elizium Lately Discouered, by a New Way Ouer Parnassus* (London: Thomas Harper for John Waterson, 1630). All references are to this edition and are cited hereafter parenthetically in the text.

18. Thomas Browne, *Pseudodoxia Epidemica, or, Enquiries into Very Many Received Tenents and Commonly Presumed Truths* (London: T. H. for E. Dod, 1646), 138.

19. Alexander Ross, *Arcana Microcosmi; or, the Secrets of Man's Body Discovered* (London: Tho[mas] Newcomb for John Clark, 1652), 155.

20. Graham Hammill, "Miracles and Plagues: Plague Discourse as Political Thought," *Journal of Early Modern Cultural Studies* 10 (2010): 85–104.

21. David Norbrook, *Poetry and Politics in the English Renaissance*, rev. ed. (Oxford: Oxford University Press, 2002), 214–15.

22. Norbrook, "Levelling Poetry," 219.

23. John Walter, "The Social Economy of Dearth in Early Modern England," in *Famine, Disease, and the Social Order*, 75. See also Post, *Food Shortage, Climatic Variability and Epidemic Disease in Pre-Industrial Europe*, who argues the English, unlike their neighbors, did not experience full-fledged famine.

24. Walter and Schofield, "Famine, Disease, and Crisis Mortality in Early Modern Society," 9. For a different view of "two Englands," one susceptible to famine, the other immune to it, see Andrew Appleby, "Disease or Famine? Mortality in Cumberland and Westmorland, 1580–1640," *Economic History Review* 26 (1973): 403–31.

25. Walter, "Social Economy of Dearth," 81.

26. Walter, 76.

27. William Shakespeare, *The Arden Shakespeare Works*, ed. Richard Proudfoot, Ann Thompson, and David Scott Kastan (New York: Bloomsbury, 2011).

28. See, for example, T[homas] D[ekker], *Canaans Calamitie, Jerusalems Misery, or The Doleful Destruction of Faire Jerusalem by Tytus* (London: John Bayly, 1618); Josephus Ben Gorion, *The Wonderful, and Most Deplorable History of the Latter Times of the Jews with the Destruction of the City of Jerusalem* (London: Christopher Ecclestone, 1662).

29. See David B. Goldstein, "The Cook and the Cannibal: Titus Andronicus and the New World," *Shakespeare Studies* 37 (2009): 99–133.

30. His poetry, according to Norbrook, "breaks down barriers between prophecy, autobiography, satire, journalism, political philosophy, and lyricism, in response to political crisis" ("Levelling Poetry," 221).

31. John Webster, *The Duchess of Malfi*, ed. Leah S. Marcus (London: Bloomsbury, 2009).

32. Graham Hammill, *The Mosaic Constitution: Political Theology and Imagination from Machiavelli to Milton* (Chicago: University of Chicago Press, 2012).

33. Andrew McRae, *God Speed the Plough: The Representation of Agrarian England, 1500–1660* (Cambridge: Cambridge University Press, 1996), 12–13. See also William F. Ruddiman, *Plows, Plagues, and Petroleum: How Humans Took Control of Climate* (Princeton: Princeton University Press, 2005).

34. McRae, *God Speed the Plough*, 299.

35. See Arthur H. Nethercot, *Abraham Cowley: The Muse's Hannibal* (New York: Russell and Russell, 1931), 51.

36. General studies of Cowley's life and works include Nethercot and Robert B. Hinman, *Abraham Cowley's World of Order* (Cambridge: Harvard University Press, 1960). On Cowley's training as a physician and his contributions to the Royal Society, see Achsah Guibbory, "Imitation and Originality: Cowley and Bacon's Vision of Progress," *Studies in English Literature, 1500–1900* 29 (1989): 99–120. See also Timothy Dykstal, "The Epic Reticence of Abraham Cowley," *Studies in English Literature, 1500–1900* 31 (1991): 95–115.

37. Abraham Cowley, *The Works of Abraham Cowley*, 2 vols., 12th ed. (London: J. Tonson, 1721). All references are to this edition.

38. Alexander Pope, *The Major Works*, ed. Pat Rogers (Oxford: Oxford University Press, 2008), 346.

39. On voluntarism in seventeenth-century England, see particularly Robert Markley, *Fallen Languages: Crises of Representation in Newtonian England, 1660–1740* (Ithaca: Cornell University Press, 1993).

40. Nethercot raises the possibility that the plague poem and Cowley's "The 34 Chapter of the Prophet Isaiah" provide "opportunities for allegorical interpretation," possible parables written in preparation for his career as a spy (154–55).

41. Nethercot, "Abraham Cowley's Essays," *Journal of English and Germanic Philology* 29 (1930), 124–25.

42. Goodman, *The Fall of Man*, 219.

43. Cowley, "Inconstancy," 64.

44. Abraham Cowley, *The Poetical Works of Abraham Cowley Vol. III* (Edinburgh: Apollo Press, 1784), 43. Hereafter cited parenthetically in the text.

45. On "collective identity" and modern environmental consciousness, see Robert Watson, *Back to Nature: The Green and the Real in the Late Renaissance* (Philadelphia: University of Pennsylvania Press, 2007), 32.

46. John Ray, *The Wisdom of God Manifested in the Works of the Creation*, 7th ed. (London: R. Harbin, 1717), 373.

47. Ray, *Wisdom of God*, 374.

48. Ray, 374–75.

49. Ray, 375.

50. Ray, 375.

51. Frank N. Egerton, "Ancient Sources for Animal Demography," *Isis* 59 (1968): 175–89.

52. Egerton, "Ancient Sources," 181.

53. Watson, 32.

54. Thomas Molyneux, *A Letter from Dr. Thomas Molyneux, Fellow of the Royal Society, to the Right Reverand St. George, Lord Bishop of Clogher; Concerning Swarms of Insects, That of Late Have Much Infested Some Parts of the Province of Connought in Ireland*, Philosophical Transactions, Vol. 19 (1695–97): 741–56. (http://www.jstor.org/stable/102408). Accessed 12/17/2012, 744. Hereafter cited parenthetically in the text.

55. In 1885, the amateur naturalist Vincent M. Holt questioned our reliance on mammalian flesh in a book called, modestly, *Why Not Eat Insects?* Addressing directly the prejudices against what he regards as the consumption of wholesome and delicious insects and small mollusks, Holt recommends the "poor" increase their income and vary their diet by "hand-picking destructive insects" from the crops and "partaking of toothsome and nourishing insects dished at home." Vincent C. Holt, *Why Not Eat Insects?* (London: Field and Tuer, 1885), 15. Holt's question—if not his work program—has been renewed in recent years by the UN's Food and Agriculture Organization (FAO), which estimates that two billion of the world's population already eat insects as part of their normal diet.

Chapter 3

1. Thomas Shadwell, *The Virtuoso* (1676), ed. Marjorie Hope Nicolson and David Stuart Rodes (Lincoln: University of Nebraska Press, 1966), I.ii.12–13. All references are to this edition and are cited parenthetically in the text.

2. Andrew Black, "The Orator in the Laboratory: Rhetoric and Experimentation in Thomas Shadwell's *The Virtuoso*," *Restoration* 37 (2013): 1–18. See also John Shanahan, "Theatrical Space and Scientific Space in Thomas Shadwell's *Virtuoso*," *Studies in English Literature 1500–1900* 49 (2009): 549–71.

3. Francis Bacon, *Sylva Sylvarum: Or, The Natural History in Ten Centuries*, in *The Works of Francis Bacon*, ed. James Spedding, Robert L. Ellis, and Douglas D. Heath (rpt. New York: Garrett Press, 1968), 2: 557. Hereafter cited parenthetically in the text.

4. On Southall and the cultural significance of bedbugs in eighteenth-century England, see Lisa Sarasohn, "'That Nauseous Venomous Insect': Bedbugs in Early Modern England," *Eighteenth-Century Studies* 46 (2013): 513–30.

5. Hooke, *Micrographia, or, Some Physiological Descriptions of Minute Bodies* (London: Printed by Jo. Martyn and Ja. Allestree, 1665), preface unnumbered. See also Janice Neri, *The Insect and the Image: Visualizing Nature in Early Modern Europe, 1500–1700* (Minneapolis: University of Minnesota Press, 2011).

6. Tita Chico, "Gimcrack's Legacy: Sex, Wealth, and the Theatre of Experimental Philosophy," *Comparative Drama* 42 (2008): 29–49. On Behn's *Emperor of the Moon*, see Al Coppola, "Retraining the Virtuoso's Gaze: Behn's *Emperor of the Moon*, the Royal Society, and the Spectacle of Science and Politics," *Eighteenth-Century Studies* 41 (2008): 481–506, and Katherine Mannheimer, "Celestial Bodies: Readerly Rapture as Theatrical Spectacle in Aphra Behn's *Emperor of the Moon*," *Restoration* 35 (2011): 39–60.

7. Chico, "Gimcrack's Legacy," 29–33.

8. Thomas Sprat, *The History of the Royal Society*, ed. Jackson Cope (St. Louis: Washington University Studies, 1958), 113.

9. On Shadwell's dramatic satire, see Christopher Wheatley, *Without God or Reason: The Plays of Thomas Shadwell and Secular Ethics in the Restoration* (Lewisburg, PA: Bucknell University Press, 1993).

10. See Jacques Derrida, *The Animal That Therefore I Am*, trans. David Wills, ed. Marie-Louise Mallet (New York: Fordham University Press, 2008); and Giorgio Agamben, *The Open: Man and Animal* (New York: Stanford University Press, 2003). Some animal studies scholars detect a residual Cartesianism in their approaches. See, for example, Erica Fudge, "The Dog, the Home and the Human, and the Ancestry of Derrida's Cat," *Oxford Literary Review* 29 (2007): 37–54.

11. Erica Fudge, *Brutal Reasoning: Animals, Rationality, and Humanity in Early Modern England* (Ithaca: Cornell University Press, 2006), 180.

12. Laurie Shannon, *The Accommodated Animal: Cosmopolity in Shakespearean Locales* (Chicago: University of Chicago Press, 2013), 2.

13. On English anti-Cartesianism in the seventeenth and eighteenth centuries, see Robert Markley, *Fallen Languages: Crises of Representation in Newtonian England, 1660–1740* (Ithaca: Cornell University Press, 1993), 194, 200–4; and Alvin Snider, "Cartesian Bodies," *Modern Philology* 98 (2000): 299–319.

14. Alvin Snider points out that "what remains most striking about Descartes's position from a historicist perspective is not his dualism per se but his account of physical bodies as defined entirely by their mechanistic qualities. Organic processes undergo detailed analyses without recourse to postulating the existence of entities such as the 'vegetative' and 'sensitive' souls" ("Cartesian Bodies," 306).

15. Thomas, Willis, *Two Discourses Concerning the Soul of Brutes* (London: Thomas Dringe, 1683), Preface, unnumbered. Hereafter referred to parenthetically in the text as *AB*.

16. Robert Boyle, *Of the Usefulnesse of Experimental Natural Philosophy* (Oxford, 1663).

17. Shanahan, "Theatrical Space and Scientific Space in Shadwell's *Virtuoso*," 559.

18. The Latin edition of *Cerebri Anatome* was published in 1664, then translated into English by S. Pordage in 1681. I will be using a reset version of the original English edition, Thomas Willis, *The Anatomy of the Brain, the 1681 Edition, Reset and Reprinted, with the Original Illustrations by Sir Christopher Wren* (Tuckahoe, NY: USV Pharmaceutical Corp, 1971.) Hereafter referred to parenthetically in the text as *CA*.

19. Such reassessment has occurred mostly by medical historians. See the foundational text by F. J. Cole, *A History of Comparative Anatomy: From Aristotle to the Eighteenth Century* (1949; rpt. New York: Dover, 1979). The most thorough study of Willis is Hansruedi Isler, *Thomas Willis 1621–1675: Doctor and Scientist* (New York and London: Hafner, 1968). A reliable shorter account is Alfred Meyer and Raymond Hierons, "On Thomas Willis's Concepts of Neuropsychology, Part One," *Medical History* 9 (1965): 1–15; and Meyer and Hierons, "On Thomas Willis's Concepts of Neuropsychology, Part Two," *Medical History* 9 (1965): 142–55. Meyer and Hierons emphasize Willis's debt to Gassendi, whose reputation in Willis's time "was almost equal to that of Descartes" (Part One, p. 5). See also William Bynum, "The Anatomical Method, Natural Theology, and the Functions of the Brain," *Isis* 64 (1973): 444–68.

Recent popular texts include Carl Zimmer, *Soul Made Flesh: The Discovery of the Brain—and How It Changed the World* (New York: Free Press, 2004); and Francis Crick, *The Astonishing Hypothesis: The Scientific Search for the Soul* (New York: Touchstone, 1994). For relations between Willis and literary figures, see George Rousseau, "Nerves, Spirits, and Fibres: Towards Defining the Origins of Sensibility," in *Nervous Acts: Essays on Literature, Culture, and Sensibility* (New York and Basingstoke: Palgrave, 2004), 160–84. See also Raymond Martin and John Barresi, *Naturalization of the Soul: Self and Personality in the Eighteenth Century* (London: Routledge, 2000).

20. Noga Arikha argues Willis's ideas crossed the channel quickly. See "Form and Function in the Early Enlightenment," *Perspectives on Science* 14 (2006): 153–88. On Willis's influence on John Locke, see B. C. Lega, "*An Essay Concerning Human Understanding*: How the *Cerebri Anatomi* of Thomas Willis influenced John Locke," *Neurosurgery* 58 (2006): 567–76.

21. Although Shadwell attended Cambridge and left without a degree, his son, Sir

John Shadwell (1671–1747) matriculated at University College, Oxford in 1685, studied medicine under former students of Willis's, and went on to become physician to Queen Anne and George I. (DNB)

22. Zimmer, *Soul Made Flesh*, 228. On Willis's debt to Gassendi, see Meyer and Hierons, "On Thomas Willis's Concepts of Neuropsychology," 5–6.

23. For descriptions of passages in the play that echo actual experiments, see the Introduction by Marjorie Hope Nicholson and David Stuart Rodes to their edition of *The Virtuoso*, xxi–xxv, which supersedes earlier studies by Claude Lloyd, "Shadwell and the Virtuosi," *PMLA* 44 (1929): 472–94, and F. P. Wilson, "English Letters and the Royal Society in the Seventeenth Century," *The Mathematical Gazette* 19. 236 (1935): 343–54. See also Nicholson, *Pepys' Diary and the New Science* (Charlottesville: University of Virginia Press, 1965), 170–75. Robert Boyle, Robert Hooke, and Martin Lister have all been advanced as possible models for Sir Nicholas Gimcrack.

24. On the role of animals in English experimental philosophy, see Anita Guerrini, *Experimenting With Humans and Animals: From Galen to Animal Rights* (Baltimore: Johns Hopkins University Press, 2003). See also Peter Harrison, "Reading Vital Signs: Animals and the Experimental Philosophy," in *Renaissance Beasts: Of Animals, Humans, and Other Wonderful Creatures*, ed. Erica Fudge (Champaign: University of Illinois Press, 1994), 186–207.

25. Rousseau, *Nervous Acts*, 18.

26. Zimmer, *Soul Made Flesh*, 60.

27. Rousseau, *Nervous Acts*, 26.

28. Rousseau, 165.

29. Zimmer, 187.

30. Meyer and Hierons, Part One, 2.

31. On the status of cats in the early modern period, see Karen Raber, "How to do things with Animals: Thoughts on/with the Early Modern Cat," in *Early Modern Ecostudies: From the Florentine Codex to Shakespeare*, ed. Raber, Ivo Kamps, Thomas Hallock (Bastingstoke: Palgrave, 2008), 93–114.

32. Isler, *Thomas Willis*, 94–95

33. Consequently, Willis claims, these "slow and gentler beasts" are "less docile or apt to learn," a fact he knows functionally (rather than anatomically) because, unlike humans, cows are "born seeking their food," or knowing what to eat and how to get it; "what is congruous for them," he claims, "they readily know" (*CA* 100).

34. Isler, 6.

35. William Congreve, *William Congreve: Letters and Documents*, ed. John C. Hodges, (New York: Harcourt Brace, 1964), 183.

36. See the discussion of Rochester in chapter 4.

37. John Dryden, Preface to *Annus Mirabilis, The Year of Wonders, 1666* (London: Henry Harriman, 1667), unnumbered.

38. William Davenant, *Gondibert* (London: John Holden, 1651), 28.

39. Davenant, *Gondibert*, 28.

40. See Joanna Piciotto, *Labors of Innocence in Early Modern England* (Cambridge: Harvard University Press, 2010), 398–99.

41. Bruno Latour, *We Have Never Been Modern*, trans. Catherine Porter (Cambridge: Harvard University Press, 1993), 13.

42. Latour, *We Have Never Been Modern*, 39.

43. Robert Boyle, *The Works of Robert Boyle*, 5 vols. (London: A. Millar, 1744), 4: 363.

44. René Descartes, *A Discourse of a Method for the Well Guiding of Reason, and the Discovery of Truth in the Sciences* (London: Thomas Newcombe, 1649), 96.

45. Meyer and Heirons, 6.

46. Bynum, "The Anatomical Method, Natural Theology, and the Functions of the Brain," 447.

47. Zimmer's *Soul Made Flesh* was published in England with the subtitle *The English Civil War and the Mapping of the Mind*.

48. Thomas Browne, *Sir Thomas Browne's Religio Medici*, ed. William Alexander Greenhill (London: Macmillan, 1904), 55. Arguing that neither Descartes nor Kenelm Digby, one of the few English Cartesians, "satisfie[s] a mind desirous of truth" (3), Willis aligns himself with the vitalism of Gassendi. While Gassendi is willing to include nonhumans as self-conscious beings, Willis (although agreeing that animals have "a certain kind of Reason") claims Gassendi "passes over a knot"—namely, how reason can be attributed to souls "so slenderly gifted as their substances," so far "from the flame of life" (*AB* 3).

49. See, for example, A. N. Williams, "'Of Stupidity or Folly': Thomas Willis's Perspective on Mental Retardation," *Archives of Disease in Childhood* 87 (2002): 555–57.

50. Zimmer, 226.

51. Walter Charleton, *The Darknes of Atheism Dispelled by the Light of Reason* (London: Printed by J. F. for William Lee, 1652), 64. Both *Cerebri Anatome* and *De Anima Brutorum* are foundational to Charleton's anti-Cartesian argument in *A Natural History of the Passions* (London: Printed by T. N. for James Magnes, 1674) that humans are composed of "*two distinct Souls*, coexistent, conjoined, and cooperating," one rational, one sensitive, "hotly contending about the conduct of our Will" (Preface). So closely is his account of the sensitive soul "borrowed from that elaborate work of our Learned Dr. *Willis De Anima Brutorum*, lately published," that Charleton is "bound here to ingeniously acknowledge, lest otherwise [the reader] might justly condemn me as a *Plagiary*" (Preface).

52. Charleton, *Darknes of Atheism Dispelled*, 66–67.

53. As Rina Knoeff argues, "Just as Aristotle had anatomized animals to discover how the soul expresses itself in the organs of the body, so Willis now anatomized the brain and nerves to explain the workings of the soul in humans." Rina Knoeff, "The Reins of the Soul: The Centrality of the Intercostal Nerves to the Neurology of Thomas Willis and Samuel Parker's Theology," *Journal of the History of Medicine and Allied Sciences* 59 (2004): 426.

54. On alchemy in early modern science, see Betty Jo Teeter Dobbs, *The Janus Faces of Genius: The Role of Alchemy in Newton's Thought* (Cambridge: Cambridge University Press, 1991).

55. Latour, *We Have Never Been Modern*, 23–24.

56. In odd ways, Willis's "Amphibious Animal" prefigures and anticipates the posthuman recognition that the human cannot be defined along purely Cartesian lines. In *The Open: Man and Animal*, Giorgio Agamben argues the human is not a "biologically defined species" (12), but "exists historically" only in a tension between the human and the animal: "[man] can be human only to the degree that he transcends and transforms the anthropophorous animals which support him, and only because, through the action of negation, he is capable of mastering, and eventually destroying, his own animality" (12).

57. Shadwell's patron, William Cavendish, Earl of Newcastle, had an abiding interest in natural philosophy, and had conversed with Descartes and Gassendi during the 1650s in Paris. Newcastle, in the 1620s and 30s, had been Ben Jonson's patron, and Shadwell deftly negotiates the problem of satirizing natural philosophy by turning Sir Formal and Sir Nicholas into figures indebted to the humours tradition.

58. Martin Lister, *Tractatus de Araneis* (London: Royal Society, 1678). On the influence of Lister, see Anna Marie Roos, *Web of Nature: Martin Lister (1639–1712), The First Arachnologist* (London: Brill, 2011).

59. On the August 1675 riots by silkweavers, see Richard M. Dunn, "The London Weavers Riot of 1675," *Guildhall Studies in London History* 1 (October 1973–April 1975), 13–23.

60. Anonymous, *A True Narrative of All the Proceedings Against the Weavers* (London: [no publisher], 1675), 3–4.

61. Brown, *Homeless Dogs and Melancholy Apes*, 9.

Chapter 4

1. Gary A. Rendsburg demonstrates how this question divided medieval rabbis; the interpretation of the fourth plague as blood-sucking flies, rather than as jackals, wolves, leopards, lions, and other warm-blooded beasts of prey, was stabilized in 1611 with the King James Bible. See "Beasts or Bugs: Solving the Problem of the Fourth Plague," *Bible Review* 19: 2 (2003): 19–23. Cowley acknowledges the etymological ambiguity between a "swarm of flies" and a "mixture of beasts" but, following St. Hier, suggests the swarm is composed of "dog-flies," or *Canina Musca*. See *The Works of Abraham Cowley*, 2 vols. 12th ed. (London: J. Tonson, 1721), 252.

2. Daniel Defoe, *Journal of the Plague Year* (1727), ed. John Mullan (London: Pickering and Chatto, 2009), x.

3. Mark Jenner, "The Great Dog Massacre," in *Fear in Early Modern Society*, ed. William G. Naphy and Penny Roberts (Manchester: St. Martin's Press, 1997), 49. See also

Charles F. Mullett, "Some Neglected Aspects of Plague Medicine in Sixteenth-Century England," *The Scientific Monthly* 44, 4 (1937): 325–37.

4. Bernard Mandeville, *The Fable of the Bees* (London: Printed for J. Roberts, 1714), 3. A succinct account of the role of bees in Augustan literature is James W. Johnson, "The Neo-Classical Bee," *Journal of the History of Ideas* 22 (1961): 262–66. On Mandeville's relationship to this tradition, see Philip Harth, "The Satiric Purpose of *The Fable of the Bees*," *Eighteenth-Century Studies* 2 (1969): 321–40; and Danielle Allen, "Burning *The Fable of the Bees*," in *The Moral Authority of Nature*, ed. Lorraine Daston and Fernando Vidal (Chicago and London: University of Chicago Press, 2004), 74–99. Harold Cook argues that Mandeville's "defense" of parasitical society was not actually considered scandalous until the spring of 1723 when it was republished with what was considered as an attack on the clergy and charity schools. See "Bernard Mandeville and the Therapy of 'The Clever Politician,'" *Journal of the History of Ideas* 60 (1999): 101–24.

5. On classical sources for the parasite in the English tradition, see E. P. Vandiver, Jr., "The Elizabethan Dramatic Parasite," *Studies in Philology* 32 (1935): 411–27.

6. Ben Jonson, *The Workes of Benjamin Jonson* (London: Printed by W. Stansby, 1616), III.1.8–13.

7. Michel Serres reminds us that the scientific vocabulary of the parasite is borrowed (or "imported") from a much broader literature about customs and manners located in fables like "The Fly and the Ant," "The Crow and the Fox," and "The Country Mouse and the City Mouse." To regard the dog as part of the parasitical system requires a shift away from contemporary scientific definitions of the parasite. "For the science called parasitology," writes Serres, "a rat, carrion-eater like the hyena, a man, be he peasant or high official, are not parasites at all"; for scientists, parasites are required to live on, rather than beside, the host (6). *The Parasite*, trans. Lawrence R. Scher (Baltimore: Johns Hopkins, 1982; reissued Minneapolis: University of Minnesota, 2007).

8. Clifford Davidson, "*Timon of Athens*: The Iconography of False Friendship," *Huntington Library Quarterly* 43 (1980): 181–200. Davidson provides several examples of the dog as untrustworthy flatterer, including Henry Peacham, *Minerva Britanna, or a Garden of Heroical Devises* (London: Wa. Dight, 1612), 206–7, quoted here (189). See also James L. Jackson, "Shakespeare's Dog-and-Sugar Imagery and the Friendship Tradition," *Shakespeare Quarterly* 1 (1950): 260–63.

9. Henry Hartflete, *The Hunting of the Fox: or, Flattery Displayed* (London: Printed by A. M[athewes] for Philemon Stephens and Christopher Meredith, 1632), 16.

10. Davidson, 189. Davidson cites the English translation of Caesar Ripa, *Iconologia* (London: Benjamin Motte,1709), a text that was reprinted several dozen times in the eighteenth century.

11. Davidson, 189.

12. Mandeville, *Fable of the Bees*, 187.

13. A. O. Exquemelin, *Buckaniers of America* (London: William Crooke, 1684), 52–53.

14. Anders M. Gullestad, "Literature and the Parasite," *Delueze Studies* 5 (2011): 301–23, 305. See also the discussion by Karen Raber, *Animal Bodies, Renaissance Culture* (Philadelphia: University of Pennsylvania Press, 2013), esp. 109–23.

15. Mandeville, 187.

16. See P. F. Vernon, "Social Satire in Shadwell's *Timon*," *Studia Neophilologica* 35 (1963): 221–26.

17. Thomas Shadwell, *The History of Timon of Athens, the Man-Hater* (London: Printed for H. H. [Henry Herringman] and sold by W. Davies, 1703), 1. Hereafter cited parenthetically in the text.

18. Thomas Nashe, "Summer's Last Will and Testament," *Works of Thomas Nashe*, Vol. III, ed. Ronald B. McKerrow (London: Sidgwick and Jackson, 1910), 255.

19. See Proverbs 26:11 on dogs returning to their vomit. A succinct account of the failings of dogs can be found in Wolfgang Franz, *The History of Brutes* (London: Printed by E. Okes, for Francis Haley, 1670), 176: "He is a very filthy, uncleane creature, coupling himself publickly in the streets; and hath a very greedy stomach after his meat, and exceedingly loveth carrion; he satisfieth his lust with the Bitch that puppyed him."

20. On the "unclean" feeding habits of dogs, see Jenner, "The Great Dog Massacre," 52–54.

21. Alan S. Fisher, "The Significance of Thomas Shadwell," *Studies in Philology* 71 (1974): 225–46. See also Vernon, "Social Satire in Shadwell's Timon," 221–26.

22. According to Meredith Ann Skura, the "link between prostitutes and dogs" via flattery "is proverbial." See *Shakespeare the Actor and the Purposes of Playing* (Chicago: University of Chicago Press, 1994), 175. Jackson discusses spaniel imagery in "Shakespeare's Dog-and-Sugar Imagery," 260–61.

23. See Steven D. Brown, "In Praise of the Parasite: The Dark Organizational Theory of Michel Serres," *Porto Alegre* 16 (2013): 92.

24. Brown, "In Praise of the Parasite," 92.

25. Shadwell dedicated *Timon* to the Duke of Buckingham, Rochester's libertine companion, who had retired to the country after 1675. During the Exclusion Crisis (1679–82), Buckingham and Rochester both supported the First Earl of Shaftesbury's efforts to block the Catholic James, Duke of York, from succeeding to the throne.

26. Brown, 92.

27. *The Complete Poems of John Wilmot, Earl of Rochester*, ed. David Vieth (New Haven: Yale University Press, 1968), lines 129–32. All citations are from this edition.

28. Thomas Hobbes, *The Questions Concerning Liberty, Necessity, and Chance* (London: Printed for Andrew Cook, 1656), 142.

29. Hobbes, *Questions*, 142.

30. Jonathan Swift, "On Poetry," *The Essential Writings of Jonathan Swift*, ed. Claude Rawson and Ian Higgins (New York: W.W. Norton and Co., 2010), 654.

31. John Gay, "Man and the Flea, Fable xlix," *Poetry and Prose*, 2 vols. ed. Vinton A. Dearing and Charles Beckwith (Oxford: Clarendon Press, 1974), 2: 368.

32. Kirk Combe, *A Martyr For Sin: Rochester's Critique of Polity, Sexuality, and Society* (Newark and London: University of Delaware Press 1998), 18.

33. Josué V. Harari and David F. Bell, "Introduction" in Michel Serres, *Hermes: Literature, Science, Philosophy*, ed. Harari and Bell (Baltimore: Johns Hopkins University Press, 1982), xxvii.

34. Jenner, 53.

35. Mullett, "Neglected Aspects of Plague Medicine," 337.

36. Nan H. Drehrer, "The Virtuous and the Verminous: Turn-of-the-Century Moral Panics in London's Public Parks," *Albion* 29 (1997): 246–67, 249. On London's public parks, see L. R. Sadler (Jacob Larwood), *The Story of the London Parks* (London: Chatto & Windus, 1881); and Cynthia Wall, *The Literary and Cultural Spaces of Restoration London* (Cambridge: Cambridge University Press, 1998). On the parks as a feminized space, see Mona Narain, "Libertine Spaces and the Female Body in the Poetry of Rochester and Ned Ward," *ELH* 72 (2005): 553–76.

37. Sadler, *Story of London Parks*, 345–46.

38. John Evelyn, *The Diary of John Evelyn*, 2 vols., ed. William Bray (Washington & London: M. Walter Dunne, 1901), 2: 2–3.

39. Evelyn, *Diary*, 3.

40. Puget de la Serres, "Histoire de L'entrée de la Reine Mere dans la Grande Bretagne, 1683," 42. Reported in Sadler, 331.

41. Sadler, 349.

42. Sadler, 349.

43. William Austin, *Epiloimia Epe. Or The Anatomie of a Pestilence. A Poem in Three Parts. Describing The Deplorable Conditions of the City of London under its Merciless Dominion* (London: Nathaniel Brooke, 1666), 68.

44. Daniel Defoe, *Journal of the Plague Year* (1722), ed. John Mullan (Pickering and Chatto, 2009), 146.

45. Robert Boyle, *Essays of the Strange Subtilty, Great Efficacy, Determinate Nature of Effluviums* (London: Printed by W. G. for M. Pitt, 1673), 30.

46. Boyle, *Essays*, 30.

47. John Donne, *Donne's Satyr Containing 1. A Short Map of Mundane Vanity 2. A Cabinet of Merry Conceits, 3. Certain Pleasant Propositions and Questions with their Merry Solutions and Answers* (London: Printed by R.W. for M. Wright, 1662), 118.

48. Wolf mating exhibits considerable intraspecific variation, depending on group and habitat. See Rudd Denx, Jan Van Hoof, Han De Vries, and Joep Wensing, "Male and Female Mating Competition in Wolves: Female Suppression vs. Male Intervention," *Behavior* 127 (1993): 141–74.

49. On violence in "Ramble," see Ken Robinson, "The Art of Violence in Rochester's Satire," *The Yearbook of English Studies* 14 (1984): 93–108. On rivalry and the male homosocial order, see Harold Weber, "'Drudging in Fair Aurelia's Womb': Constructing Homosocial Economies," *The Eighteenth Century: Theory and Interpretation* 33 (1992):

99–117; Duane Coltharp, "Rivall Fopps, Rambling Rakes, Wild Women: Homosocial Desire and Courtly Crisis in Rochester's Poetry," *The Eighteenth Century: Theory and Interpretation* 38 (1997): 23–42; and James Grantham Turner, *Libertines and Radicals in Early Modern London: Sexuality, Politics and Literary Culture, 1630–1685* (Cambridge: Cambridge University Press, 2002), 221–27.

50. To Rochester in London from Henry Bulkely, May–June, 1676, in *The Letters of John Wilmot, Earl of Rochester*, ed. Jeremy Treglown (Oxford: Blackwell, 1980), 124–27.

51. John Trapp, *A Commentary or Exposition upon the Minor Prophets* (London: Printed by R. N. for Philemon Stevens, 1654), 459.

52. See Franz, *The History of Brutes*, 176: Dogs "cannot hunt if the South-wind bloweth, for it is the moistest of all the four winds, and all moisture hindereth the smelling."

53. Seventeenth-century writers, following Hippocrates, suggested that *furor uterinus* was capable of transforming women into men. See James Ferrand, *Erôotomania, or A Treatise Discoursing of the Essence, Causes, Symptomes, Prognosticks, and Cure of Love, or Erotique Melancholy* (Oxford: Printed by L. Litchfield for Edward Forrest, 1640), 11–13.

54. Nathaniel Highmore, *The History of Generation* (London: Printed by R.N. for John Martin, 1651), 120: "A Bitch lined with several kindes of Dogs, though in the dark, where her phansie could not operate to the assimulating of her births, brings forth her whelps fashioned and coloured, like to all those she coupled with."

55. Attributed to Rochester in *Collected Works of John Wilmot, Earl of Rochester*, ed. John Hayward (London: Nonesuch Press, 1926), 92.

56. Carol Fabricant, "Rochester's World of Imperfect Enjoyment," *Journal of English and Germanic Philology* 73 (1974), 343.

57. Combe, *A Martyr for Sin*, 117.

58. Richard Blackmore, *A Satyr against Wit* (London: Printed for Samuel Crouch, 1700), 54.

59. On the relationship among beastliness, madness, and drunkenness, see Erica Fudge, *Brutal Reasoning: Animals, Rationality, and Humanity in Early Modern England* (Ithaca: Cornell University Press, 2006), 62–74.

60. John Brydall, *Non Compos Mentis or The law Relating to Natural Fools, Mad-folks, and Lunatic Persons* (London: Printed by Richard and Edward Atkins for Isaac Cleave, 1700), 53.

61. Brydall, *Non Compos Mentis*, 53.

62. Brydall, 53.

63. Brydall, 55, 57, 60.

64. Laura Brown, *Homeless Dogs and Melancholy Apes: Humans and Other Animals in the Modern Literary Imagination* (Ithaca: Cornell, 2010). Brown argues that in the misogynist tradition of the 1680s and 90s, "the lapdog seems to be both an inappropriate or perverse sexual partner for the woman and also a metonym for female sexuality" (82). My reading of dogs in antifeminist satire is compatible with her account. Brown cites Robert Gould's *Love Given O're, A Satyr Against the Pride, Lust, and Inconstancy*

of Women (1682) as an example of misogynist satire. Gould's poem is structurally and thematically connected to Rochester's by virtue of male-male rivalry figured through canines: "How curst is *Man*! When *Brutes* his Rivals prove,/ Ev'n in the sacred business of his *Love*!" It describes lustful women retiring into their closets where "flaming *Dil—* does inflame desire/ And gentle *Lap-d—s* feed the am'rous fire." See Robert Gould, *Poems, Chiefly Consisting of Satyrs and Satirical Epistles* (London, 1689), 145. See also Pat Gill, "'Filth of All Hues and Odors': Public Parks, City Showers, and Promiscuous Acquaintance in Rochester and Swift," *Genre* 27 (1994): 333–50.

65. Laura Brown, 72.

66. See Neil Pemberton and Michael Warboys, *Dogs, Disease, and Culture, 1830–2000* (Bastingstoke: Palgrave Macmillan, 2007).

67. Daniel Defoe wrote *Journal of the Plague Year* in 1722. Here he reports, on Orders of the Lord Mayor and Alderman, that animals, including dogs were to be contained or exterminated: "no hogs, dogs, or cats, or tame pigeons, or ponies, be suffered to be kept within any part of the city, or any swine to be or stray in the streets or lanes, but that such swine be impounded by the beadle or any other officer, and the owner punished according to Act of Common Council, and that the dogs be killed by the dog-killers appointed for that purpose" (58).

68. The term "hydrophobia" pertains to the paradoxical symptom of this desiccation, an aversion to water. "Though they be very dry," writes Robert Burton, "they will rather dye, then drinke." See Burton, *The Anatomy of Melancholy* (Oxford: Printed by John Litchfield and James Short for Henry Cripps, 1621), 14.

69. William Ramsay (Ramesey), *De Venenis; or, A Discourse of Poysons* (London: Printed for Samuel Speed, 1663), 112.

70. Daniel Peter Layard, *An Essay on the Bite of a Mad Dog*, second ed. (London: Printed for John Rivington and Thomas Payne, 1763), 85.

71. Martin Lister, *A Remarkable Relation of a Man Bitten with a Mad Dog, and Dying of the Disease called Hydrophobia, Sent in a Letter to the Royal Society by the Learned Martin Lister, Esquire, dated from York March 26, 1683*, 163.

72. Lister 165.

73. Lister 169.

74. Lister 167.

75. Pierre-Joseph Desault, *A Treatise on the Venereal Distemper* (London, 1738), 211.

76. Desault, 211.

77. Desault, 211.

78. Desault, 211.

79. Laura Brown addresses this poem briefly in *Homeless Dogs and Melancholy Apes*, 72–73.

80. John Gay, *The Poetical Works of John Gay, Including His Fables*, Vol. II. (Edinburg: Apollo Press, 1784). All references are to this edition.

81. Hermann van der Heyden, *Speedy Help for Rich and Poor* (London: Printed by

James Young, for O. P. 1653), 90. On dunking or immersion as a cure for rabies, see also Daniel Peter Layard, *An Essay on the Bite of a Mad Dog*, 57–65.

82. Desault, 197–98.

83. On antifeminist satire of the period, see Felicity Nussbaum, *The Brink of All We Hate: English Satires on Women 1660–1750* (Lexington: University Press of Kentucky, 1984).

Chapter 5

1. Jonathan Watts, "Ecuador drops Poison on Galapagos Islands in Attempt to Eradicate Rats," *The Guardian*, November 15, 2012. http://www.theguardian.com/world/2012/nov/15/ecuador-poison-galapagos-islands-rats

2. See John McVeagh, "Defoe and Far Travel," in *English Literature and the Wider World, vol 1: 1660–1780. All the World Before Them*, ed. John McVeagh (London: Ashfield, 1990).

3. Garcilaso de la Vega, *The Royal Commentaries of Peru*, trans. Sir Paul Rycault (London: M. Flesher for J. Tonson, 1688), 385.

4. Samuel Clarke, *A True and Faithful Account of the Four Cheifest Plantations of the English in America* (London: Printed for R. Clavel, T. Passenger, W. Cadman, W. Whitwood, T. Sawbridge, and W. Birch, 1670), 27–28.

5. William Dampier, *A New Voyage around the World* (London: Printed for James Knapton, 1703), 281.

6. Woodes Rogers, *A Cruising Voyage round the World* (London: A. Bell and B. Lintot, 1712), 220.

7. Rogers, *Cruising Voyage*, 128.

8. Richard Steele, *The Englishman: Being the Sequel of the Guardian* (London: Samuel Buckley, 1714), 123.

9. Daniel Defoe, *The Life and Strange Surprizing Adventures of Robinson Crusoe* (1719), ed. W.R. Owens (London: Pickering and Chatto, 2008), 94. All quotations are from this edition.

10. On Crusoe and providence, see J. Paul Hunter, *The Reluctant Pilgrim: Defoe's Emblematic Method and the Quest for Form in Robinson Crusoe* (Baltimore: Johns Hopkins University Press, 1966).

11. Defoe, *A Tour thro' the Whole Island of Great Britain* (1727) (London: Printed for J. Osborn, S. Birt, D. Browne, J. Hodges, A. Millar, J. Whiston, and J, Robinson, 1742), 271.

12. Contemporary accounts of Selkirk belong to a genre of Pacific voyage literature that, in its distinctiveness from transatlantic literature, has attracted a good deal of critical attention. See Philip Edwards, *The Story of the Voyage: Sea-Narratives in Eighteenth-Century England* (Cambridge: Cambridge University Press, 1994); Glyn Williams, *The Great South Sea: English Voyages and Encounters, 1570–1750* (New Ha-

ven: Yale University Press, 1997); Jonathan Lamb, *Preserving the Self in the South Seas, 1680–1840* (Chicago: University of Chicago Press, 2001); and Robert Markley, "The Eighteenth-Century Novel and the Pacific," *The Cambridge History of the English Novel*, ed. Robert Caesario and Clement Hawes (Cambridge: Cambridge University Press, 2012), 196–212.

13. On Goodman, see chapter 2 above.

14. John Bender, *Ends of Enlightenment* (Stanford: Stanford University Press, 2012), 105. For representative readings that focus on the problem of "realism," see Paula Backscheider, *Daniel Defoe: Ambition and Innovation* (Lexington: University of Kentucky Press, 1986); Backscheider, *Daniel Defoe, His Life* (Baltimore: Johns Hopkins University Press, 1989); Maximillian Novak, *Realism, Myth, and History in Defoe's Fiction* (Lincoln: University of Nebraska Press, 1983); Novak, *Daniel Defoe, Master of Fictions: His Life and Ideas* (Oxford: Oxford University Press, 2001); John Richetti, *Defoe's Narratives: Situations and Structures* (Oxford: Clarendon, 1975); and Richetti, *The Life of Daniel Defoe* (Oxford: Blackwell, 2005).

15. Rajani Sudan, *Fair Exotics: Xenophobic Subjects in English Literature, 1720–1850* (Philadelphia: University of Pennsylvania Press, 2002), 2–4.

16. On use-value in Robinson Crusoe, see Maximillian Novak, "Robinson Crusoe and Economic Utopia," *Kenyon Review* 25 (1963): 474–90.

17. Sudan, 4.

18. On representations of agricultural labor in the Renaissance, see Liana Vardi, "Imagining the Harvest in Early Modern Europe," in *Agrarian Studies: Synthetic Work at the Cutting Edge*, ed. James C. Scott and Nina Bhatt (New Haven: Yale University Press, 2001), 86–138.

19. Keith Thomas, *Man and the Natural World: Changing Attitudes in England, 1500–1800* (London: Allen Lane, 1983), 274.

20. Stephen B. Vander Wall, *Food Hoarding in Animals* (Chicago and London: University of Chicago Press, 1990). "Two points are essential to the definition of food hoarding. First, consumption of food is deferred. The period of deferment varies greatly among food-hoarding species, ranging from a few minutes ... to as much as 2 years" (1). "Second, food items must be handled in some way that deters other organisms from consuming them. Handling encompasses a diverse array of behaviors including preparation, transportation, placement, and concealment of food items, but not all of these are exhibited in all situations" (2).

21. Vander Wall, 1.

22. "Provision" originally referred to ecclesiastical appointments made before the position was technically vacant (O.E.D.).

23. Thomas Willis, *Two Discourses Concerning the Soul of Brutes* (London: Thomas Dringe, 1683), 36.

24. John Locke, *Essay Concerning Human Understanding* (London: Printed by Eliz. Holt for Thomas Bassett, 1690), 67.

25. Everett Zimmerman, among others, has called attention to Crusoe's repetition compulsion, evident in both his desire to accumulate supplies and his fear of being devoured. "The ubiquitous references to being devoured," writes Zimmerman, "point to a generalized fear: of being dematerialized—the reversal of the desire to accumulate." Everett Zimmerman, "Defoe and Crusoe," *ELH* 38 (1971), 385.

26. Defoe, *Due Preparations for the Plague, as Well as for Soul as Body* (London: Printed for E. Matthews and J. Batley, 1722), 63–65.

27. See Thomas Kavanagh, "Unraveling Robinson: The Divided Self in Defoe's Robinson Crusoe," *Texas Studies in Literature and Language* 20 (1978): 416–32, and Geoffrey Sill, *The Cure of the Passions and the Origins of the English Novel* (Cambridge: Cambridge University Press, 2001), 86–106.

28. Daniel Defoe, *A New Voyage round the World*, ed. John McVeagh (London: Pickering and Chatto, 2009), 142.

29. Defoe, *Essays Upon Several Projects* (London: Printed and Sold by the Booksellers of London and Westminster, 1702), 31.

30. Daniel Defoe, *Mere Nature Delineated; or, a Body without a Soul* (London: Printed for T. Warner, 1726), 6–7. See Max Novak, "Crusoe's Fear and the Search for Natural Man," *Modern Philology* 58 (1961): 238–45. In an important argument to which I am indebted, Richard Nash links *Mere Nature Delineated* to the "biogeography" of Crusoe's island. See *Wild Enlightenment: The Borders of Human Identity in the Eighteenth Century* (Charlottesville: University of Virginia Press, 2003), 67–102.

31. According to Willis, "Brutes obtain only a few and more simple Notions and Intentions of Acting, yea and those always of the same Kind and not determined but to one Thing, altogether ignorant of the Causes of Things" (40).

32. Derek Hughes, *Culture and Sacrifice: Ritual Death in Literature and Opera* (Cambridge: Cambridge University Press, 2007), 95.

33. Michel Serres, *The Parasite*, trans. Lawrence R. Scher (1980) (Rpt. Minneapolis: University of Minnesota Press, 2007).

34. Daniel Defoe, *A General History of Trade* (London: Printed for J. Baker, 1713), 10.

35. Alex Mackintosh, "Crusoe's Abattoir: Cannibalism and Animal Slaughter in Robinson Crusoe," *Critical Quarterly* 53 (2011): 24–43, 29.

36. The critical literature on postcolonial approaches to *Crusoe* is extensive. For representative views, see Peter Hulme, *Colonial Encounters: Europe and the Native Caribbean 1492–1797* (New York: Routledge, 1986); Roxanne Wheeler, "'My Savage,' 'My Man': Racial Multiplicity in *Robinson Crusoe*," *ELH* 62 (1995): 821–61; Markman Ellis, "Crusoe, Cannibalism, and Empire," in *Robinson Crusoe: Myths and Metamorphoses*, ed. Lieve Spaas and Brian Stimpson (New York: St. Martin's Press, 1996), 45–61; Felicity Nussbaum, *The Limits of the Human: Fictions of Anomaly, Race, and Gender in the Long Eighteenth Century* (Cambridge: Cambridge University Press, 2003); and Daniel Carey, "Reading Contrapuntally: Robinson Crusoe, Slavery, and Postcolonial Theory," in *The Postcolonial Enlightenment: Eighteenth-Century Colonialism and Postcolonial Theory*, ed.

Daniel Carey and Lynn Festa (Oxford: Oxford University Press, 2009), 105–36. On the economic implications of this mastery, see Maximillian Novak, *Economics and the Fiction of Daniel Defoe* (Berkeley and Los Angeles: University of California Press, 1962); Wolfram Schmidgen, "Robinson Crusoe, Enumeration, and the Mercantile Fetish," *Eighteenth-Century Studies* 35 (2001): 19–40; and DeeAnn DeLuna, "Robinson Crusoe, Virginal Hero of the Commercial North," *Eighteenth-Century Life* 28 (2004): 69–91.

37. Randall Nielsen, "Storage and English Government Intervention in Early Modern Grain Markets," *The Journal of Economic History* 37 (1997), 1. Nielsen calls attention to the effects of climatic conditions on agriculture: "In the second half of the sixteenth century, Europe endured unusually severe winters, late wine harvests, and Alpine glacial advancement. The period is thought to have stabilized at the turn of the century, with further deterioration in the latter half of the seventeenth century. The chronology is thus consistent with the grain-price evidence" (27). On the "general crisis" of the seventeenth century, see Jack A. Goldstone, *Revolution and Rebellion in the Early Modern World* (Berkeley and Los Angeles: University of California Press, 1991); on climatic conditions and the problems they posed for agriculture during the early modern era, see H. H. Lamb, *Climate History and the Modern World*, second ed. (New York: Routledge, 1995), 211–41, and Brian Fagan, *The Little Ice Age: How Climate Made History 1300–1850* (New York: Basic Books, 2000).

38. In the late sixteenth century, the Crown issued its first proscriptions for the relief of dearth, demanding that private stocks be released for public consumption (Nielsen, 2). While there is considerable debate on whether or not these anti-hoarding measures were effective, it is clear that grain storage and distribution could determine the difference between a "normal" and "crisis" period.

39. Charles Davenant, *The Political and Commercial Works . . ., Relating to the Trade and Revenue of England, the Plantation Trade, the East-India Trade, and Africa Trade*, ed. Charles Whitworth, 5 vols. (London: Printed for R. Horsfield, 1771), 2: 224.

40. During the seventeenth century, grain increasingly was moved from open-air ricks, where it was subject to rain and rodents, to barns, and then (closer to the eighteenth century) to raised platforms in barns.

41. On the publication history of *Farther Adventures*, see Melissa Free, "Unerasing Crusoe: *Farther Adventures* in the Nineteenth Century," *Book History* 9 (2006): 89–130.

42. Daniel Defoe, *The Farther Adventures of Robinson Crusoe*, ed. W.R. Owens (London: Pickering and Chatto, 2008), 12.

43. Jeremias Drexel in 1703 paints images of "extream hunger" in "besieged Cities, and close rigorous Prisons" in order to provide his readers with what he calls "a Specimen" of Hell: "so low are they brought by hunger, that not only Dogs, Cats, and Horses, but also Mice, Dormice, yea, even Serpents and Toads are boil'd and eat, the very Grass is pull'd up, and the Skins torn off their Shield to serve for food; the dung of Pigeons and other Creatures is turn'd into sustenance for Men, by the force of ravenous hunger, which spares not the Bodies of the dearest Friends." Jeremias Drexel, *Considerations of*

Drexelius on the Eternity of Hell Torments (London: Printed for N. Boddington in Dick's Lane, 1703), 54.

44. In a chapter of *Cerebri Anatome*, entitled "Of the Nervous Liquor, and whether that or the bloody Humour be nutritious," Willis argues that "the blood of younger Animals" contains more of nutritive "Gelly" than the blood of "more ancient or Older creatures"; "very much of this kind of Gelly comes out of the Flesh of a Lamb or Calf being boiled or roasted," and "nothing almost from Mutton or Beef, especially if old" (*CA*, 107). While much has been written about blood in the circulation of living bodies, the scholarship surrounding debates on the nutritive powers of dead animal blood is less visible. See Domenico Bertoloni Meli, "The Color of Blood: Between Sensory Experience and Epistemic Significance," *Histories of Scientific Observation*, ed. Lorraine Daston and Elizabeth Lunbeck (Chicago: University of Chicago Press, 2011): 117–34.

45. On sensibility in the eighteenth century, see G. J. Barker-Benfield, *The Culture of Sensibility: Sex and Society in Eighteenth Century Britain* (Chicago: University of Chicago Press, 1992); John Mullan, *Sentiment and Sociability: The Language of Feeling in the Eighteenth Century* (Oxford: Clarendon, 1988); Janet Todd, *Sensibility: An Introduction* (London and New York: Methuen, 1986); and Lynn Festa, *Sentimental Figures of Empire in Eighteenth-Century Britain and France* (Baltimore: Johns Hopkins University Press, 2006).

46. Mandeville, *Fable of the Bees*, ed. Phillip Harth (London: Penguin, 2007), civ.

47. On *Farther Adventures*, see Anna Neill, "Crusoe's Farther Adventures: Discovery, Trade, and the Law of Nations," *The Eighteenth Century: Theory and Interpretation* 38 (1997): 213–30; Hans Turley, "The Sublimation of Desire to Apocalyptic Passion in Defoe's Crusoe Trilogy," in *Imperial Desire: Dissident Sexualities and Colonial Literature*, ed. Philip Holden and Richard J. Ruppel (Minneapolis: University of Minnesota Press, 2003), 3–20; Turley, "Protestant Evangelism, British Imperialism, and Crusoian Identity," in *A New Imperial History: Culture, Identity and Modernity in Britain and the Empire, 1660–1840*, ed. Kathleen Wilson (Cambridge: Cambridge University Press, 2004), 176–96; Nicole E. Didicher, "(Un)Trustworthy Praise and (Un) Governed Passions in *The Farther Adventures of Robinson Crusoe*," in *Relocating Praise: Literary Modalities and Rhetorical Contexts*, ed. Alice G. den Otter (Toronto: Canadian Scholar's Press, 2000), 75–85; and Robert Markley, *The Far East and the English Imagination, 1600–1730* (Cambridge: Cambridge University Press, 2006), 177–209.

48. See Monique Allewert, *Ariel's Ecology: Plantations, Personhood, and Colonialism in the American Tropics* (Minneapolis: University of Minnesota Press, 2013).

49. Abraham Cowley, *The Works of Abraham Cowley*, 2 vols., 12th ed. (London: J. Tonson, 1721), 653.

50. Isaac Barrow, *Of Industry, in Five Discourses* (London: Printed by W. S. for Brab. Alymer, 1700), 58.

51. See Joanna Picciotto, *Labours of Innocence in Early Modern England* (Cambridge: Harvard University Press, 2010).

52. Danielle Allen, "Burning *The Fable of the Bees*," in *The Moral Authority of Nature*, ed. Lorraine Daston and Fernando Vidal (Chicago and London: University of Chicago Press, 2004), 74–99, 75–76.

53. Virgil, *The Georgics, Book IV*, trans. A.S. Kline. Poetry in Translation (online), 2002, 207–08. See Tanya Caldwell, "Honey and Venom: Dryden's Third Georgic," *Eighteenth-Century Life* 20 (1996): 20–36.

54. *The Norton Shakespeare*, ed. Stephen Greenblatt, Walter Cohen, Jean Howard, and Katharine Maus (New York: Norton, 1997), 1461. (I.ii.187–89).

55. Henry More, *An Explanation of the Grand Mystery of Godliness* (London: Printed by J. Flesher for W. Morden, 1664), 47–48.

56. Honey is the product of the bees' digestion and regurgitation, digestive juices then stored in individual cells that comprise the honeycomb.

57. In Mandeville's work, "the meaning of the bee," writes Ann Milne, "is utterly appropriated and attributed to human society," even though his description of the hive ecosystem as a "taut balance" of cooperative forces mirrors "nature." Milne, "Fables of the Bees: Species as an Intercultural Discourse in Scientific and Literary Texts," *L'Esprit Createur* 46 (2006), 39.

58. Virgil, *The Georgics, Book IV*, 155–57.

59. On the history of beekeeping and its role in the English countryside, see Adam Ebert, "Nectar for the Taking: The Popularization of Scientific Bee Culture in England, 1609–1809," *Agricultural History* 85 (2011): 322–43. On seventeenth- and eighteenth-century discussions of bee culture and its sociopolitical implications, see Timothy Raylor, "Samuel Hartlib and the Commonwealth of Bees," in *Culture and Cultivation in Early Modern England: Writing and the Land*, ed. Michael Leslie and Timothy Raylor (Leicester: Leicester University Press, 1992), 91–129; Anne Milne, "Gender, Class and the Beehive: Mary Collier's 'The Woman's Labour' (1739) as Nature Poem," *Interdisciplinary Studies in Literature and Environment* 8 (2001): 109–29; Christopher Hollingworth, *Poetics of the Hive: The Insect Metaphor in Literature* (Iowa City: University of Iowa Press, 2001); Dror Wahrman, "On Queen Bees and Being Queens: A Late-Eighteenth-Century Cultural Revolution?" in Colin Jones and Wahrman, eds., *The Age of Cultural Revolution: Britain and France, 1750–1820* (Berkeley: University of California Press, 2002), 251–79.

60. Oliver Goldsmith, *An History of the Earth: and Animated Nature* (London: Printed for J. Nourse, 1774), 70–71.

61. See Scott Nowka, "Building the Wall: Crusoe and the Other," *Digital Defoe: Studies in Defoe & His Contemporaries* 2 (2010): 41–57.

62. John Trusler, *Proverbs Exemplified, and Illustrated by Pictures from Real Life* (London: Printed by Rev. J. Trusler, 1790), 11. On the significance of fables to the literary and cultural imagination of the period, see Jayne Elizabeth Lewis, *The English Fable: Æsop and Literary Culture, 1651–1740* (Cambridge: Cambridge University Press, 1996).

63. See Richard Grove, *Green Imperialism: Colonial Expansion, Tropical Island Edens,*

and the Origins of Environmentalism, 1600–1860 (New York: Cambridge University Press, 1995).

64. Markley, *Far East and the English Imagination*, 184–85.

65. On debates about colony collapse among North American bee populations, see Benjamin Oldroyd, "What's Killing American Honeybees?" *PLoS Biology* 5,6 (June 2007), 168.

66. Allen, 95.

67. Richard Remnant, *A Discourse or Historie of Bees* (London: Printed by Robert Young for Thomas Slater, 1637). "I call it their winter when they cannot gather food, which is their meanes to maintaine; for so soone as ever the hony gathering failes in the fields, the females kill the Drones or males, or drive them out, and suffer none in winter" (4).

68. Oliver Goldsmith, *History of the Earth*, 82.

69. Ben Jonson, *The Workes of Benjamin Jonson* (London: Printed by W. Stansby, 1616).

70. Nash, *Wild Enlightenment*, 90.

71. Serres, *The Parasite*, 10.

Afterword

1. On diet, politics, and literature, see Carol J. Adams, *The Sexual Politics of Meat: A Feminist Vegetarian Critical Theory* (1990; rpt. New York: Continuum, 2006); Timothy Morton, *Shelley and the Revolution in Taste: The Body and the Natural World* (Cambridge: Cambridge University Press, 1994); Timothy Morton, ed. *Cultures of Taste/Theories of Appetite: Eating Romanticism* (New York and Basingstokes: Palgrave MacMillan, 2004).

2. Michel Serres, *Biogea*, trans. Randolph Burks (Minneapolis: Univocal, 2012), 107.

3. Willis, *The Soul of Brutes*, 5.

4. Bernard Mandeville, *The Fables of the Bees; or, Private Vices, Publick Benefits*, 173.

5. Michel Foucault, *The History of Sexuality, Vol. 3: The Care of the Self* (New York: Vintage Books, 1988), 64–68.

6. Daniel Defoe, *Journal of the Plague Year* (1722), ed. John Mullan (London: Pickering and Chatto, 2009), 116.

7. The fear of such transformation has, of course, given rise to a host of monsters, including the vampire. Like Norway rats, vampires come like a plague from the east; they slink through the night, seek dark corners, and crawl over walls; they assume animal shapes; they reproduce through unnatural means; and they have a more-than-human appetite for blood.

8. See Cary Wolfe's introduction, "Bring the Noise: The Parasite and the Multiple Genealogies of Posthumanism," in Serres, *The Parasite*, xi–xxviii.

Bibliography

Primary Sources

Ady, Thomas. *A Perfect Discovery of Witches. Shewing the Divine Cause of the Distractions of this Kingdome, and also of the Christian World*. London: H. Broome, 1661.

Agrippa, Henry Cornelius. *Three Books of Occult Philosophy*. Trans. J[ohn] F[rench]. London: R.W. for Gregory Poule, 1651.

Agrippa, Henricus Cornelius. *On the Nobility and Pre-eminence of the Female Sex*. Trans. Albert Rabil, Jr. Chicago: University of Chicago Press, 1996.

Albin, Eleazar. *A Natural History of Spiders, and Other Curious Insects*. London: John Tilly, for R. Montagu; J. Brindley; O. Payne; J. Worrall; T. Worrall; and T. Boreman, 1736.

Andry de Bois-Regard, Nicolas. *An Account of the Breeding of Worms in Human Bodies*. London: H. Rhodes and A. Bell, 1701.

"An Eminent Poulterer." *The Compleat French and English Vermin Killer*. London: Printed for G. Conyers, [1710?].

Anon. *A True Narrative of All the Proceedings Against the Weavers*. London: [no publisher], 1675.

Anon. *Health's Preservative: Being a Dissertation on Diet, Air, and Down-beds. And of the Cause and Cure of Bugs*. London: Printed for F. Cogan, 1750.

Anon. *The Autobiography of a Flea, Told in a Hop, Skip and Jump*. London: Edward Avery, 1887.

Aristotle. *The Treatises of Aristotle, Translated from the Greek*. Trans. Thomas Taylor. London: Printed for Thomas Taylor by Robert Wilks, 1818.

Austin, William. *Epiloimia Epe. Or the Anatomie of a Pestilence. A Poem in*

Three Parts. Describing the Deplorable Conditions of the City of London under Its Merciless Dominion. London: Nathaniel Brooke, 1666.

Bacon, Francis. *Sylva Sylvarum; Or, The Natural History in Ten Centuries.* In *The Works of Francis Bacon.* Ed. James Spedding, Robert L. Ellis, and Douglas D. Heath. Rpt. New York: Garrett Press, 1968.

Barrow, Isaac. *Of Industry, in Five Discourses.* London: Printed by W. S. for Brab. Alymer, 1700.

Barrow, John. *The Lord's Arm Stretched Out in an Answer of Prayer, or A true Relation of the Wonderful Deliverance of James Barrow, the Son of John Barrow of Olaves Southwark.* London, [s.n], 1664.

Bassett, Robert. *Curiosities: or The Cabinet of Nature. Containing Philosophicall, Naturall, and Morall Questions Answered.* Trans. R. B. Gent. London, 1637.

Ben Gorion, Josephus. *The Wonderful, and Most Deplorable History of the Latter Times of the Jews with the Destruction of the City of Jerusalem.* London: Christopher Ecclestone, 1662.

Blackmore, Richard. *A Satyr against Wit.* London: Printed for Samuel Crouch, 1700.

Bodin, Jean. *On the Demon-Mania of Witches* (1580). Trans. Randy A. Scott. Toronto: Centre for Reformation and Renaissance Studies, 1995.

Bouget, Henri. *An Examen of Witches (Discours des Sorciers).* Rpt. New York: Barnes and Noble, 1971.

Boyle, Robert. *Of the Usefulnesse of Experimental Natural Philosophy.* Oxford, 1663.

Boyle, Robert. *Essays of the Strange Subtilty, Great Efficacy, Determinate Nature of Effluviums.* London: Printed by W. G. for M. Pitt, 1673.

Boyle, Robert. *The Works of Robert Boyle.* 5 vols. London: A. Millar, 1744.

Browne, Thomas. *Pseudodoxia Epidemica; or, Enquiries into Very Many Received Tenents and Commonly Presumed Truths.* London: T. H. for E. Dod, 1646.

Browne, Thomas. *Sir Thomas Browne's Religio Medici.* Ed. William Alexander Greenhill. London: Macmillan, 1904.

Burton, Robert. *The Anatomy of Melancholy.* Oxford: Printed by John Litchfield and James Short for Henry Cripps, 1621.

Brydall, John. *Non Compos Mentis or The law Relating to Natural Fools, Madfolks, and Lunatic Persons.* London: Printed by Richard and Edward Atkins for Isaac Cleave, 1700.

Charleton, Walter. *The Darknes of Atheism Dispelled by the Light of Reason.* London: Printed by J. F. for William Lee, 1652.

Charleton, Walter. *A Natural History of the Passions*. London: Printed by T. N. for James Magnes, 1674.

Clarke, Samuel. *A True And Faithful Account of the Four Cheifest Plantations of the English in America*. London: Printed for R. Clavel, T. Passenger, W. Cadman, W. Whitwood, T. Sawbridge, and W. Birch, 1670.

Congreve, William. *William Congreve: Letters and Documents*. Ed. John C. Hodges. New York: Harcourt Brace, 1964.

Cowley, Abraham. *The Works of Abraham Cowley*. 2 vols. 12th ed. London: J. Tonson, 1721.

Cowley, Abraham. *The Poetical Works of Abraham Cowley*. Vol. 3. Edinburgh: Apollo Press, 1784.

Dampier, William. *A New Voyage around the World*. London: Printed for James Knapton, 1703.

Davenant, Charles. *The Political and Commercial Works, Relating to the Trade and Revenue of England, the Plantation, the East-India, and Africa Trade*. 2 vols. Ed. Charles Whitworth. London: Printed for R. Horsfield, 1771.

Davenant, William. *Gondibert*. London: John Holden, 1651.

de la Vega, Garcilaso. *The Royal Commentaries of Peru*. Trans. Sir Paul Rycault. London: M. Flesher for J. Tonson, 1688.

Defoe, Daniel. *A General History of Trade*. London: Printed for J. Baker, 1713.

Defoe, Daniel. *Essays Upon Several Projects*. London: Printed and sold by the Booksellers of London and Westminster, 1720.

Defoe, Daniel. *Due Preparations for the Plague*. London: Printed for E. Matthews and J. Batley, 1722.

Defoe, Daniel. *Journal of the Plague Year* (1722). Ed. John Mullan. London: Pickering and Chatto, 2009.

Defoe, Daniel. *Mere Nature Delineated: or, a Body without a Soul*. London: Printed for T. Warner, 1726.

Defoe, Daniel. *A Tour thro' the Whole Island of Great Britain*. London: Printed for J. Osborn, S. Birt, D. Browne, J. Hodges, A. Millar, J. Whiston, and J. Robinson, 1742.

Defoe, Daniel. *The Farther Adventures of Robinson Crusoe*. Ed. W. R. Owens. London: Pickering and Chatto, 2008.

Defoe, Daniel. *The Life and Strange Surprizing Adventures of Robinson Crusoe*. Ed. W. R. Owens. London: Pickering and Chatto, 2008.

Defoe, Daniel. *A New Voyage round the World*. Ed. John McVeagh. London: Pickering and Chatto, 2009.

D[ekker], T[homas]. *Canaans Calamitie, Jerusalems Misery, or The Doleful Destruction of Faire Jerusalem by Tytus*. London: John Bayly, 1618.

della Porta, Giambattista. *Natural Magick*. London: Printed for Thomas Young and Samuel Speed, 1658.

Desault, Pierre-Joseph. *A Treatise on the Venereal Distemper*. London: Printed for John Clarke, 1738.

Descartes, René. *A Discourse of a Method for the Well Guiding of Reason, and the Discovery of Truth in the Sciences*. London: Thomas Newcombe, 1649.

Donne, John. *Poems, by J. D. with Elegies on the Authors Death*. London: Printed by [M]iles [F]lesher for John Marriot, 1633.

Donne, John. *Donne's Satyr Containing 1. A Short Map of Mundane Vanity 2. A Cabinet of Merry Conceits 3. Pleasant Propositions and Questions with Their Merry Solutions and Answers*. London: Printed by R. W. for M. Wright, 1662.

Drage, William. *Daimonomageia. A Small Treatise of Sicknesses and Disease from Witchcraft and Supernatural Causes*. London: J. Dover, 1665.

Drayton, Michael. *The Muses Elizium Lately Discouered, by a New Way Ouer Parnassus*. London: Thomas Harper for John Waterson, 1630.

Drexel, Jeremias. *Considerations of Drexelius on the Eternity of Hell Torments*. London, 1703.

Dryden, John. *Annus Mirabilis, The Year of Wonders, 1666*. London: Henry Harriman, 1667.

Evelyn, John. *The Diary of John Evelyn*. 2 vols. Ed. William Bray. Washington & London: M. Walter Dunne, 1901.

Exquemelin, A. O. *Buckaniers of America*. London: William Crooke, 1684.

Ferrand, James. *Eråotomania, or A Treatise Discoursing of the Essence, Causes, Symptomes, Prognosticks, and Cure of Love, or Erotique Melancholy*. Oxford: Printed by L. Litchfield for Edward Forrest, 1640.

Finch, Anne. *Miscellany Poems, on Several Occasions: Written by the Honourable Anne, Countess of Winchilsea*. London: Benj. Tooke, William Taylor, James Round, 1713.

Franz, Wolfgang. *The History of Brutes*. London: Printed by E. Okes for Francis Haley, 1670.

Gay, John. *The Poetical Works of John Gay, Including His Fables*. Vol. II. Edinburg: Apollo Press, 1784.

Gay, John. *Poetry and Prose*, 2 vols. Ed. Vinton A. Dearing and Charles Beckwith. Oxford: Clarendon Press, 1974.

Goldsmith, Oliver. *An History of the Earth and Animated Nature*. London: Printed for J. Nourse, 1774.

Goodman, Godfrey. *The Fall of Man, or the Corruption of Nature*. London: Felix Kyngston for Richard Lee, 1616.

Gould, Robert. *Poems, Chiefly Consisting of Satyrs and Satirical Epistles.* London: Printed and sold by most Booksellers in London and Westminster, 1689.

Hartflete, Henry. *The Hunting of the Fox; or, Flattery Displayed.* London: Printed by A. M[atthewes] for Philemon Stephens and Christopher Meredith, 1632.

Harvey, William. *Anatomical Exercises on the Generation of Animals [1665].* Trans. Robert Willis. London: The Sydenham Society, 1847.

Highmore, Nathaniel. *The History of Generation.* London: Printed by R. N. for John Martin, 1651.

Hobbes, Thomas. *The Questions Concerning Liberty, Necessity, and Chance.* London: Printed for Andrew Cook, 1656.

Holt, Vincent C. *Why Not Eat Insects?* London: Field and Tuer, 1885.

Hooke, Robert. *Micrographia, or, Some Physiological Descriptions of Minute Bodies.* London: Printed by Jo. Martyn and Ja. Allestree, 1665.

Hooke, Robert. *Microscopic Observations; or, Dr. Hooke's Wonderful Discoveries by the Microscope, Illustrated by Thirty-three Copper-Plates, Curiously Engraved.* Cornhill: Robert Wilkinson, 1780.

James I, *Daemonologie.* San Diego: Book Tree, 2002.

Jonson, Ben. *The Workes of Benjamin Jonson.* London: W. Stansby, 1616.

Kircher, Athanasius. *Scrutinium physic-medicum contagiosae luis [Physico-Medical Studies on a Contagious Disease Called Pest].* Romae: Typis Mascardi, 1658.

Kramer, Heinrich, and James Sprenger. *The Malleus Maleficarum of Heinrich Kramer and James Sprenger.* Trans. Montague Summers, 1486. Rpt. New York: Dover, 1971.

Layard, Daniel Peter. *An Essay on the Bite of a Mad Dog.* 2nd ed. London: Printed for John Rivington and Thomas Payne, 1763.

Lister, Martin. *Tractatus de Araneis.* London: Royal Society, 1678.

Lister, Martin. *A Remarkable Relation of a Man Bitten with a Mad Dog, and Dying of the Disease called Hydrophobia, Sent in a Letter to the Royal Society by the Learned Martin Lister, Esquire, dated from York March 26, 1683.*

Locke, John. *Essay Concerning Human Understanding.* London: Printed by Eliz. Holt for Thomas Bassett, 1690.

Lodge, Thomas. *A Treatise of the Plague.* London: Valentime Si[mmes], 1603.

M. M. *A Short Historical Account of the Several Kinds of Worms Breeding in Human Bodies.* London: J. Baker and T. Warner, 1716.

Malpighi, Marcello. *Anatomie Plantarum*. London: Impensis Johannes Martyn, 1675.

Mandeville, Bernard. *The Fable of the Bees*. London: Printed for J. Roberts, 1714.

Mascall, Leonard. *Book of Engines: Sundrie Engines and Trapps to Take Polecats, Buzards, Rattes, Mice and All other Kindes of Vermin and Beasts Whatsoever*. London: Printed by John Wolfe and Sold by Edward White, 1590.

Molyneux, Thomas *A Letter from Dr. Thomas Molyneux, Fellow of the Royal Society, to the Right Reverand St. George, Lord Bishop of Clogher; Concerning Swarms of Insects, That of Late Have Much Infested Some Parts of the Province of Connought in Ireland*. Philosophical Transactions 19 (1695–97): 741–56.

More, Henry. *An Explanation of the Grand Mystery of Godliness*. London: Printed by J. Flesher for W. Morden, 1664.

Nashe, Thomas. *Works of Thomas Nashe, Vol. III*. Ed. Ronald B. McKerrow. London: Sidgwick and Jackson, 1910.

Ovington, John. *A Voyage to Surat in the Year 1689*. Ed. H. G. Rawlinson. London: Oxford University Press, 1929.

Peacham, Henry. *Minerva Britanna, or a Garden of Heroical Devises*. London: Wa. Dight, 1612.

Pope, Alexander. *Alexander Pope: The Major Works*. Ed. Pat Rogers. Oxford: Oxford University Press, 2008.

Ramsay, William. *De Venenis, or, A Discourse of Poysons*. London: Printed for Samuel Speed, 1663.

Ramsay, William. *Helminthologia, or, Some Physical Considerations of the Matter, Origination, and Several Species of Wormes Macerating and Direfully Cruciating Every Part of the Bodies of Mankind*. London: John Streater for George Sawbridge, 1668.

Ray, John. *The Wisdom of God Manifested in the Works of the Creation*. 7th ed. London: R. Harbin, 1717.

Redi, Francesco. *Esperienze Intorno alla Generazione Degli'insetti*. [*Experiments on the Generation of Insects*]. Firenze: Nella Stampens, 1688.

Remnant, Richard. *A Discourse or Historie of Bees*. London: Printed by Robert Young for Thomas Slater, 1637.

Rochester, John Wilmot. *Collected Works of John Wilmot, Earl of Rochester*. Ed. John Hayward. London: Nonesuch Press, 1926.

Rochester, John Wilmot, Earl of. *The Complete Poems of John Wilmot, Earl of Rochester*. Ed. David Vieth. New Haven: Yale University Press, 1968.

Rochester, John Wilmot, Earl of. *The Letters of John Wilmot, Earl of Roches-ter*. Ed. Jeremy Treglown. Oxford: Blackwell, 1980.

Rogers, Woodes. *A Cruising Voyage round the World*. London: A. Bell and B. Lintot, 1712.

Ross, Alexander. *An Exposition on the Fourteene First Chapters of Genesis*. London: printed by B[ernard] A[lsop] and T[homas] F[awcett], 1622.

Ross, Alexander. *Arcana Microcosmi; or, the Secrets of Man's Body Discovered*. London: Tho[mas] Newcomb for John Clark, 1652.

Shadwell, Thomas. *The History of Timon of Athens, the Man-Hater*. London: Printed for H. H. [Henry Herringman] and sold by W. Davies, 1703.

Shadwell, Thomas. *The Virtuoso*. Ed. Marjorie Hope Nicolson and David Stuart Rodes. Lincoln: University of Nebraska Press, 1966.

Shakespeare, William. *Complete Works of William Shakespeare*. Ed. David McKay, with notes by Edmund Malone, George Steevens, et al. Philadelphia, 1887.

Shakespeare, William. *The Norton Shakespeare*. Eds. Stephen Greenblatt, Walter Cohen, Jean E. Howard, and Katherine Maus. New York: Norton, 2008.

Sprat, Thomas. *The History of the Royal Society*. Ed. Jackson Cope. St. Louis: Washington University Studies, 1958.

Steele, Richard. *The Englishman: Being the Sequel of the Guardian*. London: Samuel Buckley, 1714.

Swammerdam, John. *The Book of Nature, or the History of Insects*. Trans. Thomas Flloyd. London: C. G. Seyffert, 1758.

Swift, Jonathan. *The Essential Writings of Jonathan Swift*. Ed. Claude Rawson and Ian Higgins. New York: Norton, 2010.

Topsell, Edward. *The Historie of Foure-Footed Beastes*. London: William Iaggard, 1607.

Trapp, John. *A Commentary or Exposition upon the Minor Prophets*. London: Printed by R. N. for Philemon Stevens, 1654.

Trusler, John. *Proverbs Exemplified, and Illustrated by Pictures from Real Life*. London: Printed by Rev. J. Trusler, 1790.

van der Heyden, Hermann. *Speedy Help for Rich and Poor*. London: Printed by James Young, for O.P. 1653.

Virgil. *The Georgics, Book IV*. Trans. A.S. Kline. Poetry in Translation (online), 2002.

Walter, Richard. *A Voyage Round the World in the Years MDCCXL, I, I, III, IV*. London: Printed for the Author by John and Paul Knapton, 1748.

Webster, John. *The Duchess of Malfi*. Ed. Leah S. Marcus. London: Blooms-bury, 2009.

Webster, Noah. *A Brief History of Epidemic and Pestilential Diseases*. Hart-ford, CT: Hudson and Goodwin, 1799.

Willis, Thomas. *The Anatomy of the Brain, the 1681 Edition. Reset and Re-printed, with the Original Illustrations by Sir Christopher Wren.* Tuckahoe, NY: USV Pharmaceutical Corp., 1971.

Willis, Thomas. *Two Discourses Concerning the Soul of Brutes*. London: Thomas Dringe, 1683.

Wither, George. *Britain's Remembrancer (1628)*. Rpt. Manchester: Charles Simms, Printed for the Spenser Society, 1880.

Woodhouse, Peter. "The Flea." London: Printed by Edward Allde for John Smethwick, 1605.

Secondary Sources

Agamben, Giorgio. *The Open: Man and Animal*. New York: Stanford Uni-versity Press, 2003.

Allen, Danielle. "Burning *The Fable of the Bees.*" *The Moral Authority of Na-ture*. Ed. Lorraine Daston and Fernando Vidal. Chicago: University of Chicago Press, 2004, 74–99.

Allewert, Monique. *Ariel's Ecology: Plantations, Personhood, and Colonialism in the American Tropics*. Minneapolis: University of Minnesota Press, 2013.

Appleby, Andrew B. "Disease or Famine? Mortality in Cumberland and Westmorland, 1580–1640." *Economic History Review* 26 (1973): 403–31.

Appleby, Andrew B. "Epidemics and Famine in the Little Ice Age." *Journal of Interdisciplinary History* 10 (1980): 643–63.

Arikha, Noga. "Form and Function in the Early Enlightenment." *Perspectives on Science* 14 (2006): 153–88.

Bacci, Massimo Livi. *Population and Nutrition: An Essay on European Demo-graphic History*. Trans. Tania Croft-Murray and Carl Ipsen. Cambridge: Cambridge University Press, 1990.

Backscheider, Paula. *Daniel Defoe: Ambition and Innovation*. Lexington: University of Kentucky Press, 1986.

Backscheider, Paula. *Daniel Defoe, His Life*. Baltimore: Johns Hopkins Uni-versity Press, 1989.

Barad, Karen. *Meeting the Universe Halfway: Quantum Physics and the En-*

tanglement of Matter and Meaning. Durham and London: Duke University Press, 2007.

Barker, Shelia. "Poussin, Plague, and Early Modern Medicine." *Art Bulletin* 86 (2004): 659–89.

Barker-Benfield, G. J. *The Culture of Sensibility: Sex and Society in Eighteenth Century Britain*. Chicago: University of Chicago Press, 1992.

Barney, Richard, and Helene P. Scheck, eds. "Rhetorics of Plague." Special issue of *Journal of Early Modern Cultural Studies* 10 (2010).

Barroll, Leeds. *Politics, Plague, and Shakespeare's Theater: The Stuart Years*. Ithaca, Cornell University Press, 1991.

Beirne, Piers. "The Law Is an Ass: Reading E. P. Evans' The Medieval Prosecution and Capital Punishment of Animals." *Society & Animals* 2 (1994): 27–46.

Beirne, Piers. "A Note on the Facticity of Animal Trials in Early Modern Britain; or, the Curious Prosecution of Farmer Carter's Dog for Murder." *Crime, Law, and Social Change* 55 (2011): 359–74.

Bender, John. *Ends of Enlightenment*. Stanford: Stanford University Press, 2012.

Bergeron, Crissy. "George de La Tour's Flea-Catcher and the Iconography of the Flea Hunt in Seventeenth-Century Baroque Art." MA thesis, Louisiana State University, 2007.

Black, Andrew. "The Orator in the Laboratory: Rhetoric and Experimentation in Thomas Shadwell's The Virtuoso." *Restoration* 37 (2013): 1–18.

Boehrer, Bruce. *Shakespeare Among the Animals: Nature and Society in the Drama of Early Modern England*. New York: Palgrave, 2002.

Breidbach, Olaf, and Michael T. Ghislen. "Athanasius Kircher (1602–1680) on Noah's Ark: Baroque 'Intelligent Design' Theory." *Proceedings of the California Academy of Sciences* 57 (2006): 991–1002.

Brown, Laura. *Homeless Dogs and Melancholy Apes: Humans and Other Animals in the Modern Literary Imagination*. Ithaca: Cornell University Press, 2010.

Brown, Steven D. "In Praise of the Parasite: The Dark Organizational Theory of Michel Serres." *Porto Alegre* 16 (2013): 83–100.

Bynum, William. "The Anatomical Method, Natural Theology, and the Functions of the Brain." *Isis* 64 (1973): 444–68.

Caldwell, Tanya. "Honey and Venom: Dryden's Third Georgic." *Eighteenth-Century* 20 (1996): 20–36.

Carey, Daniel. "Reading Contrapuntally: Robinson Crusoe, Slavery, and Postcolonial Theory." *The Postcolonial Enlightenment: Eighteenth-Century*

Colonialism and Postcolonial Theory. Ed. Daniel Carey and Lynn Festa. Oxford: Oxford University Press, 2009, 105–36.

Chico, Tita. "Gimcrack's Legacy: Sex, Wealth, and the Theatre of Experimental Philosophy." *Comparative Drama* 42 (2008): 29–49.

Clarke, Stuart. *Thinking With Demons: The Idea of Witchcraft in Early Modern Europe*. Oxford University Press, 1999.

Cole, F. J. *A History of Comparative Anatomy: From Aristotle to the Eighteenth Century*. 1949; rpt. New York: Dover, 1979.

Cole, Michael. "The Demonic Arts and the Origin of the Medium." *The Art Bulletin* 84 (2002), 621–40.

Coltharp, Duane. "Rivall Fopps, Rambling Rakes, Wild Women: Homosocial Desire and Courtly Crisis in Rochester's Poetry." *The Eighteenth Century: Theory and Interpretation* 38 (1997): 23–42.

Combe, Kirk. *A Martyr For Sin: Rochester's Critique of Polity, Sexuality, and Society*. Newark and London: University of Delaware Press, 1998.

Conisbee, Philip. "An Introduction to the Life and Art of Georges de La Tour." *Georges de La Tour and His World*. New Haven: Yale University Press, 1996, 13–148.

Cook, Harold J. "Bernard Mandeville and the Therapy of 'The Clever Politician,'" *Journal of the History of Ideas* 60 (1999): 101–24.

Coppola, Al. "Retraining the Virtuoso's Gaze: Behn's *Emperor of the Moon*, the Royal Society, and the Spectacle of Science and Politics." *Eighteenth-Century Studies* 41 (2008): 481–506.

Crick, Francis. *The Astonishing Hypothesis: The Scientific Search for the Soul*. New York: Touchstone, 1994.

Dannenfeldt, Karl H. "The Control of Vertebrate Pests in Renaissance Agriculture." *Agricultural History* 56 (1982): 542–59.

Darnton, Robert. *The Great Cat Massacre and Other Episodes in French Cultural History*. New York: Basic Books, 1984.

Davidson, Clifford. "*Timon of Athens*: The Iconography of False Friendship." *Huntington Library Quarterly* 43 (1980): 181–200.

Davis, David E. "The Scarcity of Rats and the Black Death." *Journal of Interdisciplinary History* 16 (1986): 455–70.

Dawson, N. J., and A. W. Keber. "Physiology of Heat Loss from an Extremity: The Tail of the Rat." *Clinical and Experimental Pharmacology and Physiology* 6 (1979): 69–80.

DeLuna, DeeAnn. "Robinson Crusoe, Virginal Hero of the Commercial North." *Eighteenth-Century Life* 28 (2004): 69–91.

Denx, Rudd, Jan Van Hoof, Han De Vries, and Joep Wensing. "Male and

Female Mating Competition in Wolves: Female Suppression vs. Male Intervention." *Behavior* 127 (1993): 141–74.

Derrida, Jacques. *The Animal That Therefore I Am.* Trans. David Wills; ed. Marie-Louise Mallet. New York: Fordham University Press, 2008.

Didicher, Nicole E. "(Un)Trustworthy Praise and (Un) Governed Passions in *The Farther Adventures of Robinson Crusoe.*" *Relocating Praise: Literary Modalities and Rhetorical Contexts.* Ed. Alice G. den Otter. Toronto: Canadian Scholar's Press, 2000, 75–85.

Dobbs, Betty Jo Teeter. *The Janus Faces of Genius: The Role of Alchemy in Newton's Thought.* Cambridge: Cambridge University Press, 1991.

Dolan, Frances E. *Dangerous Familiars: Representations of Domestic Crime in England, 1550–1700.* Ithaca: Cornell University Press, 1994.

Drehrer, Nan H. "The Virtuous and the Verminous: Turn-of-the-Century Moral Panics in London's Public Parks." *Albion* 29 (1997): 246–67.

Drummond, David. "Unmasking Mascall's Mousetraps." *Proceedings of the Fifteenth Vertebrates Pest Conference 1992.* Ed. J. E. Borrecco and R. E. Marsh. Davis: University of California, 220–35.

Dunn, Richard M. "The London Weavers Riot of 1675." *Guildhall Studies in London History* I (October 1973–April 1975): 13–23.

Dykstal, Timothy. "The Epic Reticence of Abraham Cowley." *Studies in English Literature, 1500–1900* 31 (1991): 95–115.

Eagleton, Terry. *Against the Grain: Essays 1975–1985.* London: Verso, 1986.

Easlea, Brian. *Witch Hunting, Magic, and the New Philosophy: An Introduction to the Debates of the Scientific Revolution 1450–1750.* Brighton: Harvester, 1980.

Ebert, Adam. "Nectar for the Taking: The Popularization of Scientific Bee Culture in England, 1609–1809." *Agricultural History* 85 (2011): 322–43.

Edwards, Philip. *The Story of the Voyage: Sea-Narratives in Eighteenth-Century England.* Cambridge: Cambridge University Press, 1994.

Egerton, Frank N. "Ancient Sources for Animal Demography." *Isis* 59 (1968): 175–89.

Egerton, Frank N. *Roots of Ecology: Antiquity to Haeckel.* Berkeley and Los Angeles: University of California Press, 2012.

Ellis, Markman. "Crusoe, Cannibalism, and Empire." *Robinson Crusoe: Myths and Metamorphoses.* Ed. Lieve Spaas and Brian Stimpson. New York: St. Martin's Press, 1996, 45–61.

Evans, E. P. *The Criminal Prosecution and Capital Punishment of Animals.* London: William Heinemann, 1906.

Fabricant, Carol. "Rochester's World of Imperfect Enjoyment." *Journal of English and Germanic Philology* 73 (1974): 338–350.

Fagan, Brian. *The Little Ice Age: How Climate Made History 1300–1850*. New York: Basic Books, 2000.

Festa, Lynn. *Sentimental Figures of Empire in Eighteenth-Century Britain and France*. Baltimore: Johns Hopkins University Press, 2006.

Fisher, Alan S. "The Significance of Thomas Shadwell." *Studies in Philology* 71 (1974): 225–46.

Fissell, Mary. "Imagining Vermin in the Early Modern Period." *History Workshop Journal* 47 (1999): 1–29.

Foucault, Michel. *Security, Territory, Population: Lectures at the College de France, 1977–1978*. Trans. Graham Burchell. New York: Palgrave, 2004.

Free, Melissa. "Unerasing Crusoe: *Farther Adventures* in the Nineteenth Century." *Book History* 9 (2006): 89–130.

French, J. Milton. "George Wither in Prison." *PMLA* 45 (1930): 959–66.

Fudge, Erica. *Perceiving Animals: Humans and Beasts in Early Modern Culture*. Urbana: University of Illinois Press, 2002.

Fudge, Erica. *Brutal Reasoning: Animals, Rationality, and Humanity in Early Modern England*. Ithaca: Cornell University Press, 2006.

Fudge, Erica. "The Dog, the Home and the Human, and the Ancestry of Derrida's Cat." *Oxford Literary Review* 29 (2007): 37–54.

Fudge, Erica, Ruth Gilbert, and Susan Wiseman, eds. *At the Borders of the Human: Beasts, Bodies, and Natural Philosophy in the Early Modern Period*. New York: St. Martin's Press, 1999.

Gill, Pat. "'Filth of All Hues and Odors': Public Parks, City Showers, and Promiscuous Acquaintance in Rochester and Swift." *Genre* 27 (1994): 333–50.

Gilman, Ernest B. *Plague Writing in Early Modern England*. Chicago: University of Chicago Press, 2009.

Ginzburg, Carlo. *The Cheese and the Worms: The Cosmos of a Sixteenth-Century Miller*. Trans. John and Anne Tedeschi. Baltimore: Johns Hopkins University Press, 1980.

Girard, René. "The Plague in Literature and Myth." *Texas Studies in Language and Literature* 15 (1974): 833–50.

Girard, René. *I See Satan Fall Like Lightening*. Maryknoll, NY: Orbis, 2001.

Girgen, Jen. "The Historical and Contemporary Prosecution and Punishment of Animals." *Animal Law Review* 9 (2003): 97–134.

Goldstein, David B. "The Cook and the Cannibal: Titus Andronicus and the New World." *Shakespeare Studies* 37 (2009): 99–133.

Goldstone, Jack A. *Revolution and Rebellion in the Early Modern World.* Berkeley and Los Angeles: University of California Press, 1991.

Graham, Elizabeth. "Metaphors and Metaphorism: Some Thoughts on Environmental Metahistory." *Advances in Historical Ecology.* Ed. William L. Balée. New York: Columbia, 1988, 119–37.

Green, Edward C. *Indigenous Theories of Contagious Disease.* London: AltaMira, 1999.

Greenblatt, Stephen. "Shakespeare Bewitched." *New Historical Literary Study: Essays on Reproducing Texts, Representing History.* Ed. Jeffrey N. Cox and Larry I. Reynolds. Princeton: Princeton University Press, 1993, 108–35.

Grove, Richard. *Green Imperialism: Colonial Expansion, Tropical Island Edens, and the Origins of Environmentalism, 1600–1860.* New York: Cambridge University Press, 1995.

Guerrini, Anita. "The Pathological Environment." *The Eighteenth Century: Theory and Interpretation* 31 (1990): 173–79.

Guerrini, Anita. *Experimenting with Humans and Animals: From Galen to Animal Rights.* Baltimore: Johns Hopkins University Press, 2003.

Guibbory, Achsah. "Imitation and Originality: Cowley and Bacon's Vision of Progress." *Studies in English Literature, 1500–1900* 29 (1989): 99–120.

Gullestad, Anders M. "Literature and the Parasite." *Delueze Studies* 5 (2011): 301–23.

Hammill, Graham. "Miracles and Plagues: Plague Discourse as Political Thought." *Journal of Early Modern Cultural Studies* 10 (2010): 85–104.

Hammill, Graham. *The Mosaic Constitution: Political Theology and Imagination from Machiavelli to Milton.* Chicago: University of Chicago Press, 2012.

Haraway, Donna. *When Species Meet.* Minneapolis: University of Minnesota Press, 2007.

Harris, Jonathan Gil. *Foreign Bodies and the Body Politic: Discourses of Social Pathology in Early Modern England.* Cambridge: Cambridge University Press, 1998.

Harrison, Peter. "Reading Vital Signs: Animals and the Experimental Philosophy." *Renaissance Beasts: Of Animals, Humans, and Other Wonderful Creatures.* Ed. Erica Fudge. Champaign: University of Illinois Press, 1994.

Harth, Philip. "The Satiric Purpose of *The Fable of the Bees.*" *Eighteenth-Century Studies* 2 (1969): 321–40.

Herlihy, David. *The Black Death and the Transformation of the West.* Ed. Samuel K. Cohn, Jr. Cambridge: Harvard University Press, 1997.

Hinman, Robert B. *Abraham Cowley's World of Order.* Cambridge: Harvard University Press, 1960.

Hollingworth, Christopher. *Poetics of the Hive: The Insect Metaphor in Literature.* Iowa City: University of Iowa Press, 2001.

Hughes, Derek. *Culture and Sacrifice: Ritual Death in Literature and Opera.* Cambridge: Cambridge University Press, 2007.

Hulme, Peter. *Colonial Encounters: Europe and the Native Caribbean 1492–1797.* New York: Routledge, 1986.

Humphrey, Nicholas. *The Mind Made Flesh: Essays from the Frontier of Psychology and Evolution.* Oxford: Oxford University Press, 2002.

Hunter, J. Paul. *The Reluctant Pilgrim: Defoe's Emblematic Method and the Quest for Form in Robinson Crusoe.* Baltimore: Johns Hopkins University Press, 1966.

Hyde, Walter W. "The Prosecution and Punishment of Animals and Lifeless Things in the Middle Ages and Modern Times." *University of Pennsylvania Law Review* 64 (1916): 696–730.

Isler, Hansruedi. *Thomas Willis 1621–1675: Doctor and Scientist.* New York and London: Hafner, 1968.

Jackson, James L. "Shakespeare's Dog-and-Sugar Imagery and the Friendship Tradition." *Shakespeare Quarterly* 1 (1950): 260–63.

Jenner, Mark. "The Great Dog Massacre." *Fear in Early Modern Society.* Ed. William G. Naphy and Penny Roberts. Manchester: St. Martin's Press, 1997, 44–61.

Johnson, James W. "The Neo-Classical Bee." *Journal of the History of Ideas* 22 (1961): 262–66.

Kavanagh, Thomas. "Unraveling Robinson: The Divided Self in Defoe's Robinson Crusoe." *Texas Studies in Literature and Language* 20 (1978): 416–32.

Kelly, John. *The Great Mortality: An Intimate History of the Black Death, the Most Devastating Plague of All Time.* New York: Harper Perennial, 2006.

Knoeff, Rina. "The Reins of the Soul: The Centrality of the Intercostal Nerves to the Neurology of Thomas Willis and Samuel Parker's Theology." *Journal of the History of Medicine and Allied Sciences* 59 (2004): 413–40.

Lamb, H. H. *Climate History and the Modern World*. 2nd ed. New York: Routledge, 1995.

Lamb, Jonathan. *Preserving the Self in the South Seas, 1680–1840*. Chicago: University of Chicago Press, 2001.

Landry, Donna. *Noble Brutes: How Eastern Horses Transformed English Culture*. Baltimore, Johns Hopkins University Press, 2009.

Laquer, Thomas Walter. *Making Sex: Body and Gender from the Greeks to Freud*. Cambridge: Harvard University Press, 1990.

Latour, Bruno. "The Enlightenment without the Critique: An Introduction to Michel Serres' Philosophy." *Contemporary French Philosophy*. Ed. J. Griffith. Cambridge: Cambridge University Press, 1988, 83–97.

Latour, Bruno. *We Have Never Been Modern*. Trans. Catherine Porter. Cambridge: Harvard University Press, 1993.

Latour, Bruno. *Politics of Nature: How to Bring the Sciences into Democracy*. Trans. Catherine Porter. Cambridge: Harvard University Press, 2004.

Lega, B. C. "*An Essay Concerning Human Understanding*: How the *Cerebri Anatomi* of Thomas Willis influenced John Locke." *Neurosurgery* 58 (2006): 567–76.

Lewis, Jayne Elizabeth. *The English Fables: Æsop and Literary Culture, 1651–1740*. Cambridge: Cambridge University Press, 1996.

Lloyd, Claude. "Shadwell and the Virtuosi." *PMLA* 44 (1929); 472–94.

Mackintosh, Alex. "Crusoe's Abattoir: Cannibalism and Animal Slaughter in Robinson Crusoe." *Critical Quarterly* 53 (2011): 24–43.

Mannheimer, Katherine. "Celestial Bodies: Readerly Rapture as Theatrical Spectacle in Aphra Behn's *Emperor of the Moon*." *Restoration* 35 (2011): 39–60.

Markley, Robert. *Fallen Languages: Crises of Representation in Newtonian England 1660–1740*. Ithaca: Cornell University Press, 1993.

Markley, Robert. *The Far East and the English Imagination, 1600–1730*. Cambridge: Cambridge University Press, 2006.

Markley, Robert. "Summer's Lease: Shakespeare in the Little Ice Age." *Early Modern Ecostudies: From the Florentine Codex to Shakespeare*. Ed. Thomas Hallock, Ivo Kamps, and Karen L. Raber. New York: Palgrave Macmillan, 2008, 131–42.

Markley, Robert. "The Eighteenth-Century Novel and the Pacific." *The Cambridge History of the English Novel*. Eds. Robert Caesario and Clement Hawes. Cambridge: Cambridge University Press, 2012, 196–212.

Martin, Raymond, and John Barresi. *Naturalization of the Soul: Self and Personality in the Eighteenth Century*. London: Routledge, 2000.

McCormick, Michael. "Rats, Communication, and Plague: Towards an Ecological History." *Journal of Interdisciplinary History* 34, (2003): 1–25.

McNeill, William H. *Plagues and Peoples.* Garden City, New York: Anchor, 1976.

McRae, Andrew. *God Speed the Plough: The Representation of Agrarian England, 1500–1660.* Cambridge: Cambridge University Press, 1996.

McVeagh, John. "Defoe and Far Travel." *English Literature and the Wider World, vol 1: 1660–1780. All the World Before Them.* Ed. John McVeagh. London: Ashfield, 1990.

Meli, Domenico Bertoloni. "The Color of Blood: Between Sensory Experience and Epistemic Significance." *Histories of Scientific Observation.* Ed. Lorraine Daston and Elizabeth Lunbeck. Chicago: University of Chicago Press, 2011, 117–34.

Merriman, Mira Pajes. "Comedy, Reality, and the Development of Genre Painting in Italy." *Giusseppei Maria Crespi and the Emergence of Genre Painting in Italy.* Ed. John T. Spike. Fort Worth: Kimball Art Museum, 1986, 39–76.

Meyer, Alfred, and Raymond Hierons. "On Thomas Willis's Concepts of Neuropsychology, Part One," *Medical History* 9 (1965): 1–15.

Meyer, Alfred, and Raymond Hierons, "On Thomas Willis's Concepts of Neuropsychology, Part Two," *Medical History* 9 (1965): 142–55.

Milne, Anne. "Gender, Class and the Beehive: Mary Colliers's 'The Woman's Labour' (1739) as Nature Poem." *Interdisciplinary Studies in Literature and Environment* 8 (2001): 109–29.

Milne, Anne. "Fables of the Bees: Species as an Intercultural Discourse in Scientific and Literary Texts." *L'Esprit Createur* 46 (2006): 33–41.

Milne, Anne. *"Lactilla Tends her Fav'rite Cow": Ecocritical Readings of Animals and Women in Eighteenth-Century British Labouring-Class Poetry.* Lewisburg: Bucknell University Press, 2008.

Mullan, John. *Sentiment and Sociability: The Language of Feeling in the Eighteenth Century.* Oxford: Clarendon, 1988.

Mullett, Charles F. "Some Neglected Aspects of Plague Medicine in Sixteenth Century England." *The Scientific Monthly* 44, 4 (1937): 325–37.

Nagy, Kelsi, and Phillip David Johnson. *Trash Animals: How We Live with Nature's Filthy, Feral, Invasive, and Unwanted Species.* Minneapolis and London: University of Minnesota Press, 2013.

Narain, Mona. "Libertine Spaces and the Female Body in the Poetry of Rochester and Ned Ward," *ELH* 72 (2005): 553–76.

Nash, Richard. *Wild Enlightenment: The Borders of Human Identity in the Eighteenth Century*. Charlottesville: University of Virginia Press, 2003.

Neill, Anna. "Crusoe's Farther Adventures: Discovery, Trade, and the Law of Nations." *The Eighteenth Century: Theory and Interpretation* 38 (1997): 213–30.

Neri, Janice. *The Insect and the Image: Visualizing Nature in Early Modern Europe, 1500–1700*. Minneapolis: University of Minnesota Press, 2011.

Nethercot, Arthur H. "Abraham Cowley's Essays." *Journal of English and Germanic Philology* 29 (1930): 14–130.

Nethercot, Arthur H. *Abraham Cowley: The Muse's Hannibal*. New York: Russell and Russell, 1931.

Neustatter, Otto. "Mice in Plague Pictures." *The Journal of the Walters Art Gallery* 4 (1941), 104–13.

Nicholson, Marjorie Hope. *Pepys' Diary and the New Science*. Charlottesville: University of Virginia Press, 1965.

Nielsen, Randall. "Storage and English Government Intervention in Early Modern Grain Markets." *The Journal of Economic History* 37 (1997): 1–33.

Norbrook, David. "Levelling Poetry: George Wither and the English Revolution, 1642–1649." *English Literary Renaissance* 21 (1991): 217–56.

Norbrook, David. *Poetry and Politics in the English Renaissance*. Rev. ed. Oxford: Oxford University Press, 2002.

Novak, Maximillian. "Crusoe's Fear and the Search for Natural Man." *Modern Philology* 58 (1961): 238–45.

Novak, Maximillian. *Economics and the Fiction of Daniel Defoe*. Berkeley and Los Angeles: University of California Press, 1962.

Novak, Maximillian. "Robinson Crusoe and Economic Utopia." *Kenyon Review* 25 (1963), 474–90.

Novak, Maximillian. *Realism, Myth, and History in Defoe's Fiction*. Lincoln: University of Nebraska Press, 1983.

Novak, Maximillian. *Daniel Defoe, Master of Fictions: His Life and Ideas*. Oxford: Oxford University Press, 2001.

Nowka, Scott. "Building the Wall: Crusoe and the Other." *Digital Defoe: Studies in Defoe & His Contemporaries* 2 (2010): 41–57.

Nussbaum, Felicity. *The Brink of All We Hate: English Satires on Women 1660–1750*. Lexington: University Press of Kentucky, 1984.

Nussbaum, Felicity. *The Limits of the Human: Fictions of Anomaly, Race, and Gender in the Long Eighteenth Century*. Cambridge: Cambridge University Press, 2003.

Oldroyd, Benjamin. "What's Killing American Honeybees?" *PLoS Biology* 5, 6 (June 2007), e168.

Orent, Wendy. *Plague: The Mysterious Past and Terrifying Future of the World's Most Dangerous Disease*. New York: Free Press, 2004.

Oster, Emily. "Witchcraft, Weather and Economic Growth in Renaissance Europe." *Journal of Economic Perspectives* 18 (2004): 215–28.

Pagel, Walter. *New Light on William Harvey*. Basel and New York: Karger, 1976, 42–61.

Palmierei, Frank ed. *Humans and Other Animals in Eighteenth-Century British Culture: Representation, Hybridity, Ethics*. Burlington, VT: Ashgate, 2006.

Pemberton, Neil, and Michael Warboys. *Dogs, Disease, and Culture, 1830–2000*. Bastingstoke: Palgrave Macmillan, 2007.

Piciotto, Joanna. *Labors of Innocence in Early Modern England*. Cambridge: Harvard University Press, 2010.

Post, John D. *Food Shortage, Climatic Variability and Epidemic Disease in Pre-Industrial Europe: The Mortality Peak in the 1740s*. Ithaca: Cornell University Press, 1985.

Pritchard, Allan. "George Wither: The Poet as Prophet." *Studies in Philology* 59 (1962): 211–30.

Purkiss, Diane. *The Witch in History: Early Modern and Twentieth-Century Representations*. London: Routledge, 1996.

Raber, Karen. "How to Do Things with Animals: Thoughts on/with the Early Modern Cat." *Early Modern Ecostudies: From the Florentine Codex to Shakespeare*. Ed. Karen Raber, Ivo Kamps, and Thomas Hallock. Bastingstoke: Palgrave, 2008, 93–114.

Raber, Karen. "Vermin and Parasites: Shakespeare's Animal Architectures." *Ecocritical Shakespeare*. Ed. Linda Bruckner and Daniel Brayton. Burlington, VT: Ashgate Press, 2011, 13–32.

Raber, Karen. *Animal Bodies, Renaissance Culture*. Philadelphia: University of Pennsylvania Press, 2013.

Raber, Karen, and Treva J. Tucker, eds. *The Culture of the Horse: Status, Discipline, and Identity in Early Modern World*. New York: Palgrave, 2005.

Rawson, Claude. *God, Gulliver, and Genocide: Barbarism and the European Imagination, 1492–1945*. Oxford: Oxford University Press, 2001.

Raylor, Timothy. "Samuel Hartlib and the Commonwealth of Bees." *Culture and Cultivation in Early Modern England: Writing and the Land*. Eds. Michael Leslie and Timothy Raylor. Leicester: Leicester University Press, 1992, 91–129.

Reiter, Paul. "Climate Change and Mosquito-Borne Disease." *Environmental Health Perspectives* 109, Supplement 1 (2001): 141–61.

Rendsburg Gary A. "Beasts or Bugs: Solving the Problem of the Fourth Plague." *Bible Review* 19, 2 (2003): 19–23.

Revard, Stella R. "Cowley's 'Pindarique Odes' and the Politics of the Interregnum." *Criticism* 35 (1993): 391–418.

Richetti, John. *Defoe's Narratives: Situations and Structures*. Oxford: Clarendon, 1975.

Richetti, John. *The Life of Daniel Defoe*. Oxford: Blackwell, 2005.

Robinson, Ken. "The Art of Violence in Rochester's Satire." *The Yearbook of English Studies* 14 (1984): 93–108.

Roos, Marie Anna. *Web of Nature: Martin Lister (1639–1712), The First Arachnologist*. London: Brill, 2011.

Rousseau, George. "Nerves, Spirits, and Fibres: Towards Defining the Origins of Sensibility." *Nervous Acts: Essays on Literature, Culture, and Sensibility*. New York: Palgrave, 2004, 160–84.

Ruddiman, William F. *Plows, Plagues, and Petroleum: How Humans Took Control of Climate*. Princeton: Princeton University Press, 2005.

Sadler, L. R. (Jacob Larwood). *The Story of the London Parks*. London: Chatto & Windus, 1881.

Sarasohn, Lisa. "'That Nauseous Venomous Insect:' Bedbugs in Early Modern England." *Eighteenth Century Studies* 46 (2013): 513–30.

Schiebinger, Londa. *Nature's Body: Gender in the Making of Modern Science*. New Brunswick, NJ: Rutgers University Press, 2004.

Schmidgen, Wolfram. "*Robinson Crusoe*, Enumeration, and the Mercantile Fetish." *Eighteenth-Century Studies* 35 (2001): 19–40.

Schwartz, Janelle A. *Worm Work: Recasting Romanticism*. Minneapolis: University of Minnesota Press, 2012.

Serres, Michel. *Hermes: Literature, Science, Philosophy*. Eds. Josue V. Harari and David F. Bell. Baltimore: Johns Hopkins University Press, 1982.

Serres, Michel. *The Parasite*. Trans. Lawrence R. Scher (1980). Rpt. Minneapolis: University of Minnesota Press, 2007.

Serres, Michel. *Biogea*. Trans. Randolph Burks. Minneapolis: Univocal, 2012.

Shanahan, John. "Theatrical Space and Scientific Space in Thomas Shadwell's *Virtuoso*." *Studies in English Literature 1500–1900* 49 (2009): 549–71.

Shannon, Laurie. "The Eight Animals in Shakespeare; or, Before the Human." *PMLA* 124 (2009): 472–79.

Shannon, Laurie. *The Accommodated Animal: Cosmopolity in Shakespearean Locales*. Chicago: University of Chicago, 2013.

Sharpe, James. *Instruments of Darkness: Witchcraft in Early Modern England*. Philadelphia: University of Pennsylvania Press, 1996.

Shoulson, Jeffery S. "'Propertie in this Hebrew poesy': George Wither, Judaism, and the Formation of English National Identity." *Journal of English and Germanic Philology* 98 (1999): 353–72.

Sill, Geoffrey. *The Cure of the Passions and the Origins of the English Novel*. Cambridge: Cambridge University Press, 2001.

Skura, Meredith Ann. *Shakespeare the Actor and the Purposes of Playing*. Chicago: University of Chicago Press, 1994.

Slack, Paul. *The Impact of the Plague in Tudor and Stuart England*. Cambridge: Cambridge University Press, 1998.

Snider, Alvin. "Cartesian Bodies." *Modern Philology* 98 (2000): 299–319.

Stevenson, Ruth. "Hamlet's Mice, Motes, Moles, and Mincing Malech." *New Literary History* 33 (2002): 435–59.

Sticker, Georg. *Die Pest in Berichten der Laien und in Werken der Künstler*, Amsterdam, 1898.

Sudan, Rajani. *Fair Exotics: Xenophobic Subjects in English Literature, 1720–1850*. University of Pennsylvania Press, 2001.

Swan, Claudia. *Art, Science, and Witchcraft in Early Modern Holland: Jacques de Gheyn II (1565–1629)*. Cambridge: Cambridge University Press, 2005.

Thomas, Keith. *Man and the Natural World: Changing Attitudes in England, 1500–1800*. London: Allen Lane, 1983.

Todd, Janet. *Sensibility: An Introduction*. London and New York: Methuen, 1986.

Totaro, Rebecca. *Suffering In Paradise: The Bubonic Plague in English Literature from More to Milton*. Pittsburgh: Duquesne University Press, 2005.

Turley, Hans. "The Sublimation of Desire to Apocalyptic Passion in Defoe's Crusoe Trilogy." *Imperial Desire: Dissident Sexualities and Colonial Literature*. Eds. Philip Holden and Richard J. Ruppel. Minneapolis: University of Minnesota Press, 2003, 3–20.

Turley, Hans. "Protestant Evangelism, British Imperialism, and Crusoian Identity." *A New Imperial History: Culture, Identity and Modernity in Britain and the Empire, 1660–1840*. Ed. Kathleen Wilson. Cambridge: Cambridge University Press, 2004, 176–93.

Turner, James Grantham. *Libertines and Radicals in Early Modern London: Sexuality, Politics and Literary Culture, 1630–1685*. Cambridge: Cambridge University Press, 2002.

Vander Wall, Stephen B. *Food Hoarding in Animals*. Chicago: University of Chicago Press, 1990.

Vandiver, E. P., Jr. "The Elizabethan Dramatic Parasite." *Studies in Philology* 32 (1935): 411–27.

Vardi, Liana. "Imagining the Harvest in Early Modern Europe." *Agrarian Studies: Synthetic Work at the Cutting Edge*. Eds. James C. Scott and Nina Bhatt. New Haven: Yale University Press, 2001, 86–138.

Vernon, P. F. "Social Satire in Shadwell's *Timon*." *Studia Neophilologica* 35 (1963): 221–26.

Wahrman, Dror. "On Queen Bees and Being Queens: A Late-Eighteenth-Century Cultural Revolution?" *The Age of Cultural Revolution: Britain and France, 1750–1820*. Ed. Colin Jones and Dror Wahrman. Berkeley and Los Angeles: University of California Press, 251–79.

Wall, Cynthia. *The Literary and Cultural Spaces of Restoration London*. Cambridge: Cambridge University Press, 1998.

Walter, John. "The Social Economy of Dearth in Early Modern England." *Famine, Disease, and the Social Order in Early Modern Society*. Ed. Walter and Roger Schofield. Cambridge: Cambridge University Press, 1989, 75–128.

Walter, John, and Roger Schofield, ed. *Famine, Disease, and Social Order in Early Modern Society*. Cambridge: Cambridge University Press, 1989.

Watson, Robert N. *Back to Nature: The Green and the Real in the Late Renaissance*. Philadelphia: University of Pennsylvania Press, 2007.

Watts, Jonathan. "Ecuador drops poison on Galapagos Islands in Attempt to Eradicate Rats," *The Guardian* (15 Nov. 2012). http://www.theguardian.com/world/2012/nov/15/ecuador-poison-galapagos-islands-rats.

Weber, Harold. "'Drudging in Fair Aurelia's Womb': Constructing Homosocial Economies." *The Eighteenth Century: Theory and Interpretation* 33 (1992): 99–117.

Wheatley, Christopher. *Without God or Reason: The Plays of Thomas Shadwell and Secular Ethics in the Restoration*. Lewisburg, PA: Bucknell University Press, 1993.

Wheeler, Roxanne. "'My Savage,' 'My Man': Racial Multiplicity in *Robinson Crusoe*." *ELH* 62 (1995): 821–61.

Williams, A. N. "'Of Stupidity or Folly': Thomas Willis's Perspective on Mental Retardation." *Archives of Disease in Childhood* 87 (2002): 555–57.

Williams, Glyn. *The Prize of All the Oceans: The Dramatic True Story of Com-*

modore Anson's Voyage Round the World and How He Seized the Spanish Treasure Galleon. New York: Viking, 1999.

Williams, Glyn. *The Great South Sea: English Voyages and Encounters, 1570–1750*. New Haven: Yale University Press, 1997.

Willis, Deborah. *Malevolent Nurture: Witch-Hunting and Maternal Power in Early Modern England*. Ithaca: Cornell University Press, 1995.

Wilson, F. P. *The Plague in Shakespeare's London*. Oxford: Clarendon Press, 1927.

Wilson, F. P. "English Letters and the Royal Society in the Seventeenth Century." *The Mathematical Gazette* 19, 236 (1935), 343–54.

Wilson, Mary Floyd. *Occult Knowledge, Gender, and Science on the Shakespearean Stage*. Cambridge: Cambridge University Press, 2013.

Wolfe, Cary. *Animal Rites: American Culture, the Discourse of Species, and Posthumanist Theory*. Chicago: University of Chicago Press, 2003.

Wolfe, Cary. "Bring the Noise: The Parasite and the Multiple Genealogies of Posthumanism." Introduction to Michel Serres, *The Parasite*, xi–xxviii.

Wolfe, Cary. *What Is Posthumanism?* Minneapolis: University of Minnesota Press, 2009.

Wolloch, Nathaniel. *Subjugated Animals: Animals and Anthropocentrism in Early Modern European Culture*. Amherst, NY: Humanity Books, 2006.

Wu Lien-teh, J. W. H. Chun, R. Pollitzer, and C. Y. Wu. *Plague: A Manual for Medical and Public Health Workers*. Shanghai Station, China: National Quarantine Service, 1936.

Zimmer, Carl. *Soul Made Flesh: The Discovery of the Brain—and How It Changed the World*. New York: Free Press, 2004.

Zimmerman, Everett. "Defoe and Crusoe." *ELH* 38 (1971): 377–96.

Zinsser, Hans. *Rats, Lice, and History* (1935). Rpt. New Brunswick: Transaction Press, 2008.

Index

soul, 93; of animals, 84–88, 94–99, 110, 197n48; Aristotelian model, 84; Cartesian model, 86, 110; corporeal soul, 87–88, 102–3; of humans, 86, 96–99, 103–4, 197n51; incorporeal soul, 105, 106, 197n51; tripartite model, 84–85, 86, 94; of vermin, 95–96, 102

Southall, John: *A Treatise of Buggs*, 82

spiders, 105–6l; anthropomorphized, 92

spontaneous generation, 28–29, 33; of frogs, 56, 68; in *Macbeth*, 37; theories of dispelled, 13, 37, 82, 179n2

Sprat, Thomas, 83

Sprenger, James: *Malleus Malificarum of Heinrich Kramer and James Sprenger*, 33–34, 41–42

Steele, Richard, 144–45, 146

St. Hier, 72

St. James's Park, 126–27

Sudan, Rajani, 148

Swammerdam, Jan, 2, 82

Swan, Claudia, 31, 35

Swift, Jonathan: *Gulliver's Travels*, 104; "On Poetry: A Rhapsody," 124

Sydenham, Thomas, 5, 6, 25

systems, 22; agricultural, 71; biopolitical, 7–15, 25, 112–14, 170, 172; Crusoe's island as, 147; food, 147–63; parasites within, 15, 171, 184n44, 184n46; pestilential, 25; vermin within, 17, 22–23, 74–80, 177, 184n44, 184n46

taxonomy, 14, 17, 183n40

Thomas, Keith, 149

Topsell, Edward: *Historie of Foure-Footed Beasts*, 17, 29, 30, 35, 39, 56

Trapp, John, 130

Turks, 45, 47

Tyson, Edward: *Anatomy of a Pygmy*, 90

Vallisneri, Antonio, 14

van der Heyden, Hermann, 139

Vander Wall, Stephen, 150

Van Helmont, Jan Baptist, 13

Vega, Garcilaso de la, 144

vegetarianism, 173–75

vermin, 2, 3–4, 172; agency of, 2, 5, 8–9, 17, 19, 20, 29, 34, 43; anatomical structures of, 20, 100–101; anthropomorphic, 32–35, 92, 164, 166–67; as category, 1, 17, 29, 42, 53, 62, 68, 115, 148, 170; cats as, 148; conflation with racial and religious others, 45, 161–63; disease and, 2, 3, 5, 7, 17–18, 24–31, 36–42, 126–27; domestic animals and, 13, 22, 42, 111; as food source, 79, 173, 193n55; food supply, threat to, 3, 4–5, 39, 53, 56, 57, 143, 147, 148–49; in household, 44, 56; humans, relationship to, 77, 86–93, 172; individuated, 4, 7; moral corruption and, 7, 37–38, 64–66; native ecologies disrupted by, 143, 145; natural order, role in, 74–80; necessity of, 170; popular depictions of, 43; predators as, 163; as scapegoats, 22–23, 43–44, 45; in scientific experiments, 81–84, 105–7; on ships, 6, 30, 39, 143, 144, 176–77; supernatural and, 18, 27, 31–42; in theology, 16–17, 40–41, 50, 57–58, 95. *See also* birds; crabs; dog packs; dogs; fleas; frogs; imperfect creatures; mice; parasites; rats; snakes; spiders

vermin control, 44–47, 143, 148, 149, 161, 177, 203n67; city dogs and, 137; extermination, 3, 44, 137, 148, 170; national policies on, 4, 50–51, 60, 149; women's role in, 12, 14

vermin infestations, 13, 22, 24, 27–28, 30, 44–45, 51, 54, 60, 79, 146–47, 161; agriculture and, 72, 77; biblical, 19, 49; disease and, 5, 6, 7, 126; infection and, 6, 22, 27–28, 126; moral corruption and, 27, 42; predation related to, 161

vermin reproduction, 1–2, 4, 13, 16, 24, 30, 39, 146; through spontaneous generation, 28–29, 33, 37, 56, 68

Virgil, 163; *Aeneid*, 25

Walter, John, 59–60

Walter, Richard, 6

weather. *See* climate; Little Ice Age

Webster, John: *The Duchess of Malfi*, 65

Webster, Noah: *Brief History of Epidemic and Pestilential Diseases*, 18–19

Wilkins, John: *Essays Toward a Real Character and a Philosophical Language*, 16

Printed and bound by CPI Group (UK) Ltd, Croydon, CR0 4YY

09/06/2025

14686091-0002